Jacob Levy Moreno
1889–1974

The International Library of Group Psychotherapy and Group Process

General Editor

Dr Malcolm Pines
Institute of Group Analysis, London, and formerly of the Tavistock Clinic, London.

The International Library of Group Psychotherapy and Group Process is published in association with the Institute of Group Analysis (London) and is devoted to the systematic study and exploration of group psychotherapy.

Jacob Levy Moreno
1889–1974

Father of psychodrama, sociometry, and group psychotherapy

René F. Marineau

Tavistock/Routledge
London and New York

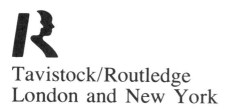

First published 1989
by Routledge
11 New Fetter Lane, London EC4P 4EE
29 West 35th Street, New York, NY 10001
with the collaboration of Editions Saint-Martin
416 boul. Saint-Laurent, Montreal, Quebec H2W 1Z3

Phototypeset in 10pt Times by
Mews Photosetting, Beckenham, Kent
Printed in Great Britain by Biddles Ltd, Guildford and King's Lynn

British Library Cataloguing in Publication Data

Marineau, René F., *1942–*
Jacob Levy Moreno, 1889–1974.
1. Medicine. Psychoanalysis. Group therapy. Group therapy in psychoanalysis. Moreno, Jacob Levy 1889–1974
I. Title
616.89′17

Library of Congress Cataloging in Publication Data
also available

ISBN 0-415-04383-2
0-415-04110-4 (pbk)

Contents

Illustrations

The author and publishers would like to thank all those listed above who gave permission to reproduce these photographs.

Foreword

Malcolm Pines

Jacob Moreno, a principal co-founder of group psychotherapy, claimed that he had been the originator of the very term group psychotherapy. Even before the First World War he had organized the prostitutes of Vienna into groups through which they could achieve their proper rights as citizens and cease to be treated as the detritus of bourgeois and aristocratic society. Through his experiences as doctor to refugee settlements he began to recognize the dynamics of the group and of social groupings, and that social tensions can be either created or reduced through the way people are put into artificial social groups. After the war, through his immersion in theatre in Vienna he began to glimpse the potentiality that man can be an actor in the theatre of his own life and thereby recognize and resolve some of his conflicts. In psychodrama and the allied science of sociometrics that he founded, he found channels for his great creative energy and both these innovations, the art of psychodrama and the quantitative science of sociometrics, are major contributions to modern psychotherapy and social psychology.

What is Moreno's place in the Pantheon of modern psychotherapy, in the company of the other creators of group psychotherapy?

The American pioneer Slavson, an engineer and educator inspired by psychoanalysis, founder of the American Group Psychotherapy Association which he dominated for years, led the way in activity group therapy for children and adolescents and enthused the first generations of American group psychotherapists. As a creative theorist he is not in the first rank, unlike his German-British counterpart, S.H. Foulkes who has left a rich heritage in the form of group analytic theory and technique. Foulkes was a psychoanalyst whose formation in Vienna and later in Frankfurt, where he was in touch with the Marxist Frankfurt sociologists, led to an integration of sociodynamics and psychodynamics which will continue to be studied and developed.

Foulkes and Slavson lived fairly conventional, middle-class, professional lives, but Moreno was a Bohemian. As a young man he lived in the world of theatre and literature, writing down tracts and verses that came to him in moments of mystical, possibly manic, inspiration. He was a child of his times, with their upsurge of new forms of literature, drama, and art. His work is part of that movement, the devising of new forms of human expression.

Myths quickly form around major creative persons. With some of them the myths come largely from others, their followers or rivals. For others, the creative person is his own principal myth-maker. The current study of Freud's life is a process of the examination of the psychoanalytic myth. The task of the historian is to penetrate the myth and to place the person and his circumstances in the perspective of history. In answer to the question 'Who am I?' the Spanish philosopher Ortega y Gasset wrote 'I am myself plus my circumstances.' In this book René F. Marineau has begun to examine the Moreno myth and I welcome the opportunity to include a book about Moreno in this series, which already includes books dedicated to S.H. Foulkes and to Wilfred Bion, the founder of the Tavistock tradition, who was a later arrival in the field than Foulkes, Slavson, or Moreno. The phenomenon of Moreno and his impact on psychotherapy is part of the as yet unwritten sociocultural and intellectual history of modern psychotherapy.

Preface

Jacob Levy Moreno, born in Bucharest in 1889, was to become famous world-wide for the development of the science of sociometry, the method of psychodrama, and his pioneering work in group psychotherapy.

Even though his work and legacy are of great importance, Moreno's story has not yet been properly told. There are many reasons for this: Moreno developed his ideas in Vienna, in the shadow of Freud and psychoanalysis; when he emigrated to the United States, he found himself again, as in Europe, at the centre of controversies; while developing his most important theories, he also expended his energies and talent in related but secondary projects; too much of a maverick, he did not give enough attention to creating a cohesive school to continue his work. None of these reasons alone is sufficient to explain the relative lack of attention given to his methods and to his own story immediately after his death. The reasons lie as much in the difficulties for people in grasping a philosophy that, as presented by Moreno himself, at times lacked unity and coherence. Furthermore, the implications of some of Moreno's ideas were challenging for his time and in that sense premature; it is only now that many of Moreno's intuitions and concepts are finally being accepted and understood, while some others still need to be tested and applied; it is only now that the concepts and techniques that he developed can be said to be gaining real ground.

The philosophy and theories developed by Moreno are not only fascinating, but ultimately much more coherent than he made them appear. Many of his concepts and ideas survived him and are now part of the psychological vocabulary, but his scientific works are often mixed with autobiographical fragments and personal claims, as he admits himself in *Preludes to the Sociometric Movement* (1953) where he concludes, 'There is no controversy about my ideas, they are universally accepted. *I am the controversy*. The fondest dream of my youth has come true, they are already used anonymously in many places.' While Moreno is right about the use of his ideas and techniques, the reference to anonymity is one of the many instances where he uses a double meaning — in fact, far from seeking anonymity, he fought long and hard for recognition, to establish fatherhood under his own name of every word and concept that he invented. This may explain why he became so much the controversy himself.

Moreno was a giant during his life, an object of love, veneration, and hatred. He is almost forgotten as a scientist or a psychotherapist. His personal life, fascinating in every aspect, explains in a large measure, the development of his scientific thinking and therapeutic techniques. His roots, Jewish, Roumanian, Turkish, and Viennese, need to be examined in order to reconcile the apparent contradictions in his personality and behaviour, and a focus on his immediate family system helps us understand the origins of his mysticism and megalomanic tendencies. The intellectual, political, and medical climate of the time was also an important factor in his development: he witnessed the fall of the Austro-Hungarian Empire; he knew Freud, Adler, Reik, Buber, Werfel, Kokoschka and many other intellectuals in post-war Vienna; he was a contemporary of the first Viennese psychoanalytical school and the expressionist movement, part of both, and yet out of the mainstream of any school or group. I hope that this biography will reveal the similarities and the differences between Moreno and his contemporaries.

The time has come, with the centennial of Moreno's birth, to re-examine his image and place him in a proper light among contributors to the well-being of mankind and the history of medical and social science. This contribution goes way beyond his technological innovations, even though his methods were ingenious and daring. He was a visionary and a creator who offered human beings a new path towards self-fulfilment: a path originating in spontaneity and creativity, culminating in genuine and meaningful encounters.

* * *

This book is in two parts, encompassing the whole life of Moreno. In Part One special attention is given to Moreno's European period (I call it 'The warm-up process', using a Morenean concept that means 'preparation for the main actions to come'). In Chapter 1 particular emphasis is put on Moreno's ancestors, since they are so much part of what he calls his psychodramatic truth. This chapter also deals with Moreno's birth, around which so many myths developed that space needs to be given to exorcize and explain them, and, finally, with the other members of his family. In Chapter 2 I deal with Moreno's childhood and adolescence in which important foundations were laid for the development of his 'megalomania' and the mystical basis for his journey was established. The third chapter focuses on his student years, in and out of the University of Vienna, a period of intense activity during which many of the ideas and techniques of the future creator of psychodrama, sociometry, and group therapy can be seen unfolding. Chapter 4 discusses the years spent in Bad Vöslau with Marianne Lörnitzo, without doubt the most creative of his European years, when he wrote *The Words of the Father* and *The Theatre of Spontaneity* at the same time as he was experimenting with the concepts he was writing about.

Part Two, called 'Action and sharing', covers Moreno's life in the United States where as a mature therapist and scientist he was able to develop an integrated philosophy of mental health, an alternative method of psychotherapy, and an objective methodology for measuring interpersonal relationships. Chapter 5 focuses on the first difficult years before he was able to make the desired 'fresh start in a new land' which was to be a more receptive environment for the 'third psychiatric revolution'. Chapter 6 shows Moreno looking for a new muse, and finally finding a companion and professional partner in Zerka Toeman: it was with her help that he was finally able to put into practice his whole system of philosophy. I will show the unfolding of Moreno's ideas in two separate chapters, the seventh one dealing with sociometry, the eighth with psychodrama. Around 1951, Moreno's conquest of psychiatry and sociology took a new turn when he started touring the world to bring his message and techniques back to Europe, and other continents: this is the subject of Chapter 9. The tenth chapter centres around Moreno's death: encountering health problems and diminishing physical capacity, Moreno chose to die according to his own philosophy, quitting the stage when he sensed that he could no longer perform, but leaving his ideas and ideals as a legacy to the world.

* * *

Writing this biography was not easy because little was known of Moreno's European period, and what was known appeared to be a mixture of legend and fact compounded to suit Moreno's megalomania. As a historian, I have had the difficult task of verifying every bit of information. While doing so, I have come to discover that many of Moreno's stories are in fact true, and that when he is not historically accurate, there is often some justification in the use that he made of what he termed the poetic and psychodramatic truth: this truth does not aim at any precise demonstration of facts, but at a subjective representation of reality.

It has taken me more than five years, many interviews, repeated reading of his books and articles, and many hours in different archives, in my attempt to understand Moreno, his actions, and his insights. I needed to get close to him, to identify with his associates and his enemies, and then to take some distance from them all to gain perspective. Using Moreno's own vocabulary, I could say that writing this biography has involved a prolonged exercise in role reversal, doubling with Moreno himself and many other people in an attempt to mirror his life and work. I hope that as a result of this process the book which follows will convey a legitimate and truthful picture of the man called Jacob Levy Moreno.

Acknowledgements

Writing this biography has taken me on a pilgrimage through Europe and America, in which I have received friendship and care from both strangers and long-established acquaintances.

A special thanks is due to the Morenean 'family' in particular to Zerka Toeman Moreno, Regina and Jonathan Moreno, Florence Bridge, Merlyn Pitzele, Anne Ancelin-Schützenberger, Gretel Leutz, Jonathan Fox, and many other members. Their dedication, openness and tolerance of my repeated requests for information will not soon be forgotten. Many of the illustrations in this book are reproduced by kind permission of Zerka Moreno. Mr Richard Wolfe, of the Harvard Archives, also showed repeated generosity and made himself constantly available to me.

I owe an incommensurable debt to many people in Austria, particularly my two Viennese hostesses, Maria and Veronika Andorfer: they not only provided me with a place to work, but with much needed friendship in the darker days of my search. Without constant guidance through the archives of Vienna and the streets of the city from Manfred Stelzig, Ernst Schwager, Andrea Heubel, Walter Reichelt, Rikki Scherr, Murray Hall, and Brigitte Marschall, I might still be looking for a way to get to the National Library. I tested the proverbial Austrian hospitality beyond reasonable limits and was never made aware of any feelings of impatience on the part of my hosts. I also wish to acknowledge the everlasting support and encouragement that I received from Karoline and Willi Hochreiter.

Many individuals volunteered interviews and archive material. Among others: in Bucharest, George Bratescu, Monica Ionescu, Ada Alistar, Theodore Blumenfeld, and Panait Panait; in Budapest, Maria Hari; in France, Juliette Favez-Boutonier, George Stoetzel, Didier Anzieu, Serge Lebovici, Yves Pélicier, and Claude Ouzilou; in London, Elisabeth Bergner, Lana Sutton, Marcia Karp, Malcolm Pines, and Ken Sprague;

and then colleagues from the United States, Russia, Denmark, Finland, Sweden, Germany, Greece, Japan, Brazil, Argentina, Canada.

I would like to thank also my assistants and critics, Francine Provencher, Christine L. Johnson, Johanne Doyon, Lucie Lafrenière, Esther Beloch, Sophie Painchaud, Jean-Marc Ménard, and Richard Desgagné, with special thanks to the photographers, Veronika Andorfer and Claude Demers. This research was done with the full support of my university department: I wish to acknowledge the technical and financial help given to me by André Pellerin, and the encouragement of the Chancellor, Jacques Parent, and the Vice-Chancellor, Paul-André Quintin. This book would not have been published without the collaboration of my Canadian and English publishers and I am particularly grateful to Richard Vézina, the editorial director of Editions St Martin, Quebec, for encouraging me to publish this shorter version in English of my full biography of Moreno in which he holds the rights.

A very special acknowledgement goes to my wife, Kristine Macchi, who supported me on a journey that was sometimes difficult, and who often acted as a much valued collaborator; thanks also to my two children, Sébastien and Christophe, who never denied me their encouragement. A last thanks to my history teachers: first, my parents, Wilfrid Marineau and Alice Carle, for giving me the meaning of roots; second, Antunas Paplouskas Ramunas who gave me the honour of choosing me as his assistant to teach the history of psychology and who was a living example of a creative, procreative, and recreative life.

Part One

The warm-up process: life in Europe

Chapter 1
Ancestors and family: the birth of a myth

20 May 1892. On a non-identified ship on the Black Sea Jacob Levy Moreno is born. So the legend says . . .

Four hundred years earlier, on 30 March 1492, an edict had been issued from the palace of Alhambra, Granada, by Isabella of Castille and Ferdinand of Aragon, the Catholic sovereigns of Spain, ordering all Jews to convert to Catholicism or to leave the country. Ferdinand and Isabella had entered Granada, the Moslem capital, a few months earlier, and were now determined to make their country an all-Catholic stronghold.

The edict was devastating to the Jewish community. The story goes that Isabella and Ferdinand were almost persuaded to revoke it in return for a substantial amount of money, and after emotional pleas from senior and influential Jews, but that Torquemada, prior of the convent of Santa Cruz, suddenly entered the royal chamber, with crucifix aloft, and thundered: 'Judas Iscariot sold his master for thirty pieces of silver. Your Highness would sell him anew for thirty thousand. Here he is, take him, and barter him away.' Ferdinand was compelled to listen and there was nothing left for the Jews but to convert to Catholicism or to prepare for the exodus.

> In the same month in which their Majesties issued the edict that all Jews should be driven out of the Kingdom and its territories, they gave me the order to undertake with sufficient men my expedition of discovery to the Indies.

Thus began the diary of Christopher Columbus.

In the next few months, Columbus, who was widely helped by the Jewish community, both financially and with human resources, prepared for his journey. He left the port of Palos, Spain, on 3 August 1492, the last day set by the authorities for the Jews to leave the country. A third of the crew on the *Nina*, the *Pinta* and the *Santa Maria* were Jews (the controversy still rages about whether Columbus himself was a Jew), but in comparison to what was going to happen to other members of their faith, these men were lucky to be aboard.

Over 200,000 other Jews prepared to leave their home and country. Those living in the south sailed to the ports of the North African coast. Twenty vessels reached the coast of Fez and were met by pirates; while negotiating for ransom, they decided to turn around: three vessels were lost in a storm, others were captured by the Spanish, and of those who finally reached Fez 20,000 died in a great fire followed by an outbreak of fever.

Others went the route of Italy. Vessels came from Genoa to pick them up and a good number of Jews were robbed, beaten, and killed. They were permitted to stay only upon receiving baptism. Some set foot on Corfu, Candia, and other Greek islands: they were sold as slaves, often to other Jews who succeeded in freeing them.

Some took the direction of Turkey. Along the way, many were killed, thrown to the sea after having their bodies gutted and searched for gold, and there were many storms to be endured. The more fortunate finally reached the Ottoman dominion where they were hospitably received by the Sultan, Bayazid II, who lent them money and gave them estates and fields to work. Among these, it seems, were the ancestors of Jacob Levy Moreno who gradually made their way to Constantinople, Plevna, and eventually Bucharest.

This story was repeated many times to the young Moreno, and was to have a great influence on him. For the Sephardic Jews, this long and rough journey was never to be forgotten over the centuries. In the minds of many, their journey also came to be associated with the one of Christopher Columbus. Their exodus was the beginning and the discovery of a new world.[1]

Moreno's ancestors settled in Turkey, in Constantinople, around 1492, under the family name Levy; the name Moreno, which Jacob used later, was one of his father's forenames. Among them were doctors and merchants, and it seems that some of the Levys converted to Islam, as we know that Moreno's great uncle married the daughter of the mayor of Constantinople and inherited a harem.[2]

We do know that Moreno's grandfather was named Buchis[3] and that he moved from Constantinople to Plevna (now Pleven in Bulgaria) and then to Bucharest, probably during the war between Turkey and Russia. This war, which was to restore Bulgaria's autonomy and Roumania's independence, saw many a Jewish Turkish citizen emigrate to more hospitable cities. The Levys became members of a Sephardic community in Bucharest, having followed Rabbi Haim Bejarano from Plevna. As merchants, they kept their ties with other Balkan countries and did not get involved in politics: the Levys always had a reputation for being on good terms with everyone.

Moreno's father, Moreno Nissim Levy was born, probably in 1856, in Plevna. This city was then part of Turkey, which explains his Turkish nationality, a nationality which he passed on to his own children; he later acquired Roumanian citizenship. Moreno Nissim was a merchant, working for himself like his father Buchis, though for a while he worked in his in-laws grain business and in the newly developed petroleum industry in Roumania. His date of birth made him a contemporary of Sigmund Freud.[4]

Moreno's mother, Paulina, was also of Sephardic descent, but the original family name is unknown. In Roumania, the family used the Roumanian name 'Iancu', and seemed well-established there, but it is highly probable that, like other Sephardic families, they had followed the same route as the Levys and had originally settled in Turkey or Greece. With the opening of ports along the Black Sea and the lower Danube for international commerce in 1829, the 'Iancu' family more than likely came to Calarasi, via the route of Constanta. Paulina's parents became rich grain merchants and were part of the Sephardic community of Cacomeanca, a small town close to Calarasi. Paulina Iancu was born on 14 November 1873.[5] Her father died when she was still a child and her two older brothers, Marcus and Jancu, took over the family business and the education of the three younger sisters. Paulina was sent to a Catholic convent in Bucharest where she was exposed to French culture and language and almost converted to Catholicism. However, the two brothers took her out of boarding school before her fifteenth birthday and began to search for a suitable husband for their sister.

The marriage of Moreno Nissim Levy and Paulina Iancu took place sometime in 1888[6] and the couple moved into an area of Bucharest where some of Moreno Nissim's relatives were already living. Their first appartment was at 50 Serban Voda Street, but they were to change appartments almost every year in the next six years, an indication of their relative instability and poverty.[7]

Life in Roumania at this time was not easy. After an emotional boost related to the proclamation of autonomy the country had to be rebuilt; a great deal of investment was undertaken and progress made, particularly in developing transport facilities by rail and sea, but this relative prosperity was not to last and at the end of the nineteenth century the country had to wrestle with an economic crisis. The situation was particularly hard for the Jews who still had to fight for equality of rights, in spite of the Treaty of Berlin which guaranteed justice and equality irrespective of religious faith. It was in this difficult context that Moreno Nissim Levy and Paulina Iancu married.

It was in many ways a marriage of convenience. Moreno Nissim Levy was thirty-two years of age, a relatively poor travelling salesman; he had reached the time in his life when it became important for a man to settle and have a family. Paulina had really nothing to say in the matter, having to accept her older brothers' choice. At fourteen, she was one day a schoolgirl in a Catholic convent, the next a wife living by herself, with a husband travelling in the Balkans. The marriage was the beginning of a difficult relationship that was to have a far-reaching effect on their son, Jacob Levy Moreno.

Soon after the marriage, Moreno Nissim left for the road again, travelling to Serbia, Greece, and Turkey, selling 'Turkish wares'. He left his pregnant wife behind and Paulina gave birth to her first child, Jacob, on 18 May 1889. She was barely fifteen-and-a-half years of age. We will talk later about the myth surrounding the date of Jacob's birth, for a long time proclaimed as 1892; for now, let us continue with the historical truth.

The child was born at four o'clock in the afternoon of 18 May 1889, in his parents' house on Serban Voda Street. His father was not present at the time of birth. The official record of the birth was signed by friends of the family and members of the Sephardic community, Avran Mitran, Salomon Alseh, and Salomon Athias.

The absence of the father's name on the birth certificate is symbolically important. This absence was to make it easy for Jacob to claim in later years that he literally started a new dynasty, being the father and son at the same time. On the certificate, his mother claims to be eighteen years old and she was to constantly change her name and her age in later years, learning like many Jews to be wary of revealing too much about her identity on official documents.

But the main interest for us remains in the exploration of the myth surrounding Jacob Levy Moreno's place and date of birth, which became universally accredited as being on the Black Sea in 1892:

> I was born on a stormy night on a ship sailing the Black Sea from the Bosphorus to Constanta in Roumania. It was on the

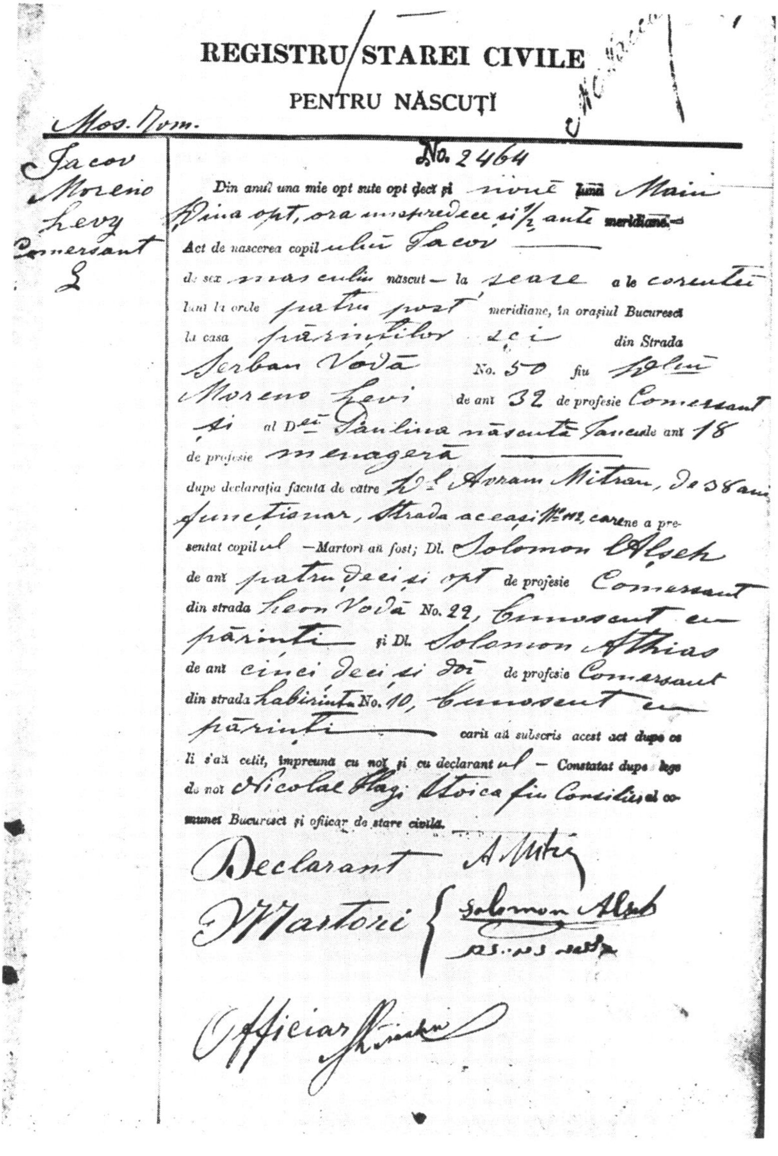

REGISTRU STAREI CIVILE

PENTRU NĂSCUŢI

Mos. Rom.

Iacov Moreno Levy Comersant

No. 2464

Din anul una mie opt sute opt deci şi nouă luna Maiu
Ziua opt, ora unsprezece şi ½ ante meridiane.
Act de nascerea copilului Iacov
de sex masculin născut la seara a le corentei
luni la orele patru post meridiane, în oraşul Bucuresci
la casa părinţilor sei din Strada
Serban Vodă No. 50 fiu Dlui
Moreno Levi de ani 32 de profesie Comersant
şi al Dnei Paulina născută Iancu de ani 18
de profesie menageră
dupe declaraţia facută de catre Dl Avram Mitran, de 38 ani
funcţionar, Strada aceaşi No 112, care ne a presentat copilul —Martori aŭ fost; Dl. Solomon Alseh
de ani patru deci şi opt de profesie Comersant
din strada Leon Vodă No. 22, cunoscut cu
părinţii şi Dl. Solomon Athias
de ani cinci deci şi doi de profesie Comersant
din strada Labirint No. 10, cunoscut cu
părinţii carii aŭ subscris acest act dupe ce
li s'aŭ citit, împreună cu noi şi cu declarantul — Constatat dupe lege
de noi Nicolae Hagi Stoica fiu Consilierul comunei Bucuresci şi oficiar de stare civilă.

Declarant A Mitran

Martori Solomon Alseh

Officiar

Figure 1 J.L. Moreno's birth certificate. (Registru Starei Civile, Bucharest.)[8]

> dawn of the Holy Sabbath and the delivery took place just before the initial prayer. My being born on a ship was due to an honorable error, the excuse being that my mother was only sixteen and little experienced in the mathematics of pregnancy. No one knew the identity of the ship's flag. Was she a Greek, a Turkish, a Roumanian or a Spanish ship? The anonymity of the ship's flag started off the anonymity of my name and the anonymity of my citizenship. When World War I broke out in 1914 no one knew whether I was a Turk, a Greek, a Roumanian, an Italian, or a Spaniard because I had no birth certificate. When I offered my services to the Austro-Hungarian Monarchy, they would not accept me at first because I had no proof of nationality. I was born a citizen of the world, a sailor moving from sea to sea, from country to country, destined to land one day in New York harbor.
>
> ('Autobiography' 1985: ch. 1: 6)

Many versions of this story exist, with minor variations, but the message is the same in all of them. What can we say about this 'story' of Moreno's birth?

The first comment to make is that the myth was created after Moreno's emigration to the United States. The records found in Europe indicate that Jacob Levy (Moreno) always used his real place and date of birth on official papers there, for example, his registration at the University of Vienna. So while he knew the historical facts, he clearly felt that he needed to create a new story when he arrived in New York. This story is an account that incorporates imagination and symbolism with reality. It represents what Moreno will call the poetic and psychodramatic truth.

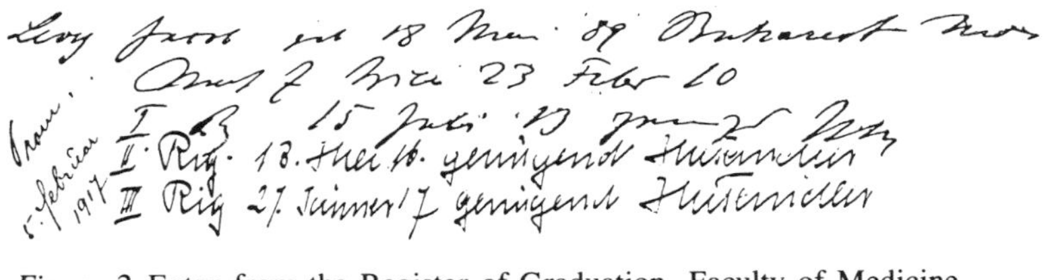

Figure 2 Entry from the Register of Graduation, Faculty of Medicine, University of Vienna for 'Levy Jacob, born 18 May 1889 in Bucharest'. (Archives of Alte Universität, Postgasse, Vienna.)

The second comment that needs to be made is that in his book *The First Psychodramatic Family* Moreno has this to say before presenting the story of his birth:

> The stories told in this book strive to be psychodramatically and poetically accurate, as they exist in the minds of the people involved and told by them. They do not strive for historic accuracy. For instance, Moreno's first name is not Johnny — which was inspired by the story of Johnny Appleseed — but Jacob, or Jacques. And so it goes for other details. A psychodramatic biography differs in this sense from an historically analytical biography.
>
> (*The First Psychodramatic Family* 1964: 7)

This text is clear, and it is interesting that it did not lead at the time to more questions about Moreno's handling of the historical truth.[9] The first story in the book, appearing just a few lines below the text quoted above, is precisely the story of his birth. For us, it is of importance to clarify why Moreno created the myth, and then let it stand. It could be argued that Moreno wanted only to grow young again in order to stand a better chance of being admitted as an immigrant to the United States and to please younger women in America. But if so, why did he choose 1892? I think that this particular date was over-determined for him.

As a child Moreno received religious instruction in Bucharest from Rabbi Bejarano. His lessons started in 1892, at the time of the 400 years' commemoration of both the exodus of the Jews from Spain and Christopher Columbus's discovery of America. The two events, as we have seen, were intimately linked for many people of the Sephardic community, and especially for the historian Haim Bejarano, director of the Bucharest Jewish School.[10] The young Jacob was no doubt impressed by the teaching that he received. That he chose later, in 1925, to sail to America like another Columbus should not surprise us. He even had a dream about it, a dream that we will refer to in a later chapter. The date of 1892 is also the date of birth of his favourite brother, William — an identification figure, but also a rival. Jacob Levy, faithful to his Biblical ancestor, could well have borrowed or stolen his brother's birth date. The rivalry and ambivalence of Jacob towards his brother William, and vice-versa, is one of the interesting aspects of the family dynamic.

In addition to the story about the date, the story about the place of

Moreno's birth is of prime importance. One can ascribe different meanings to it, but two are striking. The story of the ship that came from Spain and was *en route* to Roumania can be seen as a *recapitulation* of four hundred years of community and family history. We not only travel through the storms and suffering of his mother giving birth to her first child, but we are also invited to share the miseries and uncertainty of a larger group. Four hundred years ago Moreno's ancestors had to endure the pain of leaving their country and face the challenge of starting anew. Later in life one of the most emotional moments that Moreno will experience is receiving an honorary doctorate from the University of Barcelona, as if, representing all Sephardic Jews, he witnesses history being rewritten and justice being restored. From this perspective, the myth of his birth tells us about his very deep identification with the Sephardic Jews.

The story of his birth on a ship can also convey a quite different meaning. The fact that the ship was apparently 'flagless' allows Moreno to claim anonymity of nationality, absence of belonging to a definite country, and makes him a citizen of the world. This symbolic meaning will be very important later in understanding Moreno's philosophy and theories. The story of Moreno's birth becomes one of the finest examples of what he himself called poetic and psychodramatic truth. The myth makes sense, not for a researcher striving for historical facts, but for an analyst of Moreno's motivation. In order to understand this more fully, one could interpret many more details of the story: the absence of the father, real and symbolic, which will allow Moreno to claim and to create a new dynasty; the role of the mother, who will support the child's subjective interpretation of the story of his birth, and hence his megalomania; the time of birth, (the dawn of the Holy Sabbath) which will enrich the prophetic role of Jacob; the very name chosen for the child which is in itself full of symbolism (I will comment in Chapters 2 and 3 on the significant meaning of names in Moreno's life).

The myth of Jacob Levy Moreno's birth is so full of meaning, that one wonders why so little attention was given to the fact that it was a symbolic way of talking, and a very rich way to introduce us to his personality. When the historic truth was uncovered in 1975 by Professor Bratescu of Roumania,[11] many people were scandalized and felt cheated; very few tried to put the legend of Moreno's birth in the perspective of symbolism and *surplus-reality*.

For me, the exploration of this myth, the relationship between historical and poetic psychodramatic truth in Moreno, his reaction to his followers and enemies, all were opportunities to try to grasp the real personality of the future creator of psychodrama. Moreno did not lie: he used another channel to speak the truth, in a way that was simultaneously symbolic, and conducive to gratifications rooted in reality, giving him, for instance, all the advantages of making him seem younger than he was. Of course, this dual form of truth creates problems for others. It especially became a problem for the people who did not dare ask . . . What is certain is that as a storyteller, Moreno derived great pleasure from letting people guess and wonder!

* * *

Jacob Levy Moreno was to have five brothers and sisters; they were born in the nine years following his own birth:

- Rahel, better known as Vittoria or Victoria, was born on 29 March 1891 in Bucharest. She became a *modiste*, first in Vienna and later in New York. She was to be a great financial help to their mother after the separation of the parents. She was married in Vienna and left the city when Hitler entered Austria in 1938.
- Volf-Valerian, better known as Vily or William, was born on 2 December 1892 in Bucharest. He was the first Levy to emigrate to the United States. A great admirer of his brother Jacob, he helped him financially in Vienna, and then in New York. It is interesting to note that the name Volf is also a name used by Moreno's mother as a family name.
- Scharloti, better known as Charlotte, was born on 26 November 1893 in Bucharest. She was the only member of the family who remained in Europe. She moved from Vienna back to Bucharest after her marriage to one of her cousins, George Rosenfeld. This man was the son of Elisabetha, sister of Charlotte's mother, Paulina. Charlotte continued to live in Bucharest until her death. Her father, Moreno Nissim, also moved back to Bucharest after his separation from Paulina. Charlotte, like the rest of the family, had little contact with him.
- Clara, affectionately called Lala, was born on 7 February 1898. The first four children were born in Bucharest. Clara was the first one to be born in Vienna. She emigrated to the United States with her husband and daughter in 1938.
- Norbert, usually referred to as Buby, was also born in Vienna on 10 October 1899. The family story is that he married a Polish princess who refused to follow him to the United States in 1938. He settled in Florida and eventually remarried.

Two last points need to be stressed here: the influence of the mother's French upbringing in the names given to the children (for example, Jacob was always referred to as Jacques in the family) and the fact that the name Levy was gradually replaced by the name Moreno. Jacob was the first one to use the name Moreno as a family name and almost everybody but his father and his sister Charlotte followed his example. Moreno, it is important to remember, was the first name of Jacob's father. In a way, by appropriating his father's first name, Jacob did establish a new dynasty.

Chapter 2

A brave child and a rebellious adolescent

The parents of J.L. Moreno were very different.

Moreno Nissim Levy, when not travelling, led a very active social life outside the home, away from his wife and children. He spoke little, but retained his authority. He was in and out of the city a lot and remained quite a mystery to his children who feared him as much as they admired him. As a businessman he was good at starting projects, but they quickly failed; basically gentle, he was not good at chasing debtors and was often abused financially. He was always active in the Sephardic community, helping friends and neighbours.[1]

Paulina Iancu was a warm, cheerful, and socially active woman. She had status in the community, being multilingual and well-educated for her time, and somewhat refined. Although she was a Sephardic Jew, she was also very close to Christian values through her reading of the New Testament and the influence of the nuns at her Catholic school. Her hero, who was to become Jacob's model, was Jesus Christ. At the same time she was superstitious: she often listened to gypsies, believed in dream interpretations, and in fortune-telling. She predicted catastrophes, marriages, and wealth through coffee grounds, tea leaves, palm reading, and Tarot cards. Above all she had a tremendous sense of humour, strength in adversity, and unrelenting energy. It fell to her to take responsibility for the upbringing of the six children.[2]

The relationship of the couple seems to have been difficult right from the start, and it should be remembered that the marriage took place under pressure from Paulina's brothers. When husband and wife were together it seems that there was tension and uneasiness between both parties. It is not clear whether Moreno's father chose to travel a great deal because of unhappiness at home, but in any event the couple were to be apart most of the time. It was in this environment that the little Jacob was born and raised.[3]

Figure 3 Paulina Iancu aged fourteen-and-a-half years, wearing the convent regulation dress, just before she left school to get married. (Zerka Moreno, private collection.)

Paulina's first child was to be her favourite. In addition to being the oldest, the fact that she was often alone with him in the first few months certainly helped to create a very special bond. This bond was reinforced when, at only twelve months, Jacob suffered a severe attack of rickets: he had no appetite, lost weight, and could not walk. No doctor seemed to be able to help and it was becoming clear that the boy was not going to survive. His young mother would often cry; she became depressed and desperate. One day, as she was taking her son out in the yard, a gypsy passed by. She stopped, told Paulina to stop crying, and to apply the following treatment: 'Go and get some fine sand. At high noon, when the sun burns hot, put the baby on the sand. The sun will heal the baby.' Pointing her finger at the child, she added this prophecy: 'The day will come when this boy will become a very great man. People will come from all over the world to see him. He will be a wise and kind man.'

This story is extremely important, for it created in the mind of the mother the idea that her son was not just an ordinary baby. From that day she believed that God had given her an important mission to reinstate her child's health and prepare him for his future journey. She started to give Jacob special attention and, without realizing it, laid the foundations of his future megalomanic dream. She shared the story of the prophecy with the people around her and, as a result, the young Jacob developed a very special relationship with the people around him.[4] Paulina having followed the gypsy's advice, within a few months saw her son cured, healthy, and able to walk. The first part of the prophecy was fulfilled; the second part was already in the making.

Moreno's religious upbringing was a mixture of Jewish beliefs and Christian values. As a young boy he was taught by Rabbi Bejarano, an impressive figure in the Jewish community[5], but it was Jesus who was to become the identification model for this young Sephardic Jew. He was also a frequent witness of, and visually impressed by, the long and solemn processions that took place at the nearby Greek Orthodox San Spiridon Basilica. It was the combination of these diverse influences that led to the future religious make-up of J.L. Moreno.

As a child Moreno played games that not only reflected his religious beliefs, but also give us an idea of how he had already introjected a perception of a special destiny. His favourite game was to play the role of God. He did it often, building with other children a stage representing heaven and, while doing it, he would often break the furniture: a carpenter needed to be called in regularly to fix chairs and tables after these games. One episode of playing God particularly stuck in the boy's memory:

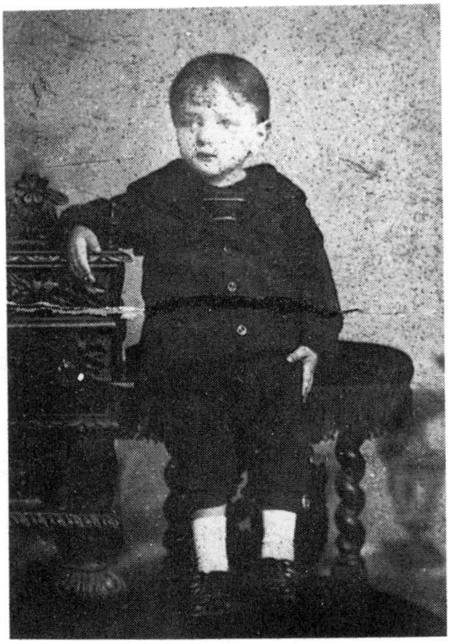

Figure 4 Jacob Levy Moreno, aged four years. (Zerka Moreno, private collection; rephotographed by Claude Demers.)

When I was four-and-a-half years old my parents lived in a house near the River Danube. They had left the house on a Sunday to pay a visit, leaving me alone in the basement of the house with neighbors' children. The size of this basement was about three times that of an average room. It was empty except for a huge oak table in the middle. The children said: 'Let's play.' One child asked me: 'What?' 'I know', I said, 'let's play God and his angels.' The children inquired: 'But who is God?' I replied: 'I am God and you are my angels.' The children agreed. They all declared: 'We must build the heavens first.' We dragged all the chairs from every room in the house to the basement, put them on the big table and began to build one heaven after another by tying several chairs together on one level and putting more chairs above them until we reached the ceiling. Then all the children helped me to climb up until I reached the top chair and sat on it. There I sat pretty. The children began to circle around the table, using their arms as wings, and singing. Suddenly I heard a child asking me: 'Why don't you fly?' I stretched my arms, trying it. A second later

I fell and found myself on the floor, my right arm broken.
(*Psychodrama, volume 1* 1946: 2)

This story became a legend among Moreno's students and was narrated in different versions. One has it that Moreno's mother went to see a gypsy to ask her to look at her son's arm. The gypsy renewed the prophecy about the boy's important future mission to the world and recommended him not to break the left arm because it would be a bad omen.

Moreno later commented on the learning process that took place that particular Sunday: he acknowledges being both director and protagonist in this first private psychodrama; he makes a connection between the future psychodramatic stage and the heavens; he sees the different roles played by other children as being the same as future auxiliary egos; above all, he recognizes his need to play God.

I would like to add a few comments of my own here. First, I found through my research that this God-playing game was repetitive and systematically supported by Moreno's mother.[6] Second, this role was for Moreno a 'warm-up' for his future mission: through it, he was preparing to be the important cosmic person who would later associate his name with that of God the Creator. Third, this theme — playing God, being almighty, becoming the Father — makes sense not only in relation to religious belief, but also secures him a place as a creator of a new down-to-earth dynasty; in the child's mind, he is his own God and his own father. This first psychodrama (Moreno often called it 'The Psychodrama of the Falling God') can also be seen as the formative moment in the child's megalomania, his first megalomanic episode. It was to leave doubts in his young mind about being an indestructible God and to make him question his own strength.

Let us now turn to Moreno's first few years and expand on the theme of the early influences in his life, for Moreno cannot be understood if one does not grasp his relationship both to his parents and to God. In fact, one has to consider his ties with his environment at two levels: that of the family and his relationship to his father, mother, brothers and sisters, and that of the religious realm which can be seen as a kind of symbolic meta-system.

The most important relationship in Moreno's life seems to have been with his father. Even though his father was often far away, unsuccessful in his projects, and unhappy with his family, the young Jacob still loved and idealized him. He idealized him to the point of making him a god. He sided with him against his mother and uncles, and as the eldest of the family introjected the behaviours expected from a young man in a respectable family. But this relationship with his father was not grounded in the reality of daily life: occasionally he would travel with his father, and these would be moments to cherish, but more often it was through his imaginary life that he could identify with him. The most interesting aspect of this is the way in which the young Jacob *incorporated* his father: and I think that the word incorporate, used here in the psychoanalytical sense, is the best term to describe Jacob Levy Moreno's internalization of his father, Moreno Nissim Levy. It seems that the quasi-physical and symbolic process of 'letting the father in', took place very early in life. This probably came about through the mother's belief in the gypsy's prophecy that her 'son' would have a special mission, as a prophet or messiah, reinforcing the tendency to megalomania in the child. The inner representation of 'the father' took on a mystical aspect and would later be confused with the one of God.

The mother also reinforced the dyads Paulina/Jacob, Mary/Jesus. In the second dyad, the father, Joseph, is very secondary, just as, later, Moreno Nissim would seem almost an accessory in Jacob's life. Jacob was eventually to call himself the father of a new dynasty, and having said this, it becomes evident how Jacob related to his real father by erasing him from his life, replacing him as the new 'chief of the tribe', an expression he used later to describe his relationship with Freud. There was confusion in his mind about fatherhood, creation, and God. It began with the story of his birth, and was never to be resolved.[7]

Soon after entering school the young Jacob confirmed this identification of Father–God, by refusing to be called by his given name, even by his brothers and sisters: nobody, he said, calls God by his name.

It is evident that very early in his life Jacob Levy Moreno chose to experience his immediate family on two levels: one concrete and down-to-earth, the other symbolic, reinforcing his inner representation of himself as a messiah or prophet.

When he later borrows the name of his own father, Moreno, and sees himself as the creator of a new dynasty, Jacob Levy Moreno will have gone full circle, the child becoming his own father. What this meant in reality will become clearer later.[8]

* * *

As young Jacob's health improved and while he was being given special attention by his mother, the couple was still experiencing financial problems: by the time Jacob was five, he had three siblings and the family had moved four times. The economic situation was difficult in Bucharest and in 1895 or 1896 Moreno Nissim took the opportunity to move to Austria to work for a company whose main offices were located in Vienna. This was when Jacob was six or seven years of age.[9]

The move to Vienna was a mixed blessing for the family. The father did not find it easy to emigrate to a German-speaking country. He did not learn new languages easily and was not at ease with the lifestyle of the Viennese. He was never to feel really at home in either Austria or Germany, and took every opportunity to travel in the Balkans where he felt he really belonged. Moreno's mother, on the other hand, adapted to life in the 'second district' of Vienna, among Jews and other refugees, much more easily than her husband, even though she always felt like a refugee herself when dealing with the Viennese. She rapidly learned German and took her family in the park nearby, either the Augarten or the Prater. After four years without pregnancies, she gave birth to her last two children in 1898 and 1899.

Jacob rapidly adjusted to the new surroundings. Vienna was a city that he would come to enjoy even though he, too, always felt like a refugee among true Viennese. One must not forget how much had already taken place in Bucharest, and how the main thrust of Moreno's personality was already cast and evident.

Jacob, or Jacques as his mother called him, started school in Vienna. He took the habit of sitting in the front row: in this way he could listen more easily to the teacher, but also be chosen as an assistant. He kept this habit throughout his studies and rapidly became a favourite pupil because of his curiosity and intelligence. he did well at school, becoming the pride of his parents. His mother did not yet know what to make in practice of the old gypsy prophecy. His father, more pragmatic, suggested to his son that he should become a doctor of medicine following in the footsteps of an uncle who had just died in Constantinople. From now on, the young Jacques was often referred to as 'Doctor', a form of address used by his patients, students, and colleagues throughout his career.

With his brothers and sisters his relationship was quite different. He did not want to be called by his first name. If one of them used the name Jacob, or Jacques, he would simply ignore them. He waited to answer until he was referred to as 'you'. This was the beginning of the 'anonymity' to which he gave so much importance. This anonymity was rooted, as we saw, in his sense of being a special case of God. It later took on another significance when he extended this refusal to be called by his name to his playmates.[10]

The young Jacques had a very special relationship with his brothers and sisters, and was helped in this by his mother who viewed him as a special child. Even though he would play with his siblings, he always remained somewhat distant. When he suggested games, they would always be highly symbolic and meaningful. One night, for example, he got up with his brother William and created a whole universe in dough. This was for him an alternative to his earliest 'God' play: here he could be creator. Many years later he would write *The Words of the Father* and base his philosophy on the responsibility of everyone to continue the works of the creator. He would stress action before words, remembering that he first created a universe in dough before talking about it.[11]

Moreno's childhood was, in his own words, the happiest time of his life. He studied and played without being aware of his parents' drama around him. He also had a chance to travel alone with his father, a special treat. He made two trips, one to Calarasi where his mother's brothers had their business and one to Constantinople; this second trip was to be one of the most beautiful memories of his life. The trip to Calarasi gave him a chance to make one last visit to his homeland and to reconnect with his maternal language, Roumanian. It also gave him the opportunity to be alone with his father and to experience a different man to the one he was used to at home. He listened for hours to his father telling stories and was very impressed as the train made its way through the mountains of Transylvania and the plains of Roumania. Unfortunately, during the visit he contracted malaria and had to return to Vienna feverish and pale.

A few months later his father took him to Constantinople. The Levys had many relatives there and their ancestors had lived in the city for many generations. It was on this occasion that Jacob had an opportunity to visit the harem belonging to his uncle. He was fascinated by naked young women, bathing and being massaged; he was also impressed by the architecture of the building, the structure of the organization, and the role of the eunuchs. It was an adolescent fairy-tale come to life. He also spent considerable time in the bazaar, where he was overwhelmed by the number of people, the infinite choice of goods, and the well organized system behind the apparent lack of structure. Above all it was the deep knowledge his father displayed of human nature and different lifestyles that impressed him most. Jacob did not have many opportunities to be close to his father, but when the opportunity arose, he discovered a man who had the dimensions of a god: he had experience, knowledge, and wisdom. Secretly, he envied him. Later, after his father's death, when Jacob emigrated to the United States, he would remember that Moreno Nissim was the 'real Moreno, the one that had all the ideas'.[12]

Around 1905 the family moved to Berlin. It seems that Moreno Nissim started a new financial venture with a partner: it still had to do with Turkish wares, ornaments for religious celebrations and funerals, and possibly the manufacture and sale of coffins. The start of this enterprise was a new challenge, and at the onset things seemed promising. Perhaps this time his father would succeed.[13]

Jacob was fourteen years old, very involved with his own projects and friends. He moved to Berlin, only to find after three weeks that he could not bear to leave Vienna. After a discussion with his parents, he received their permission to return and live with friends of the family. He was never to live with his own parents again. He went back to school, but rapidly, as we shall see, turned rebellious. Meanwhile, for some mysterious reason, Moreno's father got into trouble with the police in Berlin: he was ordered to leave the city and settled in Chemnitz.

At about this time Jacob made another trip, this time with one of his uncles on his mother's side of the family. They travelled extensively throughout Italy. His uncle, who called him 'Doctor' all the time, was very proud of his nephew. He tried to teach him the value and management of money, but found that Jacob only laughed at him. There were two high points to this trip. First, Moreno met a young and beautiful woman in Florence named Pia with whom he immediately fell in love; for days, his heart beat only for her in the extremely beautiful surroundings of the city. Jacob had already had physical and sexual relations with many girls in his life but Pia was the first to become his 'muse', replacing his mother as the person who would motivate him to surpass himself.[14] In addition, Moreno met a group of students on the train with whom he held long and heated philosophical and existential debates; as a result, for the first time, he got a sense of some of the directions in which he wanted to take his life.

This journey left him full of questions, depressed by the separation from Pia and worried about his own future. He went to visit his parents in Chemnitz, but the situation was even more difficult than before: the relationship was on the point of breaking up. He tried to bring his parents together, to make them communicate, but to no avail. The young therapist, full of idealism, encountered his first failure. The final separation was soon to follow. He would then take sides with his father who would literally disappear from his children's life. The family legend has Moreno Nissim returning to Constantinople where he fathered many more children before returning to Roumania. What is certain is that he did go back to Bucharest where he died in 1925, completely forgotten by his family.[15]

The separation of his parents was hard for Jacob to handle. He was very angry with his mother and became very cynical about marriage. As the oldest child, he felt the responsibility of taking the 'father' role, but could not see himself carrying out the day-to-day job of raising a family.

Resentment and disappointment at the loss of his father found various outlets. Previously a well-behaved student, Jacob now started arguing with his teachers and missing classes. He was later to quit the gymnasium altogether without completing his 'matura'. He felt the injustice of the situation as a sign that God was letting him down. He challenged God Himself: here is an imaginary monologue that took place, according to the young adolescent:

> Why did you create the universe in the first place? You could have saved us all from life.
> Why did you separate light from darkness? There should have been only light.
> Why did you create rocks and volcanoes, oceans and stars? There should have been solid ground only . . .
> Why did you not start with me? And why did you finally create me? I don't feel good. I don't like myself. I have to eat. But the best food goes out the rear end. I have to walk, but I may slip and fall. I have to grow old, become sick and die. Why? You must have created me when you were sick and old, when your energy had been spent.
> Why did you split me in half? I know that I am an imperfect and unworthy being. When you saw that I was incomplete you tore me to pieces and brought forth another being, a woman. I was inferior enough, but she was still more inferior.
> This was the beginning of endless misery and futility, the chain of birth and death . . .
>
> ('Autobiography' 1985: ch. 2: 7–9)

This cry of pain illustrates the deep feelings of depression and despair in the young Moreno, the first indication of the reasons for his later participation in the expressionist movement. His rebellion against God was parallel with his rebellion against school, the political system, authority in general. God had to be killed and society destroyed in order to bring about a new order of things, a new world. Moreno was a fervent reader of Nietzsche, Dostoievski, Kierkegaard, and Whitman. Without being in any way systematic in his reading, he was looking for an answer to his metaphysical questions about life and his own role in the universe. He would read and re-read the Old and New Testament, the works of St Paul, St Augustine, St Francis, Blaise Pascal. . . . He identified with the life of Buddha and of Swedenborg. The prophet in him, asleep during his early teens, suddenly reawoke, searching for a new path.[16]

One day, Jacob had a vision:

> It was in my fourteenth year that I came to my epiphany. There was a night when I walked aimlessly through the streets of Chemnitz, the provincial German city where we then lived. I remember the time as being the end of my school vacation; a time when one looks ahead at the approaching change in one's routine and responsibilities. As I paced the dark and empty streets, I tried to sort out my incoherent thoughts and feelings, such as are not unknown to the intelligent and young. Looking up, I found myself in a little park standing in front of a statue of Jesus Christ illumined by the moon's faint light. It drew my gaze and I stood transfixed. In the intensity of this strange moment I tried with all my will to have that statue come alive, to speak to me. I wanted Jesus to move out of the stone and act out his life there in the park for the people of Chemnitz. Then it seemed to me that the statue was about to speak and I listened intently.
>
> Standing there in front of the statue, I knew that I had to make a decision, one which would determine the future course of my life. I believe that all men have to make such a decision in their youth. This was the moment of my decision. The question was, how would I choose: was my identity the universe, or was it with the particular family or clan from which I had sprung? I decided for the universe, not because my family was inferior to any other family, but because I wanted to live on behalf of the larger setting to which every member of my family belonged and to which I wanted them to return.
>
> My decision meant that all men and women were my brothers and sisters, that all mothers and fathers were my mothers and fathers, that all children, whoever their parents, were my children, and that all women were my wives, that all the property in the world was my property, and, in reverse, that all my property was the property of the world.
>
> The small statue before me symbolized that Jesus had gone the way of the universe and had taken all the consequences which were involved. It meant, for me, an end to just drifting,

that from now on all actions, all decisions and all encounters would have to be patterned to conform with this view of life. My mother, my father, my sisters, my brothers, my relatives, my friends could never understand it, but I followed my course and no one has ever been able to sway me away from it.

Standing before the Christ in Chemnitz, I began to believe I was an extraordinary person, that I was here on the planet to fulfill an extraordinary mission. This state of mind is usually called megalomania. That is a nasty name. It's really name calling. Actually, megalomania is a natural state of the human being from birth on. Megalomania is nothing exceptional. It has, like any other natural states, normal and pathological forms. Normal megalomania is just as fundamental to man's spiritual nature as are his lungs for breathing and the blood vessels for nourishing the cells of the body to his physical nature. All men are endowed with the idea of their grandeur. The problem is not megalomania. The problem is why we, in our culture, try to suppress it and hail those who practice modesty. Why do we disapprove of men who claim that they have been chosen to do extraordinary things?

From that time on there was a new surplus of meaning in everything I did, and in everything which was done around me. There was an excess of feeling, of joy or depression, or love or of anger. It was the way lovers feel in their first excitement at finding one another. The sun, the stars, the sky, the trees seemed bigger. Colors seemed brighter. All events seemed more dynamic to me than they seemed to other people. If a child was born, if a man died, if a fire broke out, if a stranger came in the door, it all seemed so deeply significant, bursting with riddles and questions, and a challenge to my most interior sense of values.

('Autobiography' 1985: ch. 1: 1–3)[17]

This vision, like the God-playing episode of his childhood, can be seen as the formative moment of Moreno's second period of megalomania. Having wished to destroy the world in his period of revolt and depression, he now wanted to build a new one. Moreno carried this new vision with him throughout the years to come.

Chapter 3
The university years

It is around 1906: Moreno lives in Vienna and his parents have moved from Berlin to Chemnitz. The father is blamed for every kind of problem; he cannot support the family financially and has developed relationships with other women while travelling in the Balkans. Finally, the parents separate and the father drifts away.

Meanwhile, Jacob Moreno has also completed his own separation from the family. His vision in the park has been a clear indication of a new path to follow: he leaves his own intimate circle to become more available to everyone. The separation is not easy. His family, and especially his mother, need him, he feels bad about being unable to substitute for his father, but at the same time is very angry with his mother: she is the one responsible for the separation. He goes through a period of revolt, even accusing his uncles, who help financially, of interfering in family affairs.[1] But the separation is also an opportunity for a bigger revolt: the school system is full of hypocrites, society has lost its sense of fairness and basic ethics; as for God, his creation is a mess and doesn't reflect Beauty and Justice. The young adolescent has no other choice but to take his future and the future of mankind in his own hands.

In addition to revolt, Jacob goes through a period of depression. He now knows that he needs to reconnect with his 'mission', but is alone and powerless. He leaves school and spends considerable time by himself meditating and reading. To support himself financially, he does some tutoring in order to survive in Vienna. His mother moves back to the city, but he refuses to go and live with her and the family. He also refuses financial help from his two uncles and is determined to lead an independent life.

Moreno acts at times in strange ways and people worry about him: some openly suggest that he might be mentally insane. His mother does not seem to understand the problem when told about her son's behaviour.

One day, for example, he appeared naked in front of the family where he lived, and then proceeded out of the door on to the street. Perhaps, he wanted to test the story about the emperor's clothes by Hans Andersen. Evidently he had a strong desire to provoke, something which was going to become a trademark in his later life. He may also have wanted to test the hypothesis about the return of Jesus Christ. We will talk more about this later. In addition to this provocative behaviour, he also stopped relations with women at this time, after a period of intense sexual activity.[2]

Moreno now began to read mystical authors. He was particularly interested in the notion of heaven and compared Dante's concept of heaven with that of Swedenborg, while trying to make sense of the notion of the soul. He found it easy to identify with the mystics and Swedenborg, a scientist turned theologian, was a particularly good role model. Later, Moreno the doctor was to remember the case of Swedenborg, a scientist chosen by God to transmit his message to the world, when he wrote his first major work, *The Words of the Father*.[3]

There followed a two-year period of intense soul-searching — two years devoted to trying to become God himself, or make sense of the mission that he felt God wanted him to fulfil. The young adolescent did not know who God was, whether He existed, or what one could do in His name. In order to find an answer, Jacob did all kinds of reading, with no supervision: one day he saw himself as a servant of God, the next as a replica of the Almighty, and even as God himself. The vision had taken him away from everybody, but no closer to any one religion. Throughout he remained convinced that action was more important than words, experience a better teacher than books.[4]

Slowly he started to reconnect with the world. He often walked past the university, listening to groups of students representing the left or right politically, or the opposing Christian and Jewish movements, but he himself was to stay away from factions, remembering that his family was now the world, and his kingdom the universe. It was during this period that he decided to enter the university and developed a friendship with Chaim Kellmer, a man who was going to have a lasting influence on him.

* * *

Moreno entered the University of Vienna in 1909. He had been seen around the faculty for some time, always dressed in a green cloak of the kind worn by Austrian peasants. He went without a hat, which was very rare at this time, and had let his beard grow long and wild. He circulated anonymously among the students, and was noticed by everybody. A philosophy student, who had been watching him for a while approached him one morning. This was Chaim Kellmer and the two young men felt an immediate rapport: together they founded a cult called 'The Religion of Encounter' and established a community based on its principles.

Chaim Kellmer, tall and broad-shouldered, looked older than his years. He had been born two years before Moreno and was in many ways his opposite. Jewish, and raised in the Hasidim tradition, he was studying philosophy in the hope of finding answers to existential questions, but regular meditation just led to further questions: he was not basically attracted by action. On the other hand, the young Moreno was not only to preach action, but was to say that nothing was worth discussing before it was put to a test: his life was a testimony of his beliefs.

An enduring friendship developed between the two men. Chaim Kellmer was to model his life after Moreno, and to become a follower and disciple, while Moreno admired the naïveté, idealism, and purity of Chaim's philosophy. Three more students in sympathy with the ideals of Moreno and Kellmer — Andras Petö, Hans Feda, and Hans Brauchbar — joined with them to found the 'House of Encounter' for new immigrants and refugees. A sign read: 'Come to us from all nations. We will give you shelter.' Newcomers were helped to fill out papers, file for official documents, and find temporary or permanent jobs, but the house also functioned as a community. Every night there were discussions about the practical problems encountered in and outside the house, a great deal of singing, and plenty of fun. The reputation of the group spread quickly and more and more people joined the community.

The founding of the House of Encounter meant more than the day-to-day running of a small institution. The group as a whole adopted a policy of anonymity. We know that Moreno had already developed such a philosophy around his own name. He took this opportunity to go one step further: everyone would abandon their name, a trend that was not exclusive to this group. It is clear that this policy was in the old Christian tradition and had a meaning of sharing everything in the name of charity.[5] Another feature of the House of Encounter was the spontaneous leadership of Moreno; even though no-one had asked him to be the director of the house, he just assumed the role. But perhaps the most important feature of the group was its spiritual beliefs and discussions. Members often met to talk about subjects such as the return of Jesus Christ and everyone had his hypothesis. Moreno claimed that Jesus would come back nude, or jump from a tree, and tried out these hypotheses himself. It is even possible that he might have thought of himself as Jesus at one period.

The five founders of the house, one student of philosophy and four students of medicine, got along well, but Moreno's favourite remained Chaim. It was Chaim who would visit the Moreno family, acting as an intermediary between Jacob and his mother, and Chaim who would accompany Moreno to the park and join in playing with the children.

By the end of his studies[6] Chaim was agonizing about his decision to teach philosophy or to move to Israel to organize settlements. After discussing it with Moreno, he decided to stay in Austria and work the land with an old peasant in Kagran. In making this decision he was following Moreno's philosophy of action. He also decided to be a Jew among gentiles, a decision that Moreno had made earlier. It is no exaggeration to say that the two men 'doubled' for each other and were almost alter egos. Under the influence of Moreno, Kellmer became a farmer, while Moreno, a future family doctor, was ultimately to become the 'teacher' of a new philosophy.

The House of Encounter was closed at the beginning of the war and the five members of the group went their separate ways. Chaim Kellmer, with whom Moreno kept in close contact, died of tuberculosis during the war as a result of overwork and Moreno lost his closest ally and disciple. What followed for Moreno was a new bout of revolt and depression. Meanwhile, however, he had completed his medical studies and begun all sorts of other activities.

* * *

Moreno's entrance to the University of Vienna in 1909 was complicated. He had left school before obtaining his diploma, the 'matura', and because of this, he could not enter the faculty of medicine. He was instead admitted in philosophy, under a temporary status, and before becoming a full-time student had to pass both the written and oral examinations related to the secondary school diploma. He took the written part before entering university in the autumn of 1909 and the oral examination took place during his first semester.

Moreno's course of study was quite traditional. From 1909–10, he studied the history of philosophy with Professor Stöhr, in addition to taking courses in metaphysics, cosmology, and Kant's philosophical idealism. However, at this time he was also registering for classes in anatomy, bacteriology, and biology. When he acquired full-time status in 1910 he transferred to the faculty of medicine to start the first of ten semesters.

In this classical course he attended basic seminars in anatomy and biology held by Professors Hochstetter and Tandler and acted as an assistant to the latter, becoming a 'buffer' between the professor and his rebellious class. He again found himself in the leadership role, defending the comparatively powerless students against the professor. He did his surgical training with Professor Eiselsberg and gynaecology with Professor Wertheim, known world-wide for the development of techniques still in use today. Ironically, Moreno always had difficulty delivering babies, making a special arrangement with colleagues to leave that part of medical practice to them. Because of it he even failed his entrance examination when he applied for recognition as a doctor of medicine after his move to the United States in 1927.[7]

In psychiatry the official course of study was limited. He studied basic diagnosis and pathology with Professors Stransky, Berze, and Redlich and also took a two-hour a week seminar for one semester with Professor Pötzl. Pötzl was at that time an assistant to Wagner von Jauregg, a future Nobel prize winner for his work on the cure of syphilis, but also an enemy of Freud and hostile to psychoanalysis. Pötzl himself was more open to the new science, having research assistants such as Paul Schilder and Helene Deutsch. Even though the student records do not mention it, it seems that Moreno also worked as a research assistant for Pötzl. Moreno's memories about the various projects are so clear that there seems little doubt about this; in particular, he worked on research centred on dreams with Deutsch and Schilder. This gave him an expertise in a subject that was at the heart of psychoanalytical writings.[8]

According to Moreno, his relationship with Pötzl, the son of an editor-in-chief of the newspaper *Freie Presse*, was very stimulating. He found him to be refined, warm, humorous, and sociable. Pötzl was a specialist in neuropathology and climbed the university ladder quite rapidly. Even though he was very close to Wagner von Jauregg's perspectives, he kept an independent mind, open to new ideas, and for a while was active in psychoanalytical circles.

The association with Pötzl gave Moreno a chance to work in the university clinic on Lazarettgasse and at the Steinhof Psychiatric Hospital, his first experience of institutions for the mentally ill. He did not particularly like what he saw: patients entering the wards went to stay and die; they were used and abused in research, injected with viruses and alcohol; no therapy was taking place. Moreno observed what he saw without commenting. This was not his usual style, but he felt that it was the only way for him to survive the then tyrannic and powerful grip of Wagner von Jauregg. One has to remember that in 1913 Moreno had no idea that he would one day work in the field of mental health himself; he was basically preparing himself to become a family doctor.

* * *

It was at about this time that Moreno had his encounter with Freud and psychoanalysis. According to Moreno, it happened in 1912, even though the year 1914 would seem a more accurate date if one looks at Moreno's university career. We have an account of the meeting only from Moreno himself, since nowhere do we find in Freud's writings any reference to the future creator of psychodrama. I do not think one need doubt that the meeting took place, but the details given by Moreno may encompass his own psychodramatic experience and truth. We must remember in this context that Moreno was an unorthodox student trying to establish himself as a new prophet and saviour. In addition to his medical study, he had been running a house for refugees, and, as we will see, would be very much involved with children and writing. He was well acquainted with Freud's ideas and work through his association with Otto Pötzl, Paul Schilder, and Helene Deutsch.

By this time Freud had already attained international recognition and acclaim. He had visited the United States with Jung and Ferenczi; *The Interpretation of Dreams* was in its fourth printing; the International Association of Psychoanalysis was very active, even though it was also plagued with dissension; Adler was out and Jung would soon be gone. Psychoanalysis was becoming popular among intellectuals in Vienna, but for its founder, the pains associated with the growth of a movement were felt daily.

Let us now turn to Moreno's account of his meeting with Freud:

> While working at the Psychiatric Clinic of Vienna University, I attended one of Dr Sigmund Freud's lectures. Dr Freud had just ended his analysis of a telepathic dream. As the students filed out, he asked me what I was doing. I responded, 'Well, Dr Freud, I start where you leave off. You meet people in the artificial setting of your office. I meet them on the street and in their homes, in their natural surroundings. You analyzed their dreams, I try to give them courage to dream again. I teach

people how to play God.' . . . . Dr Freud looked at me as if puzzled and smiled.

(*The First Psychodramatic Family* 1964: 16–17)[9]

The apparent boldness of the young student's address to Freud on being singled out by him is entirely consistent with Moreno's approach to people throughout his life. However, it is worth noting that Moreno was probably not so much singled out by Freud as singled out by himself, because of his eccentric mode of dress. It is clear that at this period Moreno was trying to establish his own revolutionary ground. Freud himself was occupying a lot of new territory and, through his disciples, was a new Moses bringing down new tablets. That Moreno opposed him should come as no surprise, especially as he saw Freud as a disguised traditionalist, using a revolutionary vocabulary.

It is interesting to see the comments that Moreno makes in his autobiography about this meeting. He sees Freud as a king of a large territory, and himself as a chief of a tribe. 'In that sense', he says, 'we are both "fathers" '. And Moreno adds: 'Except for my biological sonhood, I was never able to be a "son" to anyone. In my early life, I tried and succeeded in becoming a "father" very early.' That comment tells us a lot about Moreno's ever-present desire to be first, even in the field of psychiatry.

Moreno also made a very legitimate comment, consistent with his later theories concerning psychotherapy, about Freud's fears around acting out. Moreno felt that healers should be at ease enough to live among their patients and that they should provide a place in which patients could act out their conflicts. He did not advocate an acting out in reality, but on the stage. The stage, especially during this period, was the community, the streets, the parks. This is quite a departure from the classic attitude of Freud on acting out. It is not surprising that Freud should have been puzzled and amused by this young student, especially as there was no opportunity for elaboration or explanation on Moreno's part.

The meeting with Freud set the scene for Moreno's later attitude towards psychoanalysis. He probably suffered a lot at this time from not having space to develop his own ideas and was also probably envious of Freud, just as Jacob in the Bible was envious of his older twin. His view of psychotherapy and Freud's view of psychoanalysis were so completely different that it was difficult for him to discuss psychoanalysis from Freud's standpoint. Moreno was more interested in the conscious process, the here and now, the creativity of the person, than the unconscious process, the past and the resistance of the 'patient'.

A final point to make about this meeting concerns the content of Freud's lecture. We know about Freud's teaching at the University of Vienna through his publication of the *Introductory Lectures on Psychoanalysis* in 1916. We also know that thought transference and telepathic dreams were not a preoccupation for Freud at this time. He later became very interested in the subject, but remained uneasy about it. He may have made a passing reference to it in 1912 or 1914, but even that remains doubtful. It is interesting to note that the man who later developed the notions of *tele* and *co-unconscious* remembered only the topic of telepathic dreams when he remembered his meeting with Freud. This could make for a case of identification with Freud through a subject, telepathic dream, that evidently had more meaning for the young student than the master.[10]

Moreno's short encounter with Freud never developed directly beyond this point, but later he became friendly with Theodor Reik and through him tried unsuccessfully to reach Freud again.[11] He also struck up a long-lasting relationship with Alfred Adler, based in part, almost certainly, on a common competition with and dislike of Freud.[12]

Moreno's aggressive stance against psychoanalysis was rooted in epistemological differences. It was also related to his immediate experience of meeting Freud. Moreno was never able to confront Freud directly, just as he was never able to go back to Roumania to confront his father. However, he was to do battle with some of Freud's disciples with an energy that gives evidence of an earlier unresolved problem with another master, another father.

* * *

Moreno was quite proficient in his medical studies. Like every medical student, he had to prepare for three gruelling exams, the 'rigorosas'. He passed the first on 15 July 1913. He was not drafted during the war because of his ambiguous national status and consequently was able to present himself to the examination board for the second 'rigorosa' on 13 February 1916, and the third on 27 January 1917. In all three exams he received the pass mark and took his medical degree on 5 February 1917.

When we look at his student records we see nothing outstanding, but, while studying, Moreno never foresaw himself as a specialist in medicine; he was preparing himself for his own 'mission'. His reasons for becoming a medical student probably lay both in his desire to fulfil his father's wish and in his desire to become a healer.

We will now go back to 1909 to look again at Moreno as a young student engaging in all kinds of parallel activities during the course of his studies.

* * *

As we already know, Moreno started to gather a group of friends and disciples around him in 1908. Together they created a 'religion' which centred around creativity, encounter, and anonymity. They helped refugees and the poor, they let their beards grow, and devoted a lot of time to discussing theological and philosophical questions. It is interesting to see how this came about, how the young Moreno started to pull out of his narcissistic and self-centred behaviour, and, after the inner debate of late adolescence, set about fulfilling the old gypsy prophecy of his childhood:

> My becoming a prophet was not sudden. It was a slow, gradual growth whose determinants could be traced to my early childhood. This may explain the firmness and the stability of my conduct and why it never resulted in mental aberrations of crippling proportions.
>
> I began to play the part. I wanted not only to become a prophet, but to look like one. That a first beard grew was unavoidable for an adolescent approaching eighteen, but that I did not shave it had the mark of an important departure from the norm. By means of the beard I made the point that one should not interfere with the healthy spontaneity of the body. Nature should be allowed to take its course. My beard was reddish blonde and sparse. In the course of years it took the form which some medieval painters ascribed to Christ. Unconsciously I must have approved of its appearance and of the effect the beard would have on people living in a Christological culture. Looking fatherly and wise, anticipating old age, was exactly what a young God would like . . . .
>
> My eyes are blue. I was told that they were very large and smiling with gentleness and love. Looking into my eyes, people would feel that I could read all that was on their minds. My affectionate bearing and overt kindness seemed to be deeply concerned with the affairs of the person just facing me . . . .
>
> I wore a dark green mantle which fell almost to my ankles. Everyone began to identify me with it, 'the Prophet's Mantle'. I wore it summer and winter, perhaps with the intention of making

> myself easily identifiable, like an actor who wears the same costume at every performance. At times it seemed to me that I was creating a type, a role, which once encountered, could never be forgotten.
>
> I had the *idée fixe* that a single individual had no authority, that he must become the voice of a group. It must be a group, the new word must come from a group. Therefore, I went out to find friends, followers, good people. My new religion was a religion of being, of self-perfection. It was a religion of helping and healing, for helping was more important than talking. It was a religion of silence. It was a religion of doing a thing for its own sake, unrewarded, unrecognized. It was a religion of anonymity.
>
> I felt that, even if my modest effort should remain entirely ineffective and be forgotten, it would have been important from the point of view of eternity that such things were tried and existed, that such things were cultivated, and that such purity was maintained regardless of whether it paid off. The new religion required a mood of resignation, of just being and having the immediate satisfactions of such a state of being. If love and comradeship should arise, it should be fulfilled and retained in the moment without calculating the possible returns or without expecting any compensation.
>
> ('Autobiography' 1985: ch. 2: 13–17)

In this quotation from the autobiography we find a good indication of the direction of Moreno's thinking. He now began to open himself to others in a way that incorporated both the idea of anonymity and that of the collective responsibility of the group. We will have an opportunity later to see how these two ideas were developed in Moreno's life. However, the quest to become a prophet was not as easy or as pure in motivation as Moreno implies. He still had the urge to be in the limelight, to be the first and the best. He said he wanted to be anonymous, but always chose ways of achieving this that elevated his own position. This inconsistency, symptomatic of inner conflict, was evident to observers and one often wonders if he was not in fact playing a game. All his life he had difficulty in convincing some people of his sincerity. His inner ambivalence, between being a star or remaining anonymous, turned every one of his moves into a paradox. But his closest associates had faith in him and entered his world. The group became active in Vienna and, as in the case of Andras Petö,[13] their reputation spread beyond their immediate circle.

Meanwhile, Moreno and his friends were still busy debating the identity of the messiah, the returning Christ; they wondered if Moreno might not be Him:

> Adolescent men are nearer to Christ than are mature or older men. Christ is a symbol of youth. He came for children and young people. We (the group of five) looked with curiosity and suspicion at every man who walked by. Then we looked at our own reflections, at our own shadows. Who could tell? It could be one of us. Once when we were speculating on the coming of Christ, Kellmer and Feda suddenly looked at me with an expression of awe and reverence. They expected it from me. They pushed me forward to the great deed, the transformation.
>
> ('Autobiography' 1985: ch. 2: 19)

This period of Moreno's life was engrossed in mysticism, but at about the same time he also became interested in the world of children. There were two reasons for this: one, more mystical, was related to Christ's interest in children and to Moreno's belief that a revolution needed to start with the youth; the other was more practical. His mother had debts with a family called Bergner: in order to pay them, Moreno was asked to become tutor to the three children of the family. Here is Moreno's account of this story:

> One day a distraught mother came to see me. Deeply concerned about her child who was a pathological liar and mischief maker, she poured out her story and pleaded with me to work with her daughter, Liesel. The girl was on the verge of being thrown out of school where she was always in trouble. She told fantastic lies to her father about her mother, causing terrible scenes in the household. The father, Herr Bergner, was a tailor and the family was rather poor. Word of my saintly, prophetic mien had passed around the neighborhood. Although I was quite young, people in trouble turned to me.
>
> Liesel prospered under my tutelage. I discovered that she had incredible dramatic talent and I encouraged her mother to give the girl dramatic training, which she did. Liesel became Elisabeth Bergner, one of the most famous actresses of the German stage in the twentieth century.
>
> ('Autobiography' 1985: ch. 2: 15)

We have many accounts of this story. We also have the account of Elisabeth Bergner herself, which corroborates Moreno's version.[14] However, it is important to note that Moreno created different feelings among the three children; although Liesel responded well to Moreno's way of teaching, her brother and sister would have nothing to do with him. There were to be many other instances of children either becoming mesmerized by Moreno, or completely turning away. Let us see how he worked with Elisabeth around the age of ten: it will give us some insight into his future work and philosophy:

> Jacob Moreno, medical student at the University of Vienna, approximately twenty, but at most twenty-three years old. To me he looked more like a hundred because he had a beard. In those days only very old men wore beards. My father had a mustache. Moreno had a Christbeard, as I recognized much later. He was tall and slender, had grippingly beautiful blue eyes that always smiled and dark hair. I believed he was wondrously beautiful. I still believe that today. Most fascinating was his smile. That was a mixture of mockery and kindness. It was loving and amused. It was indescribable. . . .
>
> Thus, with Moreno a new era begins. The ease and speed with which the schoolwork was accomplished was soon no longer the most important thing. I was given poems to learn. And not just 'The Bell' and 'The Hostage' and such things from the school reader, but the wildest, most beautiful 'unknown' poems: 'The moon is risen, the little golden stars are resplendent'; 'Ride, ride, ride through the day, through the night, through the day'; 'Many must surely die there where the heavy rudders of ships are streaking'; 'Thus far too many things there are at which we smile with confidence, because our eyes do not see them'. Oh, it was a new world.
>
> Or, when Moreno went with us to the Prater, we did not go to the 'Wurschtel' but very deep, far away into the main avenue where the beautiful large meadows are.
>
> 'But you don't need a skipping rope for skipping! Come, let's give the skipping rope to a poor child who never had one!'
>
> 'But you don't need a ball to play ball! Come, I'll toss the sun to you, catch it!' 'Ow, I burnt myself!' 'Come, come, I'll make a bandage for you until the sunburn has cooled.'
>
> (Bergner 1978: 11–17)

The results of tutoring Liesel were astonishing. She started to like

Figure 5 Elizabeth Bergner as 'Miss Julie' in Strindberg's play of that name. (René F. Marineau, private collection; rephotographed by Claude Demers.)

school, to pay attention to other children, to give place to her imagination. She was amongst the first group of actors and actresses in Moreno's children's theatre. It was also on Moreno's recommendation that she entered drama school and she was always very grateful to him. An interesting footnote to Elisabeth Bergner's story is the fact that she was also to know Freud quite intimately, especially through her future husband, Paul Czinner. Comparing Moreno and Freud, she praised the first for giving her a chance to develop her creativity and credited the second with putting order in her mind. She was also acquainted with Alfred Adler, who was at one point her therapist, but disliked him a great deal.[15]

As a teacher Moreno was very open and tolerant. He called upon his pupils' creativity, imagination, and spontaneity; the learning process for him had to be a global and highly motivating experience. He succeeded with certain types of student, but had difficulty with others: this would carry over later, into his professional life. In order to work with him, people had to be in touch or recapture their spontaneity and, as we would say today, be in contact with the child inside themselves. The episode with Elisabeth Bergner was repeated with many other students and is a good introduction to Moreno's work with children.

Moreno always enjoyed spending time in the Augarten, a large public park in which he had played as a child when his family moved to Vienna. About 1908 Moreno started to meet children there and would tell stories and play games with them in a way which gives us some idea of the basis of his future philosophy:

> One day I walked through the Augarten, a garden near the Archduke's Palace, where I saw a group of children loafing. I stopped and began to tell them a story. To my astonishment other children dropped their games and joined in, nurses with their carriages, mothers and fathers and policemen on horseback.
>
> From then on, my favorite pastime was to sit at the foot of a large tree in the gardens of Vienna and let the children come and listen to fairy tales. The most important part of the story was that I was sitting at the foot of a tree, like a being out of a fairy tale, and that the children had been drawn to me as if by a magic flute and removed bodily from their drab surroundings into the fairy land. It was not as much what I told them, the tale itself, it was the act, the atmosphere of mystery, the paradox, the unreal becoming real. I was in the center, often I moved up from the foot of the tree and sat higher, on a branch; the children formed a circle, a second circle behind the first, a third behind the

second, many concentric circles, the sky was the limit.
(*Who Shall Survive?* 1953: xviii)

It is very clear from this extract from *Who Shall Survive?* how Moreno called upon children's imagination. It is also interesting to see the reference to the 'heaven-like' situation or 'stage', taking us back to the psychodramatic stage. Note how Moreno occupies the central place as storyteller, a God-like place. He acknowledges this when he concludes: 'The only way to get rid of the "God syndrome" is to act it out.'[16]

Moreno not only told stories. He played games with the children, games that called upon children's spontaneity, but also challenged the values inherited from their parents and teachers. He would get them to invent tales, or find new names for themselves, and even new parents. In a few weeks the person of Moreno became very invested by children. Stories about his origin, his residence, started to spread around: he was a king, he was living in a tree, he did not need to eat like ordinary people. The medical student succeeded in capturing the children's imagination. At times, his own friends would join in. One day, for example, when he suggested to the children that they should go around the park finding 'new parents', his friend Chaim Kellmer took part in the search and chose Moreno as his new father. These games were revolutionary and through them Moreno challenged parents and teachers alike. On one occasion the children at a certain school refused to go to see a film. The teacher was surprised and could not understand why, instead, they were asking to go outside into the 'real' nature: Moreno's influence was behind it. The children did not know the name of their mentor but let their teacher know that playing in the park was much more educative than going to see a film about the Swiss Alps. The school administration and the police started to search for the man who was having such a strong influence. A rumour started to circulate that he might even be a paederast. At this point Moreno understood that it might be better for him to leave the world of children, not because of the children themselves, but because the adults were so insecure about what he was teaching.[17]

Meanwhile, Moreno had also created a theatre for children. He had a regular group of young actors, including Elisabeth Bergner. They invented and improvised plays like *Thus spake Zarathustra* and even presented classics such as Molière's *Le Malade Imaginaire*. The presentations took place either in the park, or in a small hall turned temporarily into a theatre.[18]

Both the experience of playing games with children and the theatre group came to an abrupt end, the latter because of the war, the former because of the attitudes of the parents and teachers. On this subject, Moreno concludes:

> Behind the screen of telling fairy tales to children I was trying to plant the seeds of a diminutive creative revolution . . . .
>
> Gradually the mood came over me that I should leave the realm of the children and move into the world, the larger world, but, of course, always retaining the vision which my work with the children had given me. Therefore, whenever I entered a new dimension of life, the forms I had seen with my own eyes in that virginal world stood before me. Children were my models whenever I tried to envision a new order of things or to create a new form. When I entered a family, a school, a church, a parliament building, or any other social institution, I rebelled. I knew how distorted our institutions had become and I had a new model ready to replace the old: the model of spontaneity and creativity learned from being close to the children.
>
> ('Autobiography' 1985: ch. 2: 34)[19]

* * *

Another of Moreno's favourite pastimes during his medical studies was to go to the courts and witness trials. He would then go back home and with his friends or family reconstruct the drama and the trial. He would play all the different roles, including judge and jury, and on this basis would predict the outcome of the trial, giving the reasons why the lawyer would fail, how this witness was convincing, and so on. People would wait for the results of the trial and be amused at the high percentage of correct predictions Moreno had made.[20] Here one has a first glimpse of two of the future techniques of psychodrama — *doubling* and *role reversal*. We can see already, in addition to Moreno's intuition, his tremendous diagnostic ability and capacity for observation and identification.

At about this time an event took place that led Moreno to appreciate another dimension to the work of a therapist:

> One afternoon I walked through the Praterstrasse when I encountered a pretty girl, smiling at me. She wore a striking red skirt and white blouse with red ribbons to match it. I had hardly begun to talk to her when a policeman came between us and

took her away. I followed and saw them entering a police station. After a while she came out and I asked her what had happened. 'Well', she said, 'they told me that we are not permitted to wear such striking clothes as this during the day, as we may attract customers. It is only after sundown that we are allowed to do so.'

Vienna had at that time a red light district, a ghetto for prostitutes, in its first borough, located in the famous Am Spittelberg. Here was an entire class of people segregated from the rest of society, not because of their religious or ethnic character, but because of their occupation. They were not acceptable either to the bourgeois or to the Marxist, not even to the criminal. The criminal, after he has completed his prison sentence is again a free agent; but these women were eternally lost, they had no rights, there were no laws established to protect their interests. In 1913 I began to visit their houses, accompanied by a physician, Dr Wilhelm Gruen, a specialist in venereal disease and Carl Colbert, the publisher of a Viennese newspaper, *Der Morgen*. These visits were not motivated by the desire to 'reform' the girls, nor to 'analyse' them. They suspected this at first because the Catholic charities in Vienna had frequently tried to intervene in their lives. Nor was I trying to find among them what one may call the 'charismatic prostitute'. I had in mind that what LaSalle and Marx had done for the working class, leaving aside the revolutionary aspect of the labor movement, was to make the workers respectable, to give the working man dignity; to organize them into labor unions in order to raise the status of the entire class. Aside from the anticipated economic achievements it was accompanied by ethical achievements. I had in mind that perhaps something similar could be done for the prostitute. I suspected to begin with the 'therapeutic' aspect would be here far more important than the economic, because the prostitutes had been stigmatized as despicable sinners and unworthy people for so long in our civilization that they have come to accept this as an unalterable fact. It was easier to help the working class. Although manual labor had been and still is considered by some people as a sign of vulgarity it was still comparatively easy to give it, with the aid of skillful propaganda, the emblems of service and dignity.

But we were optimistic and started to meet groups of eight to ten girls, two or three times a week in their house. It was during the afternoon when the Viennese had what is called 'Jauze'; it is the counterpart of the English five o'clock tea. Coffee and cake were served around a table. The conferences at first only dealt with everyday incidents which the girls encountered: being caught by a policeman because they were wearing too provocative a dress; being put into jail because of false accusations by a client; having a venereal disease but being unable to find an hospital to admit them; becoming pregnant and giving birth to a baby but having to hide the child before the world under a different name and hiding their own identity as the mother towards the child. At first they warmed up very slowly, fearful of persecution, but when they saw the purpose and some benefits from them, they began to open up more. They first noticed superficial results, for example, we were able to get a lawyer for them to represent them in court, a doctor to treat them and a hospital to admit them. But gradually they recognized the deeper value of the meetings, that they could help each other. The girls volunteered to pay a few dimes a week towards the expenses of these meetings as well as towards some savings for emergencies like sickness and unemployment or old age. From the outside it looked like a prostitutes' 'union'. But we began to see then that 'one individual could become a therapeutic agent of the other' and the potentialities of a group psychotherapy on the reality level crystallized in our mind.

Four aspects of group psychotherapy struck me already then; they became later the cornerstones of all form of group psychotherapy: 1) the autonomy of the group; 2) that there is a group structure and the need to know more about it; group diagnosis as a preliminary to group psychotherapy; 3) the problem of collectivity; prostitution represents a collective order with patterns of behavior, roles and mores which color the situation independently from the private participants and the local group; 4) the problem of anonymity. When a client is treated within the framework of individual therapy, he is alone with the doctor, his ego is the only focus, he has a name, his psyche is highly valued private property. But in the group psychotherapy there is a tendency towards anonymity of membership, the boundaries between the egos weaken, the group as a whole becomes the important thing.

(*Who Shall Survive?* 1963: xxviii–xxx)[21]

This was another formative experience for the future founder of group psychotherapy. It taught Moreno many lessons, even though it seems that he had a minor role in these meetings. In terms of his own personal development, it may have contributed to his move away from a self-centred and egotistic stance. For the first time, he let other people take the lead and occupy the better portion of the stage. It is no accident that it corresponds, as we shall see, with the publication of *Invitation to an Encounter* (1914–15). We find here a more humble Moreno, but nevertheless the same man who at the same time confronted Freud.

* * *

Another episode needs to be presented now. It centres around the medical work that Moreno did during the period 1915–18. Moreno could not serve in the army because of his ambiguous national status. From his father he had inherited both Turkish and Roumanian nationality and it seems that the family, who came to Austria as refugees, never obtained Austrian citizenship. For this reason, Moreno did not have to serve in the war.

However, in about 1915, first as an advanced medical student and then as a young doctor, he secured a job in a refugee camp. In fact, he worked in two camps, one in Austria, the other in Hungary. His work in the Austrian camp, Mitterndorf, is of particular interest and can be seen as a prelude to the development of sociometry.

Mitterndorf was a camp for refugees who had to leave the South Tyrol because of the invasion of their territory by the Italians. Thousands of people left their homes and needed to be temporarily relocated. They were quartered in barracks each accommodating up to one hundred people; as more people came, they were assigned to the next empty barrack. There were many problems in the camps, mainly because no effort was made to take into consideration affinities of religion, lifestyle, social status, and so on, among the refugees.

Moreno had been assigned to the children's hospital in the camp and he started to observe the living conditions of the people in the barracks. He also developed a friendship with an Italian clinical psychologist, Feruccio Bannizone, who had been an administrator at the camp since its opening in 1914. Moreno made observations of individual barracks, between barracks, of the local factories created within the camp, of associations of people within religious and political groups; he also initiated many discussions, a lot of them with Bannizone. After a while

Moreno realized the importance of taking into consideration people's preferences and affinities if they were to be happier in inherently difficult situations. He started to make suggestions to the authorities of the camp, and even wrote a letter to the Minister of the Interior. A draft of this letter has been preserved, and can be seen as the first initiative in the formal creation of the science of sociometry. This draft letter was written on 6 February 1916. It starts as follows:

> To the Austro-Hungarian Minister of the Interior:
> The positive and negative feelings that emerge from every house, between houses, from every factory, and from national and political groups in the community can be explored by means of sociometric analysis.
> A new order, by means of sociometric methods is herewith recommended . . .
>
> (*Who Shall Survive?* 1953: inner cover)[22]

No-one has been able to establish so far whether this letter was actually sent to the Minister. However, this issue is somewhat secondary; what is of more interest is that the experience of Mitterndorf was the foundation for Moreno's work to come in the early 1930s in the United States. Moreno was showing for the first time his ability to observe large groups and to suggest remedies for social problems at the micro level. He was helped in doing this by the psychologist, Bannizone, whose contribution should not be ignored.

For the young doctor this early confrontation with daily misery and suffering was a very good 'warm-up' for his future work not only as a family doctor, but also as a sociodramatist.

Moreno's next job in a camp in Znolnok, Hungary, seems to have given him the opportunity to practise medicine on a daily basis. The camp received refugees from Transylvania, a territory that belonged to the Austro-Hungarian empire, was now under siege from Roumania, and was later to become a part of that country. Moreno was an assistant to a 'brain surgeon', Dr Wragasy, and also in charge of about thirty convalescent soldiers. Moreno worked in this camp until the end of the war.

A note on Moreno's publications

Moreno valued experience more than books, action more than words, and had an antipathy towards what he termed *cultural conserves*; that he wrote at all is only another contradiction that we have to deal with. Before giving a conference he would meditate and warm up to a spontaneous state, hoping to find something new to say, something that he had never told an audience before, but he was not as spontaneous in his writing. He often repeated himself and used part of one publication in the next. This is why his books are not the best way to get acquainted with him. He was a prolific writer and felt compelled to use words to convey his ideas, but he always preferred to write about an experience after he had actually acted it out.

In the period 1908–17 Moreno wrote a few essays and booklets. All of them reflect aspects of Moreno's philosophy and follow 'actual' experiences. For example, he wrote about his experience with children after he had tried all kinds of different games with them; he published 'The Godhead as Comedian' after his confrontation with an actor (see below).

During the period that we are dealing with, a series of three booklets was published under the title *Invitation to an Encounter* and under the name Jacob Levy. Other essays, 'Homo Juvenis', 'The Realm of Children', and 'The Godhead as Comedian', were apparently first published anonymously between 1908 and 1911, but were never found: they resurfaced as parts of other publications at a later date.

The first of Moreno's publications are simple, almost naïve tales, but in them one can already see the dominant themes to come. If we take, for example, the text 'The Godhead as Comedian or Actor' we can see in it the origins of what Moreno was to call *axiodrama*. In this book an actor, confronted with himself, has to give up the role that he is playing; beyond the immediate shock felt by the actor, it is the whole idea of the theatre that Moreno is questioning here. Axiodrama is really a preliminary stage in the development of sociodrama and psychodrama.[23] Through criticism of the generally accepted values of society, leading to the abolition of *cultural conserves* in the fields of religion, politics, and the arts, its aim is to get back to a more spontaneous stage of expression. Moreno eventually wrote an axiodramatic trilogy, adding 'The Godhead as Orator or Preacher' and 'The Godhead as Author.'

In 1911 Moreno was in a very active period of his life. He was working hard at his medical studies, was very much involved with his friends in the Religion of Encounter group, and was spending time with children in the parks of Vienna. His direct and confrontational approach to life led to further activity and, in turn, to further developments in his thinking. One day he entered a theatre with a friend: the play being presented was *Thus Spake Zarathustra*, based on Nietzsche's book of that name. Moreno and his friend stopped the actor who was about to play Zarathustra and objected that nobody but Zarathustra himself could play the role. The director of the play and the author rapidly came to the defence of the actor. Finally Moreno announced that they were witnessing the end of traditional theatre and that the time as ripe for the birth of the only real theatre in which every actor would play himself, not a role. The police were called in, Moreno and his friend went before a judge, and they had to promise not to interfere again in other people's plays. This is one version of the story; another version, saying that this incident that happens at a play put on by Moreno himself for the children in the Augarten, is less dramatic, but the basic scenario remains the same.

It was this story that formed the basis of the protocol, 'The Godhead as Comedian or Actor,' first published, perhaps in 1911 but definitely in 1919, in the journal *Daimon*. The protocol is interesting in both presentation and content and gives us some of Moreno's basic thinking. Moreno wanted to do away with the artificial roles that people play; he confronted them, urging them to abandon their masks and to present their real 'selves'. He did this with the actor from the play as a metaphor of a much larger social problem to be solved.

He was later to take the same approach with other representatives of the social and religious hierarchy.[24] Axiodrama as an idea was born and experienced. It was to be a favourite tool of the expressionist movement, in the sense that old ways have to be abandoned to create a new society, a new world.

There are two additional comments to be made here. Moreno was a student and admirer of Socrates and in these protocols he uses the Socratic method of discussion. He even reminds us of the story about Socrates going to the theatre to confront the person who was playing his role. We have in the protocol of 'The Godhead as Comedian' a superb example of how the young Moreno adapted Socrates' method of teaching and was already able to use some *role reversal*, putting himself in the role of Zarathustra's 'self'.[25]

We should perhaps also compare how Moreno treated the actor who played someone else's role with his treatment of Freud: in both cases there was the same criticism, the same confrontation. Moreno was to criticize Freud for his inability to let his real 'self' out in the open.[26]

We now come to another publication, *Invitation to an Encounter*, published in three parts from 1914–15.

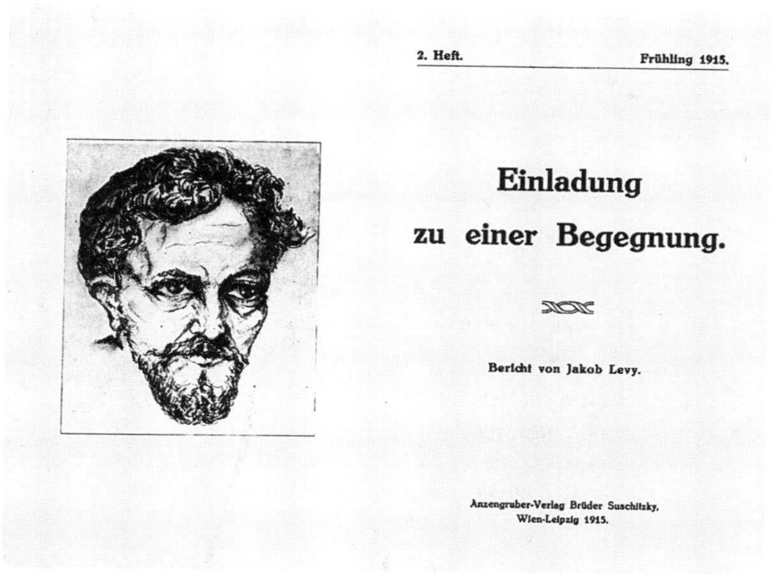
2. Heft.
Frühling 1915.
Einladung
zu einer Begegnung.
Bericht von Jakob Levy.
Anzengruber-Verlag Brüder Suschitzky,
Wien-Leipzig 1915.

Figure 6 Sketch of Moreno by Johannes Fischer on the title page of the 1915 edition of *Invitation to an Encounter, Part 2*. (Photograph by Claude Demers.)

These three small booklets represent the totality of Moreno's philosophy up to 1915. He published the first in the spring of 1914, the second in the spring of 1915, and the third in the autumn of the same year. They contain a number of essays and poems, including 'The Realm of Children' and 'Homo Juvenis', a philosophical text that presents a cycle that goes from birth to old age. We also find a text on 'Silence' and 'The Philosophy of Silence'. It is in the second booklet that we find the poem that was to become Moreno's 'motto' and also be the origin of Moreno's controversy with Martin Buber:

More important than science is its result.
One answer provokes a hundred questions.

More important than poetry is its result,
one poem invokes a hundred heroic acts.

More important than recognition is its result,
the result is pain and guilt.

More important than procreation is the child.
More important than evolution of creation is the
evolution of the creator.

In the place of the imperative steps the imperator.
In the place of the creative steps the creator.
A meeting of two: eye to eye, face to face,
And when you are near I will tear your eyes out
and place them in place of mine,
and you will tear my eyes out
and will place them instead of yours,
then I will look at you with your eyes
and you will look at me with mine.

Thus even the common thing serves the silence and
our meeting remains the chainless goal:
The undetermined place, at an undetermined time,
the undetermined word to the undetermined man.
(*Invitation to an Encounter, Part* 2 1915: 2)

This poem is a good illustration of three ideas that are important to Moreno. The first is that the person is more important than what he produces: Moreno will repeat often that the creator is more important than his creation. From this perspective, he will take issue with Henri Bergson who had published *L'Evolution Créatrice* in 1906.[27]

The second idea has to do with a vivid representation of what will become Moreno's most important therapeutic technique, role reversal. Nowhere, it seems to me, was it expressed better than here: changing eyes, so that one can see the world from the other's point of view. Of course, we can argue that this process is still pretty rational and calls for only one sense, sight. It would be much stronger to say: 'I will tear your ears out, your nose, your skin, your guts . . .' and so on. But we do have here a sense of the process: to enter someone else's world, we have to change places in a very physical sense.

The third idea is the notion of 'meeting', of 'encounter'. Moreno has argued that Martin Buber, who wrote an article in the magazine *Der Neue Daimon* (see page 56) in 1919, was influenced by his own concept of 'Begegnung' (encounter) of 1914. It would be very interesting to establish the exact nature of the relationship between the two authors and clarify the extent of their mutual influence. There seems to be no historical basis for putting too much emphasis on direct influences. Buber's thinking developed gradually, but can be traced back to his own childhood. His contribution to the journal *Daimon* was minimal. But Moreno and Buber did have common friends and relations in the persons of Max Brod and Franz Werfel.

The two men also had a lot of other things in common. Both read Socrates, Dante, Kierkegaard, and Nietzsche. Both acknowledged the primacy of the original 'encounter': Moreno says that at the beginning was action and the group, while Buber says that at the beginning was the relationship. Both stress the necessity to alter the form taken by culture to arrive at a more 'fruitful chaos'. Both also stress the importance of 'experiencing' reality as a means of change rather than just talking about it. Both were highly emotional people, giving prime importance to the body: Buber, still smarting from the loss of his friend and companion Landauer forty-five years after his murder, told Carl Rogers: 'Now once more, I was compelled to imagine this killing, not only visually, but with my *body*.' Moreno, equally sensitive to bodily experience, developed the concept of *tele*.[28]

* * *

At this point we conclude our discussion of Moreno's nine years as a student, a period vital to the 'making' of the future sociometrist and psychotherapist.

Chapter 4
Marianne, Bad Vöslau, and the first promises

The end of the war left Moreno depressed and discouraged. He was now a doctor, a rather traditional one: he had cut off his beard, was earning a good living in the refugee camps, and was practising his trade. At the same time, as the war came to a close, like his compatriots he was in disarray: Austria was dismantled, there was a lack of direction in terms of the future of the country and everyone was trying to take advantage of any political leverage that was left. On a more personal basis, Chaim Kellmer was gone, and with him the idealism of 1909. The other members of the Religion of Encounter were scattered in different directions. The year 1918 was for Moreno an opportunity to take a good look at his own future. This depression did not last long — the man of action soon took over again — but before talking about this, let us go back to the Vienna that Moreno grew up in.

Vienna: 1880–1925

The Vienna that Moreno had known was a tapestry of contradictions. Moreno was born during the long reign of Emperor Franz Josef I (1848–1916), a reign that lasted longer than that of any other European monarch. Through the years Franz Josef became a symbol of longevity, but also of immobility. His own life was a succession of tragedies, even though a sense of duty to his people tended to mask this: his wife was assassinated, his son committed suicide, and, finally, the assassination of his nephew at Sarajevo was the occasion of the First World War.

Franz Josef was himself a traditionalist, but, politically opportunistic, he was not entirely averse to progress. In many ways, he was a 'rubber stamp' monarch responding to whichever political faction seemed dominant at any given time. In this way, he was able to remain in power, worshipped by the people, but assailed by the politicians. He always found room for compromise and superficial accommodation. This ability to govern in difficult times was praised by many, but more sensitive observers of the political scene like Robert Musil and Stefan Zweig foresaw that the disintegration of the empire was not far off.

The contradictions in the personality of the emperor were reflected at all political and cultural levels. At the same time as there were political changes giving more freedom to Jewish citizens, for example, a new social class began to practise anti-Semitism. Factions from all sides forced confrontations along the line of political and religious beliefs. But the political leaders of the time, and Franz Josef himself, had no wish to face this disturbing reality. While the social fabric of the country was slowly crumbling, it was still possible for the Viennese painter Makart to organize historical reconstructions and endless processions of allegorical floats. Even as political resentment brought the conflicts of communists or nationalists into their own palaces, the aristocracy were still waltzing to the music of the Strausses, father and son.

The empire, with its numerous nationalities and languages, could still pretend to a semblance of unity around its leader, but discontent and criticism were close to the surface. This was not overtly expressed since everyone tended to protect his own position and suffered from the national malaise often called 'Protektion': people had learned to perpetuate a system which, by use and abuse of personal influence, served their ends and guaranteed their survival. The important element was not what you did for your country or city, but who you knew and who could help you continue to take advantage of social and political leniency. In this context, the overall degeneration of Austrian institutions was only a matter of time, since discontent was bound to surface in one way or another. The redesign of the Vienna Ring and other massive architectural projects brought only temporary relief.[1]

In this system the Jewish population had a very special place. It was almost impossible for Jewish citizens to exert a direct influence politically as they were not allowed to attend military functions or hold high-level political appointments. In reality, however, they had considerable influence through journalism, arts, medicine, and commerce. Political leaders and many a citizen resented the Jews for their relative success and power. Even though the Jews were officially free citizens, harassment was frequent. Dedication and will power had put Jews at the top of the cultural, social, and musical scene; the liberal professions were their territory. In the city of Vienna, where they represented less than ten per cent of the population, more than half the medical students were

Jews. Jewish influence was also felt in law, journalism, and commerce.

The young Jacob Levy Moreno grew up in the second district of Vienna, the Jewish district: he was therefore identified as a Jew, even though, for philosophical reasons, he always made an effort to play this down. His family was not very active within the Sephardic community which represented only about five per cent of Jews in Vienna, small by all counts when compared with the much larger Ashkenazic community.[2]

While preparing to become a doctor, Moreno did not have in front of him a professional role model and embarked on his studies without expectations about his future career in the medical world of Vienna. His future method and place of practice were to be more in line with his own upbringing as the son of a merchant, offering a service to 'ordinary' people. During adolescence, Moreno also became very interested in philosophy, art, and the theatre: here again, he did not belong to any particular school of thought, but drifted in and out of groups, forging his own identity during the course of his encounters.

In the general context of life in Vienna at this time two fields are of particular interest to us in relation to Moreno: art and psychiatry.

In the field of art, it was people like Otto Wagner and Gustav Klimt who were to create a new movement aimed at regenerating culture in Austria and bringing Vienna into the circle of *art nouveau*. The movement was called 'Secession' and a building was designed for it by Josef Olbrich, 'using the form of a modernized temple to suggest the function of art as a surrogate religion for Vienna's secular intellectual elite'. The motto of the group was: 'To the age its art, to art its freedom.' The group succeeded in getting the emperor to open the house officially and preside over the first exhibition. The creation of the movement was a turning point in the development of the arts in Vienna and the Olbrich building became a gathering place for artists, along with the Café Museum not far away.[3]

Similar initiatives had already been taken in other areas. In the political arena, in late 1870, 'Jung-Wien' was the name chosen by rebels of the new left. 'Jung-Wien' was also the name chosen by a new literary movement set up to challenge the moralistic values of the nineteenth century: the movement called for an adherence to authentic sociological and psychological truth, and for a greater openness in society, especially in the area of sexual mores. Above all it seemed that the movement called for the 'death' and replacement of the 'fathers' by rebellious 'sons'. Plays by Schnitzler, Wedekind, and Strindberg were to echo these themes.

The revolt came later in the field of architecture and painting, probably because of the numerous projects relating to the reconstruction of the

Ring boulevard. These projects took much of the time and energy of artists, but by the mid-nineties the Secession movement was born. The poster announcing the first exhibition was designed by Klimt: it showed Theseus, symbol of youth, killing the Minotaur. Here again, the theme is destruction of a figure in the past and, indirectly, parricide. In the musical arena, the movement also had a protagonist in Gustav Mahler.

The first generation of 'Jung-Wien' drew from existing foreign ideals, as expressed by Nietzsche, Dostoievski, the impressionist school, and Rodin. The movement may already have been too institutionalized. For the extremists, it compromised too much with tradition, but for the classicists it had already broken away too far.

More radicalism was to follow. In painting and architecture the leaders were Oskar Kokoschka, Egon Schiele, and Adolf Loos; in music, Arnold Schoenberg, Anton von Webern, and Alban Berg; in literature and poetry, Franz Kafka, Franz Werfel, Peter Altenberg, and Heinrich Mann. Above all, Karl Kraus was the epitome of the critic who will not compromise with anyone. This new movement embraced the creed of subjectivism, and called for the representation of life as it is experienced in the 'here and now': it is most often referred to as expressionism. This term covers a wide spectrum of artists' work. It was a call for a new ethic and aesthetic to project a vision of a new world that would encompass the needs of everyone.[4]

Even though the young Moreno always defies categorization, it is clear that he was close to many of those who were proposing this new order of things. He had many friends who were to be part of the expressionist movement.

Let us now turn to psychiatry. Revolution in this field began with the work of Philippe Pinel (1745–1826) which for the first time gave proper status to mental illness and pioneered the humane treatment of the insane. This could only have happened in a time and space open to a reforming spirit which soon spread. The mental patient was no longer classified as a criminal and much was needed to understand his inner world.

In Vienna much of the research work was done by neurologists. Theodore Meynert (1833–92), a leading European histopathologist, identified many of the structures lying deep within the brain and proposed a systematic classification of mental illness based on his studies. He was later criticized and accused of creating 'brain mythology'; he was also one of Freud's teachers. Another teacher of the future founder of psychoanalysis was Richard von Krafft-Ebing (1840–1902) who described aberrations of the sexual drive in his *Psychopathia Sexualis* (1886). With the Englishman, Havelock Ellis (1859–1939), and the Swiss, Auguste Forel (1848–1931), Krafft-Ebing contributed to the growing awareness of man's emotional and instinctual life.

Meanwhile, in Germany, Emil Kraepelin (1856–1926), a student of Wundt, had started the tremendous task of classifying mental illness. He gathered thousands of case histories and from them evolved a system of descriptive psychiatry. His treatise (*Lehrbuch*) was first published in 1883 and went to nine editions until 1927, when it came out in two volumes with a total of 2,500 pages. Kraepelin's classification did not address the question of the psychodynamic development of mental illness, nevertheless it became the bible for generations of psychiatrists, including Moreno's professors.

In Paris, Jean-Martin Charcot (1825–93) studied hypnotism and hysteria. Even though Charcot maintained that hysteria was caused by a weakness in the nervous system, he was able to demonstrate that it could be cured by psychological means. This was a breakthrough that would later be picked up and developed by Freud.

The psychiatry taught at the University of Vienna had nothing revolutionary about it in the 1880s. It was still rooted in neurology. Even the contemporary of Freud, Julius Wagner von Jauregg (1857–1940), used an approach essentially rooted in neurological research and aimed at the disappearance of symptoms. It was left to Sigmund Freud (1856–1939) to bring about a second psychiatric revolution by giving back to the patient his right to speak. Freud's conceptualization of the unconscious, enabled him to interpret thought processes and behaviour from a psychodynamic perspective, based on an understanding of repression and other defence mechanisms.

The development of psychoanalysis extended over a period of about thirty years, and it took decades before it became acceptable in Vienna, but Freud's theories were not disconnected from the world he lived in. Vienna, the world of people like Robert Musil, Arthur Schnitzler, Stefan Zweig, and Gustav Klimt, was a world of Victorian values where façade was still predominant. Like the writers and artists around him, Freud, in his own way, set out to bring about a much truer representation of the self. The importance that he gave to the interpretation of dreams and the focus that he put on psychosexual development were a breakthrough in the treatment of mental illness and in understanding human behaviour. The findings of psychoanalysis came as a shock and a threat, even to Freud's closer colleagues. The professors at the faculty of medicine, with a few exceptions like Otto Pötzl, ridiculed him and put psychoanalysis aside. Eventually, however, the theories of psychoanalysis began to gain ground and, perhaps not surprisingly, first became popular with philosophers, artists, and writers, who avidly read *The Interpretation of Dreams* long before the medical profession. As a medical student in 1910, Moreno had not heard much good about psychoanalysis. However, he made friends with many psychoanalysts, including Helene Deutsch, Paul Schilder, Theodor Reik, and the dissident Alfred Adler.[5]

The *Daimon*

During the war Moreno had developed an interest in literature and regularly visited some of the well-known cafés patronized by the young intellectuals of the time. At the Café Herrenhof he met a group of writers who, like himself, needed a forum to express their vision of the world. The group was a loose-knit association of poets, philosophers, and sociologists. They were all dismayed by the war and its consequences and were also desperately looking for alternatives to the disintegrating society in which they found themselves. It was in this context that the idea of a new journal took shape. The group itself did not have a leader. Most of the participants, all men, were to drift in and out, partly because they had other commitments, but also because of their wide ranging interests and geographical dispersion. They came from Czechoslovakia, Hungary, and Austria. The journal they created was called the *Daimon*.

There was no core group to the *Daimon* circle, even though some individuals were to cooperate on different projects. Franz Werfel, the writer, was often associated with Blei, the poet; Fritz Lampl was a close friend of Friedrich Kiesler; Max Brod was the intimate of Franz Kafka; Emil Rheinhardt was often seen with Arthur Schnitzler; Alfred Adler, then an active member of the Socialist party, was associated with Moreno's former professor, Julius Tandler. Every member of the *Daimon* group had his own social circle or, to use Moreno's terminology, his *social atom*. It was a network of almost all the intellectuals of Austria at that time.

Moreno himself was in touch with most of those who contributed to the ferment of ideas during the war and after. However, even though he was part of the intellectual circle in Vienna, in some respects he remained an outsider. There were two reasons for this: first, during the war he spent a lot of time in the practice of medicine and, when not working, would try to forget the war and enjoy himself; second, Moreno was never quite at ease within intellectual circles — he was a man of action who rapidly became impatient with people who spent so much time discussing ideas. This was a paradox in someone who was about to create a journal that had nothing to do with concrete action, but paradox was an essential part of Moreno.

In February 1918 the first issue of the journal was published. The title, *Daimon*, was taken from Socrates. The Greek word 'daimon' can mean both a good and evil spirit; it also refers to an individual's genius. The daimon is every individual's 'interior double', his inspiration and secret adviser. The daimon, associated with the creative power of the individual, allows a person to transcend rules, enabling him to achieve greater knowledge and bring about a new order in the world. The title chosen for the new journal thus succinctly expressed the aspirations of its founders.

What exactly was the role of Moreno in founding this journal? He was its editor, and in this capacity did a lot of the necessary 'running around' between publishing houses and authors. In many ways he was the organizing force behind the project. However, it seems that no intellectual leadership was assumed, either by Moreno or any other contributor. There were two centres from which the articles originated, Vienna and Prague. (Max Brod lived in Prague and so did Franz Werfel at that time.)

The journal was published for five years and appeared under different names: in 1918 as *Daimon*, in 1919 as *Der Neue Daimon*, and from 1920 as *Die Gefährten*. The structure was changed in 1919 when the journal became a 'collective' of six owners: Jacob Levy Moreno, Alfred Adler, Fritz Lampl, Albert Ehrenstein, Hugo Sonnenschein, and Franz Werfel. During the period of its existence, the journal was able to obtain contributions from the best known writers of Austria and Europe. The list is very impressive, and includes Max Brod, Gütersloh, Emil A. Rheinhardt, Friedrich Schnack, Jakob Wassermann, Franz Werfel, Franz Blei, Paul Claudel, Blaise Pascal, Iwan Goll, Egon Wellesz, André Suarès, Martin Buber, Ernst Bloch, Fritz Lampl, Ernst Weiss, Oskar Kokoschka, Heinrich Mann.[6]

Moreno was mainly involved in the founding of the journal and its first two years. During that time, he was directly and indirectly in touch with all the leading intellectuals of Vienna and Europe. In spite of this, he remained an observer of the literary scene and never felt at ease in a world he was soon to leave.

What did Moreno himself contribute to the journal? By 1918 he had published a few articles and was now looking for a vehicle for his ideas. In fact, the publication of the *Daimon* produced hardly any new major work from Moreno, except *Das Testament des Vaters* (The Words of the Father) in 1920. But it gave him a public and an audience as never before. He published, for example, the three protocols: 'The Godhead as Author', 'The Godhead as Preacher' and 'The Godhead as Comedian'. These three early texts are classics and very good illustrations of axiodramatic protocols. He also reproduced part of *Invitation to an Encounter*, 'Homo Juvenis', and 'The Realm of Children'. Looking at Moreno's publications at this time, we can see how he was reconnecting with the mystical aspect of his personality.

This period in Moreno's life is very important: it is a period of clarification, of consolidation. The young doctor could easily have chosen to enter the world of poets and writers on a permanent basis. His connections with Wellesz brought him close to Schoenberg, his relationship with Kokoschka and Werfel could have introduced him to Alma Mahler. But Moreno was uneasy with the world of intellectuals and artists and slowly he drifted away. Some controversies were to contribute and accelerate his departure (see page 81).

Before returning to Moreno's medical career, two points should be noted. First, Moreno is now using the name Jacob Moreno Levy, integrating his father's first name, Moreno, with his own. Second, setting up the *Daimon* is only one example of Moreno's activities as an originator and creator at this time: he had already founded the House of Encounter, and in future was to create publishing houses, journals, professional associations, a hospital, two theatres, training institutes . . . Moreno was like the orchestral conductor who can play all the instruments at his disposal, but, as we shall see, he lacked the patience to become a virtuoso of most of them.

Bad Vöslau and Marianne

After the war Moreno was free to start his medical practice. He showed no particular inclination as yet for the field of psychiatry and psychotherapy. His short experience at the Steinhof hospital for the mentally ill had been disappointing; patients were treated by medication and no attention was given to their feelings — Steinhof was not a place for treatment, but for 'confinement'. Even the meeting with Freud failed to ignite an interest in psychoanalysis.[7] From a philosophical standpoint, Moreno's interests as a doctor at this time lay in family practice. At the same time, as we have seen, he was involved with artists and writers, a part-time practitioner in two areas.

His first position as a doctor was that of a health officer in Kottingbrunn. After a few months he moved to Bad Vöslau, again as health officer, and was appointed by the mayor as medical director of the local textile industry, the Kammgarkfabric. Bad Vöslau is situated about forty kilometres south of Vienna. Moreno rented a house there from the city council, at 4 Maithal Street, from which he could see the beautiful valley of Vöslau. The basement was connected with the wine cellars of the Schlumberger company, and a plaque indicates that it was on this site that the first bottle of Austrian champagne was produced. The baths from which the city takes its name, famous throughout Europe, were a few yards from Moreno's house. It was here that Mozart's wife, Constanze, came to take the waters and for psychological rest.

Moreno was appointed by the city of Vöslau on 17 October 1919. The mayor, Franz Pexa, was a social democrat and a factor in the appointment must have been Moreno's friendship with socialists such as Franz Werfel and Alfred Adler. At first Moreno had an easy time with the city council, but Franz Pexa soon left office and the new mayor was less cooperative.

In Bad Vöslau, Moreno resumed his role of an extraordinary man. He was receiving a salary from the textile mills and the city and had plenty of money, so he decided not to charge for his services to the people of the town. He visited people in their homes, making himself available at all times, especially to the poor. He soon had a reputation for achieving miracles. Luck and dedication helped him to be very successful at first; as word spread, people started to come to Vöslau from further afield to see the 'Wunderdoctor'.

However, Moreno's skills did not extend to delivering babies; for this aspect of his medical practice he had to make a special arrangement with another doctor in the town. Neither was he successful in an attempt to introduce radiotherapy into his practice for which he bought an expensive X-ray machine. He was refused permission to use the equipment and told that he did not have the expertise to conduct that kind of treatment. Family practice was beginning to look less attractive, but let us go back to Moreno's first months in Bad Vöslau.

Shortly after his arrival an important event took place: he met a young woman by the name of Marianne Lörnitzo. She was a Catholic, dedicated to her family, and engaged to a young Vöslauer. She was also an energetic teacher. When Moreno saw her in the street, he loved her at first sight. When, a few weeks later, she came to consult him for a minor medical problem, the two felt very strongly drawn towards each other. She soon became his medical assistant, his secretary, his lover, and above all his muse. Not since his infatuation with his mother and his platonic romance with Pia had Moreno felt this kind of love.

Figure 7 Photograph of the house at 4 Maithal Street. At the bottom is the entrance to the wine cellar where the first Austrian champagne was made. (Photograph by Veronika Andorfer.)

Figure 8 Marianne Lörnitzo. Photograph taken at the entrance to 4 Maithal Street. (Gertrude and Veronika Selb, private collection; rephotographed by Peter Selb and Claude Demers.)

Marianne, like Dante's Beatrice, became Moreno's *raison de vivre*. She moved in to 4 Maithal Street and for a while the two were completely bound up in each other. Moreno did not go as often to Vienna and drifted away from the *Daimon* group. The year 1920 saw him enjoying Vöslau and his romance with Marianne. The relationship was not a typical love affair. Here is how Moreno described it:

When I went to Vöslau I became celibate again. The Godplayer was again ascendent. The intense sexuality I had felt and experienced during the war was put behind me. All of the lovely, gentle young women I had relationships with had never entered into my real, my very complicated lovelife. They did not touch my life as a Godplayer. I had gone through periods of intense sexual activity followed by periods of celibacy before. But what I really wanted was a woman who would put up with my fantastic utopian ideas, one who would love me both physically and spiritually, a Muse.

Most women would not accept the physical lover and the Godplayer as well. To some, I was a confused lover. To others, I was a confused Godplayer. Gradually I began to realize that I was not a unique case. There have been many men before me who have tried to play a double game, who have gone through similar comedies and tragedies of love. I have heard about many extraordinary men, although I do not intend to compare myself with them, who looked for women who could fulfill the two functions at the same time, to be a man's lover and to be a Godplayer's lover; to bear him children, as all women try to do, and to help him produce children of a different sort, paintings, sculptures, poems, books, inventions. And I heard that a name was given to such women, Muse, the goddess or the power regarded as the source of inspiration to the poet. I heard of Dante's Beatrice. I heard of Tasso's Princess, rich and beautiful, young and unhappy, a native of Florence, who enjoyed helping him write those great poems of eternity. I heard of Petrarch's Laura, and of many others, usually women of noble birth or noble character who were, perhaps, themselves confused, themselves playing two roles.

The Godplayer makes two demands of his Muse, that she makes love to him physically and that she makes love to him spiritually. She must be a woman and a Goddess in one. I found, after many trials and errors, that such women are very rare, but it was only they who could fulfill me. Only they could make my life meaningful. In other words, the Godplayer, to become real, has to find a muse. Otherwise he becomes a frustrated failure. Only two or three of the women I have known in my lifetime gave my search as a Godplayer some concrete anchorage. Without them I would have failed.

Then I found another such rare creature when I was in Vöslau.

('Autobiography' 1985: ch. 7: 8)

Moreno goes to some length to describe his relationship with Marianne. There is no doubt that she was instrumental (and perhaps the word is too weak) in making Moreno refocus on what he had perceived as his mission in his encounter with Jesus in the park at Chemnitz. The next few years were very productive for Moreno, both in trying out new methods and in developing new ideas: the presence of Marianne played a major role in helping him recapture the ideals of his youth.

In 1920, Moreno's existential megalomania 'ripened and came to fruition'[8] when messianic fever overtook him again, to be expressed in a book called *Das Testament des Vaters* (The Words of the Father).

This work seems to have come at the end of a long process for Moreno. He admits that as a child he heard voices. He had always kept this secret, thinking that people might laugh at him or find it 'abnormal', but sharing the 'secret' with Marianne he found her very sympathetic. Not only did she see nothing wrong with him, she even shared some of her own inner 'voices'. After a while, Marianne and Jacob came to think 'in harmony'. They would both hear 'voices'. They would both expect the 'voices' to come. Their life started to revolve around this 'inner and mutual experience'.

Moreno talked about this experience as a rebirth and as the experience that finally gave his philosophy its coherence. It is interesting that he needed the presence of a woman beside him to 'give birth' to, and to finally come to terms with, his philosophy of spontaneity and creativity, a philosophy which came to fruition within an 'encounter' with a woman. Here is his own way of expressing it:

> I suddenly felt reborn, I began to hear voices, not as a mental patient does, but as one who feels that he can hear a voice that reaches all beings and speaks to all beings in the same language, a language that is understood by all men, gives us hope, gives us direction, gives our cosmos direction and meaning. The universe is not just a jungle or a bundle of wild forces. It is, basically, infinite creativity. And this infinite creativity which is true on all levels of existence, whether on the physical, social or biological, whether it is in our galaxy or in other galaxies far away from us, whether it is in the past or in the present or the future, ties us together. We are all bound to one another by responsibility for all things. There is no limited, no partial responsibility. And our responsibility makes us, automatically co-creators of the world . . . .
>
> It was in such a mood of utter inspiration that I rushed into

the house in the Valley of May. The only thing I heard was a voice, words, words, coming, going through my head. I didn't have the patience to sit and write them all down. I grabbed one red pencil after another, went into the top room of the house near the tower and began to write upon the walls. I wrote all the words I heard, all the words which were spoken aloud by myself:

O open yourself
Valley of May
To the One who created you.

Delightful gifts
I bring to you.
Flamings herbs,
Dreaming dark green,
Moon-white treetrunks
In the forest.

Upon your hill
The house of stone,
New twigs and hedgerows,
Full of new wine . . .

What happened to Marianne and me during those days of revelation is deeply impressed upon my mind. . . .

Marianne and I waited night after night to hear the voice. Then, one night, we heard the Voice singing more clearly than we had heard it before. It was as if God was communicating to us from infinite horizons. . . .

I walked down the hill, up the hill, stimulated by the scent of flowers and the silent air wanderings of the nightbirds. I was marching through space and space was marching through me, on and on and on, no stop. Millions of other people were marching through space at the same time, on and on and on, no stop. It was as if the universe was in movement in an unlimited number of dimensions. Wherever I turned a new dimension would open up. I saw sky, stars, planets, oceans, forests, mountains, cities, animals, fishes, birds, flies, protozoa, stones and hundreds of other things. Then I saw each opening its mouth, each man, each tree, each stone, each particle of the universe shouting in unison:

I AM GOD,
THE FATHER,
THE CREATOR OF THE UNIVERSE.

THESE ARE MY WORDS,
THE WORDS OF THE FATHER.

HOW CAN ONE THING
CREATE ANOTHER THING
UNLESS THE OTHER THING
CREATES THE ONE THING?
HOW CAN A FIRST THING
CREATE A SECOND THING
UNLESS THE SECOND THING
ALSO CREATES THE FIRST? . . .
HOW CAN A FATHER BEGET A SON
UNLESS THE SON
ALSO BEGETS HIS FATHER? . . .

THE FIRST CREATED THE LAST
AND THE END CREATED THE BEGINNING.
I CREATED THE WORLD
THEREFORE MUST I HAVE CREATED MYSELF.

I AM THE FATHER
AND NO ONE IS MY FATHER.
I AM THE CREATOR
AND NO ONE IS MY CREATOR.
I AM GOD
AND NO ONE IS MY PROPHET.

I AM NOT YOUR GOD.
I AM GOD.
I AM NOT THIS NATION'S GOD.

NOR THAT NATION'S GOD.
I AM GOD.
I AM NOT THE GOD OF THIS CLASS
OR OF THAT CLASS,
I AM GOD.

I AM NOT CALLED BY NAME.
I AM.

I AM
ONLY TO CREATE,
ONLY TO CREATE YOU.

I AM UNNAMED.
I ONLY AM TO BE.
I WAS UNNAMED
UNTIL YOU SPOKE TO ME . . .

('Autobiography' 1985: ch. 7: 58–65; *The Words of the Father*, new ed. 1971: 49–57)

This was the beginning of the long poem that Moreno first published in *Die Gefährten* of 1920 under the title: 'Das Testament des Vaters'.

To this day, this book remains the most fascinating that Moreno wrote: fascinating because of the philosophy that he preached, a philosophy of co-creativity and co-responsibility; also fascinating because of the way it was written — clearly it came into being like a child, needing the help of a mother and a midwife. It was the logical conclusion of Moreno's childhood and adolescence, a long search for life's meaning and a truthful representation of the universe. If we read this book as an expression of a philosophy of the cosmos, we find in it the concepts of Moreno's future theories: surplus-reality, spontaneity, co-responsibility and co-creation, creation as an on-going process, 'encounter' of I and You as the basis for significant meetings. At the beginning was action, at the beginning was the group, says Moreno. At the beginning was the relationship, says Buber. All of this is exemplified here in *The Words of the Father*, starting with the role of women in Moreno's life: in addition to being the poet's inspiration, his muse, Marianne was in many ways a mother, a midwife who allowed the words to be spoken. She was also the significant other through whom Moreno could 'be': the creator of a new 'dynasty' could not exist without a woman . . . 'I was unnamed until you spoke to me.'

We cannot ignore the central theme of the father in this book. We know that the name Moreno was the first name of Jacob Levy's father and that it means the 'teacher'. Up to the end of his university years, Moreno always signed his name 'Jacob Levy'. When he created the *Daimon* and moved to Vöslau, he started to integrate the given name of his father, 'Moreno', with his own and signed himself 'Jacob Moreno Levy'. Slowly, as his father disappeared from his life, Jacob started to 'take his place'. He would adopt his father's name definitively only after Moreno Nissim Levy's death. The book is published anonymously in

1920, even though it is evident even in *Die Gefährten* that it has been written by Jacob *Moreno* Levy. In the book, there is a symbolic attempt by Moreno to become his own father. It is a call to all readers to believe that they will become someone only when they realize and take responsibility for their own creativity and involvement in the cosmos. To do this it is necessary to look at our origins in a different way, acknowledging that we are already a part of them: we are the roots, the tree, and its fruits. Transposing this to the level of reality, one wonders about the place of the biological father in Moreno's life: at times, he claims that his father was the 'real' Moreno; elsewhere, he sees himself as the creator of a new dynasty. Paradox, ambivalence, confusion? There are probably all of these in Moreno's mind, making some people wonder who this man really was who wrote *The Words of the Father*. Enemies, especially, were quick to talk about narcissism and megalomania.

In addition to publishing this poem in *Die Gefährten*, Moreno also published *Das Testament des Vaters* with his new publisher, Kiepenheuer, in Potsdam. He also started a new collection with Kiepenheuer, *Verlag des Vaters*. It clearly showed the obsession Moreno had with the theme of the father, his 'paternity syndrome'.

The Words of the Father can be read and understood from different perspectives. First, it represents Moreno's new effort to disseminate his ideas about religion. This can be explained if we remember Moreno's vision of being a new saviour. In Bad Vöslau, he even recreated a new religion of encounter and had his own followers. He apparently accosted a Catholic priest in front of his church and said he should preach on the street: this story was later published in 'The Godhead as Preacher'. The incident created quite an uproar and was instrumental in isolating him and Marianne from the majority of the community. The confrontation with the priest, as before with the actor and with God himself, was quite typical of Moreno. It was what he himself called axiodrama, a direct confrontation with *cultural conserves*.[8]

The book can also be seen as an expression of Moreno's philosophy about man and nature: we are all gods, creators and co-creators of the never-finished universe. Let us create with joy, energy, and spontaneity, and let imagination be the basis for action. Let everybody be creators in their own right. It does not have to be in the realm of children, poets, or scientists — everyone has a place on this planet, a place from which he can be and act as creator. This kind of thinking was the same that Moreno put to Freud earlier, and was to become the basis of his psychological theories.

The Words of the Father still raises questions today: some of Moreno's disciples see this book as the most important he ever wrote, others are quite uneasy about it. Moreno's enemies quote it as a proof of his lack of mental equilibrium. It seems fair to acknowledge that the book was written in a great state of excitement, probably bordering on loss of touch with reality. This does not mean that its content is without value. The book might make sense in itself, and need not to bring about the disturbance it once created among psychiatrists. Put in its proper context, it may, in fact, be the best way that Moreno found to transmit his message, which does not exclude a temporary loss of 'boundaries' on his part. Following Swedenborg's example, Moreno, the doctor of medicine, was allowing his inner 'voices' to speak, in an attempt to unite religion and science. Later, when developing his philosophy in the United States, Moreno was to insist on the importance of this revolutionary task of integrating religion and science.

Let us now return to Moreno's life in Bad Vöslau. Moreno was quite a disturbing figure and we can imagine how unsettling it must have been for people in a small town like Bad Vöslau to understand a man who spoke the words of God, 'stole' a young woman from her fiancé, and entertained friends like Peter Altenberg or Elisabeth Bergner. The bourgeois citizens of Bad Vöslau, many of whom were active in pro-Nazi groups, did find the young doctor disturbing; his natural allies were the workers, mainly communists. His Jewishness aggravated the situation and made life quite difficult for Marianne. Conflict became inevitable. On one occasion, as Moreno was waiting for a train in Baden with Marianne, a group of youths surrounded them. One youth came close up to Moreno and with disdain called him a Jew. We know how Moreno considered himself a citizen of the world, a cosmic person, but at this moment he could only feel an intense identification with his Jewish heritage. After knocking down his opponent, he looked him right in the eye, and then into the eyes of the crowd. No-one challenged him. He left on the train and the day after was the talk of the town, worshipped by his followers, hated more than ever by his enemies.

* * *

During this period Moreno was still practising as a family doctor. He had a reputation as a doctor who cared for his patients and who used an original approach to treatment. In or around 1921, he met a patient who was instrumental in teaching him something about mental health. As Moreno looked back many years later, he saw that this patient may have represented a turning point in his career and his subsequent decision to become a psychotherapist. The incident occurred at a time when he was slowing down considerably in his general practice and his efforts to use radiotherapy were encountering considerable opposition.

The patient who came to see him was a wealthy, but unhappy man. He wanted Moreno to help him die and asked him to be a partner in his suicide; he was even ready to make Moreno his heir. Moreno made it clear that, as a doctor, he dedicated his life to helping people live and feel better about themselves. He then started a course of therapeutic treatment, entering the man's inner world. For weeks they talked about planning death: the man wrote his last will, discussed at length different ways of killing himself, ate with renewed appetite knowing it might well be his last meal, and acted out different scenarios. He did this with the help of Moreno and Marianne; she was then what came to be called in psychodrama an *ego auxiliary*. The patient was the *protagonist*, and Moreno the *director*. Moreno talked about this patient as his first 'residential patient'. It is a beautiful illustration of the techniques of *psychodrama*. The patient spent many weeks in Vöslau, living in a local hotel.

Here, Moreno is giving psychodramatic treatment for the first time, and discovering the value of imaginary acting out: this was going to become an essential part of the future method. The fact that this man was able to act out every detail of his fantasy and have somebody direct him in his search, to do it in the presence of an audience (small as it was), determined the direction of his cure: somebody was ready to listen to him, to take his feelings seriously enough to have him represent them on a 'stage' and share with him afterwards. This experience contributed at firsthand to Moreno's knowledge about depression and its cure. It also gave him confidence in the kind of intervention he was making almost intuitively, contrary to the popular principles of psychotherapy at that time, in which acting out, even on a stage, was considered detrimental to the patient. This case, instructive as it was, did not immediately persuade Moreno to take up psychotherapy systematically.[10]

However, at this time, Moreno often helped families in difficulty by discussing their problems and possible solutions openly with them, repeating his experience with the prostitutes in Vienna. He called this spontaneous approach *theatre reciproque*. Moreno would use his own office or go to people's homes in order to explore new ways of emerging from difficult psychological situations. He would call upon members of the immediate family and the larger community. He would re-enact situations that had initially brought pain, and found that the re-enactment leads to de-dramatization and that liberation often occurs through laughter. This observation was in line with that of Karl Marx who also suggested that tragedies could seem much lighter, even funny at times, if they are repeated.[11] *Theatre reciproque* is based on systems theory and is an ancestor of family and community therapy. This kind of intervention is a mixed breed between psychotherapy, religious beliefs, and a sense of community. It is connected with the Religion of Encounter where everyone felt a responsibility for the group. Here again, we see Moreno exploring a field with no preconceived model. A man of action and intuition, he is able to produce 'miracles' in the eyes of the community, without yet being able to systematize his work.[12]

Moreno had, in addition to intuition, tremendous charisma. He had a way of looking at people, a way of touching them, that made many of them instant believers, but, of course, many remained sceptical. He repeated as a doctor what had happened earlier with the children: children either liked him or were scared of him. Even in Bad Vöslau, many children feared Moreno, probably reflecting the fears of their parents. But where the charisma worked it increased people's confidence in Moreno and was in itself often sufficient to bring about a cure. Moreno became for some people a 'miracle man', provoking jealousy among other doctors. In the same way that parents and teachers had started to spread rumours in Vienna in 1911, local doctors began to say that Moreno was not a 'real doctor'. These tales were enhanced by the fact that Moreno was not using official papers to prescribe drugs and refused, in line with his philosophy of anonymity, to put up an official doctor's plate outside his house. After a while, he had a sign displaying his medical diploma from the University of Vienna placed at the entrance to his office. This demonstration *après-coup* that he was telling the truth reinforced his authority among his patients, but enraged his enemies.[13]

By 1921 Moreno's position as a doctor in Bad Vöslau was controversial. He was treating patients without asking for money, visiting them in their homes and using very unorthodox methods. He was not involved in politics even though he was the appointee of a socialist mayor. He lived with a young Catholic teacher who had left her job in order to share his life and ideals. Not content with upsetting the cherished values of the citizens in all kinds of ways, he was also mixing with some very eccentric people from Vienna.[14] Bad Vöslau was confused.

The world of spontaneous theatre

Meanwhile, Moreno was again abandoning the traditional field of medicine to enter, or re-enter, the realm of theatre. This time he was to work not with children, but with adults and traditional theatre people. As we saw, Moreno was quite active in the literary world of Vienna from 1917 to 1920. He created the *Daimon*, a journal to which *avant-garde* poets and writers contributed. However, even though he acted as editor, he was never considered part of the literary 'establishment', even the new one. There were probably many reasons for this: he was living in a small town, and could not, like many other writers, meet in cafés every night; he was not at ease with many of the poets, novelists, and painters who were practising their art full-time; he was still struggling to find his own path, away from writing, closer to action; he was still refusing to be identified by a name, still agonizing over his choice of anonymity; and, perhaps, he had to face the fact that among people like Brod, Werfel, Wassermann, Blei, and Kokoschka, his talent as a poet and a writer was limited. In any event, while the original group that had started the *Daimon* survived and extended, Moreno gradually moved away.

Instead, Moreno now became involved with a group of actors. The '*Daimon*' group was strictly for men, but this new group was made up of both actors and actresses. It met at the Café Museum, close to the opera house, the Cabaret Fledermaus, and the Secession building. The Café had been renovated by Adolf Loos and was often referred to as the 'Café Nihilismus' because the decorations had been reduced to the bare essentials.

Here Moreno met artists like Anna Höllering, Moissi, Alfred Polgar, a good friend of Elisabeth Bergner, and Ladislaus Löwenstein, who was later to be better known as Peter Lorre. Many people from the literary world also joined in: Fritz Lampl, Georg Kulka, Robert Müller, and Franz Werfel. The group met regularly starting in 1921. Moreno then suggested an initiative that was to prove both costly and instructive.

A few years after the war, Austria was still suffering from a lack of social and political leadership. Moreno thought that before regeneration, the country would have to go through a purification of ideas concerning the role of authority and leadership. The purification process would have to include everyone. Moreno envisaged a plan that would bring all kinds of people together in a truly democratic way. On 1 April 1921, he rented the Komödienhaus from Anna Höllering's father, its then director. (Anna Höllering was an actress who was to become famous in the psychodrama circle under the name of 'Barbara'.) Moreno's aim was to provoke the public into a debate about the future of Austria. From the announcement in the newspaper and the date chosen, it is not clear if Moreno really wanted that evening to be serious or not. After all, 1 April is All Fools' Day!

In any event, the theatre was packed with all kinds of people: dignitaries, politicians, regular theatre people, and friends of Moreno. Among them was Franz Werfel, a writer, living with Alma Mahler, but also one of the creators of the Red Brigades in 1918. He was an anarchist by temperament and had followers among university students and Viennese intellectuals. He came with a large group on the night of April 1st.

Moreno stood alone on the stage as the curtains opened. He was dressed as the king's jester. On the stage were a throne, a crown, and a purple mantle. Moreno introduced himself and told the audience that he was looking for the king. He was looking for the kind of person who does not crown himself, but emerges naturally from the crowd and whose wisdom makes him a natural choice as leader. He then invited people to come up on the stage, talk about their ideas of a leader, and to sit on the throne if they wished. Not being used to this kind of production, few people went up and the audience became impatient, irritated, and restless. Many left the theatre, especially the dignitaries. Werfel and his group were very supportive, but as a production the evening was a disaster. Moreno noted that 'nobody is a prophet on his own turf.' He was very disappointed.

From a historical standpoint, the evening of 1 April 1921 was the first demonstration of what Moreno called *sociodrama*. Sociodrama has been defined as 'a deep action method dealing with intergroup relations and collective ideologies'. Contrary to psychodrama, where the focus is on individual growth in and by the group, in sociodrama the real subject is the group's values and prejudices. It can be a small or a large group, or many sub-groups. The aim is to explore and solve problems that emerge between members of smaller units within a large group, or between groups. Sociodrama is also different from axiodrama which aims at the purging of *cultural conserves* and stereotypes within the individual.

In this actual sociodrama, Moreno attempted to find new organizational alternatives for Austrian people and to give power to every voice within the political and social spectrum. He failed, either because there was no will on the part of people to really look at everyone else's suggestions (meaning there was no will or readiness for role reversal), or because the neophyte sociodramatist, Moreno, overlooked the difficulty of leading such a big and heterogeneous crowd. But Moreno learned from the experience: he was to refine the technique and used it many times later.[15] This sociodrama was the predecessor to Moreno's involvement in the Vietnam war and international relations (see page 147).

For the time being, Moreno went back home rather discouraged. He lost many of his friends, especially writers and poets, who could not deal with the sarcasm of the press. It seems that Moreno had little contact, if any, after this with Franz Werfel, Oskar Kokoschka, or Franz Blei. These people had their own paths to follow in the more rareified circles led by Alma Mahler.

As Moreno became more distant from the literary group, he became closer to the stage fraternity. He already knew Anna Höllering, Georg Kulka, Robert Müller, and Peter Lorre. Others in the group were Hans Rodenberg, a friend of Fritz Lampl from the *Daimon* group, and Moissi and Robert Blum. Occasionally, when she was visiting Vienna, Elisabeth Bergner joined in.

This group was the original cast of the 'Stegreiftheater', or theatre of spontaneity. In addition to being involved with families in *theatre reciproque*, Moreno was interested in ridding the traditional theatre of its *cultural conserves*. He saw the creation of a theatre group as a way to achieve this. Later, he also created a revolutionary stage and wrote a book about his theatre concepts.

Let us talk first about the new theatre group. Sometime in 1922 Moreno rented space at 2 Maysedergasse in Vienna. This belonged to a women's group and was used to exhibit members' arts and craft work. The overall space, although it was divided into different rooms, was quite large and the main hall could hold between fifty and seventy-five people. This is where the new theatre group was to perform. The first presentation seems to have taken place in 1922. The group of actors put on spontaneous plays as suggested by the audience, did some public 're-enactments' of daily news using a technique called 'the living newspaper', or improvised on themes. Peter Lorre performed in an act of his own, soon to become a favourite of the audiences — 'How to catch a Louse.' This sketch, in addition to allowing Peter Lorre to make fun of people in the audience may have had a direct relationship to his original name, Ladis*laus* Löwenstein.

After a few weeks, and good reviews from the press, the theatre really took off. The auditorium was often packed and the audience learned to get involved. Moreno was the leader of the group and began to learn his trade as a director of 'psychodrama'. It was not yet called psychodrama, but the basic methods were in place. Psychodrama as a therapeutic technique evolved in a non-linear way, and its stages of development were often unexpected. In Moreno's life, we can trace many such stages, or 'cradles'. The first, dating back to the occasion when Moreno played God at the age of four in what he called 'The Psychodrama of the Fallen God' has often been mentioned. The second

Figure 9 Entrance to the Stegreiftheater, the sign above the door showing that the premises belonged (as they still do) to a women's group. The theatre remains very much as it was in Moreno's time. (Photograph by Veronika Andorfer.)

'cradle' can be related to his involvement with children in the parks of Vienna and the creation of the children's theatre. A third can be seen in Moreno's use of what he termed axiodrama, when for example, he challenged the priest to preach on the street and confronted the actor in the theatre. Then there is his first sociodrama in the Kömodienhaus, when Moreno invited different groups to go on stage and review their own social roles. There is also the work that Moreno did with families and communities, work that he called *theatre reciproque*. Finally, there is the individual psychodrama that took place in his office with the man who wished to commit suicide, with whom he achieved his first psychotherapeutic success.

But the real awareness of the therapeutic value of acting out a conflict on stage may well have come from his work with 'George' and 'Barbara'. Moreno presented this example many times, but let us repeat it once more to really grasp its historical value. In it one can see a clear 'passage' from the theatre of spontaneity to therapeutic theatre, another formative moment in the history of psychodrama:

> We had a young actress, Barbara, who worked for the theatre and also took part in a new experiment I had started, the extemporaneous, living newspaper. She was a main attraction because of her excellence in roles of ingenues, heroic and romantic roles. It was soon evident that she was in love with a young poet and playwright who never failed to sit in the first row, applauding and watching every one of her actions. A romance developed between Barbara and George. One day their marriage was announced. Nothing changed however, she remained our chief actress and he our chief spectator, so to speak. One day George came to me, his usually gay eyes greatly disturbed. 'What happened?' I asked him. 'Oh, doctor, I cannot bear it.' 'Bear what?' I looked at him, investigating. 'That sweet, angel-like being whom you all admire, acts like a bedevilled creature when she is alone with me. She speaks the most abusive language and when I get angry at her, as I did last night, she hits me with her fists.' 'Wait', I said. 'You come to the theatre as usual, I will try a remedy.' When Barbara came back stage that night, ready to play in one of her usual roles of pure womanhood, I stopped her. 'Look, Barbara, you have done marvellously until now, but I am afraid you are getting stale. People would like to see you in roles in which you portray the nearness to the soil, the rawness of human nature, its vulgarity

and stupidity, its cynical reality, people not only as they are, but worse than they are, people as they are when they are driven to extremes by unusual circumstances. Do you want to try it?' 'Yes', she said enthusiastically, 'I am glad you mention it. I have felt for quite a while that I have to give our audience a new experience. But do you think I can do it?' 'I have confidence in you,' I replied, 'the news just came in that a girl in Ottakring (a slum district of Vienna), solliciting men on the street, has been attacked and killed by a stranger. He is still at large, the police are searching for him. You are the streetwalker. Here (pointing to Richard, one of our male actors) is the apache. Get the scene ready.' A street was improvised on the stage, a café, two lights. Barbara went on. George was in his usual seat in the first row, highly excited. Richard, in the role of the apache, came out of the café with Barbara and followed her. They had an encounter, which rapidly developed into a heated argument. It was about money. Suddenly Barbara changed to a manner of acting totally unexpected from her. She swore like a trooper, punching at the man, kicking him in the leg repeatedly. I saw George half rising, anxiously raising his arm at me, but the apache got wild and began to chase Barbara. Suddenly he grabbed a knife, a prop, from his inside jacket pocket. He chased her in circles, closer and closer. She acted so well that she gave the impression of being really scared. The audience got up, roaring, 'Stop it, stop it.' But he did not stop until she was supposedly 'murdered'. After the scene Barbara was exuberant with joy, she embraced George and they went home in ecstasy. From then on she continued to act in such roles of the lower depth. George came to see me the following day. He instantly understood that it was therapy. She played domestics, lonely spinsters, revengeful wives, spiteful sweethearts, barmaids and gun molls. George gave me daily reports. 'Well,' he told me after a few sessions, 'something is happening to her. She still has her fits of temper at home but they have lost their intensity. They are shorter and in the midst of them she often smiles, and, as yesterday, she remembers similar scenes which she did on the stage and she laughs and I laugh with her because I, too, remember. It is as if we see each other in a psychological mirror. We both laugh. At times she begins to laugh before she has the fit, anticipating what will happen. She warms up to it finally, but it lacks the usual heat.' It was like a catharsis coming from humor and laughter. I continued the treatment, assigning roles to

> her more carefully according to her needs and his. One day George confessed the effect which these sessions had upon him as he watched them and absorbed the analysis which I gave afterwards. 'Looking at her productions on the stage made me more tolerant of Barbara, less impatient.' That evening I told Barbara how much progress she had made as an actress and asked her whether she would not like to act on the stage with George. They did this and the duets on the stage which appeared as a part of our official program, resembled more and more the scenes which they daily had at home. Gradually her family and his, scenes from her childhood, their dreams and plans for the future were portrayed. After every performance some spectators would come up to me, asking why the Barbara-George scenes touched them so much more deeply than the others (audience therapy). Some months later, Barbara and George sat alone with me in the theatre. They had found themselves and each other again, or better, they had found themselves and each other for the first time. I analysed the development of their psychodrama, session after session, and told them the story of their cure.
>
> (*Psychodrama, Volume 1* 1946: 3–5)

Several points should be noted here. The first is that Moreno developed psychodrama through a gradual process of discovery, having explored many different alternatives. He believed that an individual can achieve access to change by means of what he called *action insight*, a process of experimenting and re-experimenting with behaviour and then reflecting on it. This is the reverse of the psychoanalytic approach in which reflection precedes action, but it is important to note that the 'acting out' is done on stage. In the passage quoted above we can see Moreno in the actual process of developing his theory, experimenting himself.

Second, although Moreno was never to completely abandon his dream of using professional theatre and actors as a way of changing society, here he is gradually coming to recognize the need to focus more on people's real settings such as the community, the family, the couple . . . Such therapy is very demanding. As the actors of his company were asked to become involved in their own lives, many left the group and went back to acting in other theatres. Moreno then understood that spontaneous acting, because of the demands it makes, is only appropriate for people who really want to change their lives, and take full responsibility for them.

Therapeutic theatre as Moreno begins to develop it here is also different from psychoanalysis in that it is action-oriented, public, and rooted in immediate reality. It brings the group into the picture as an essential part of therapy. It is a completely new approach, an action-oriented revolution, taking the group as the basis for change and developing the future method of psychodrama as the means to explore individual 'truth'. (This method evolved and eventually came to be used by psychoanalysts in a way quite different from Moreno, focusing in particular on the unconscious of individuals and of the group.)

On a more immediate basis, the story of Barbara and George is instructive for other reasons. We know that Barbara, as an actress, and George, as a novelist, were both close friends of Moreno. The couple was not as happy as Moreno would have us believe. George was very temperamental and would have benefited from many sessions of psychodrama himself. Moreno, blinded by his success with Barbara, did not see this. Soon after having worked with Moreno the couple separated, and five years later George killed himself. This incident always troubled Moreno, but it was the earlier suicide of another member of the group that made him question the nature and limits of his work. He was carrying out 'stage therapy' with another couple, Robert and Diora; everything seemed to be going well, but one day Diora left her partner and Robert killed himself the next morning. This happened in 1924, at a time when Moreno was having all kinds of other problems. He went through a period of intense self-examination, reassessing the reliance he had placed on the strength of the actress and his own power of diagnosis. He had been brought up sharply against the difficulties of managing suicidal patients. There is no evidence that Moreno was responsible, directly or indirectly, for Robert Müller's suicide, but it may have contributed to his decision to leave Austria.[16]

The psychodrama of Barbara and George introduces us to the early development of psychodrama techniques and shows the powerful effects of playing therapeutic roles. The place of the *warm-up* technique is becoming evident and will gain clarity as Moreno becomes more cautious in his interventions, putting more emphasis on accurate diagnosis. The *action* part of the session is also developing: Moreno suggests the exploration of many roles, and this will eventually lead to *role reversal* and *doubling*. The *sharing* part of the session is evident in the use of 'audience-therapy'. The role of the *protagonist* is there and so, too, is the role of the *director*, the *auxiliary egos* and the *audience*. All this is still at the exploratory and experimental stage. Moreno does not really know yet how to handle catharsis or understand the limits of acting out.[17]

As well as at the theatre in Vienna, Moreno occasionally carried out spontaneity work at his home in Bad Vöslau. He also toured Germany

Figure 10 Anna Höllering, the 'Barbara' of Moreno's psychodrama protocols. (Lana Sutton, private collection; rephotographed by Claude Demers.)

with his group. But by the end of 1924 he had not yet come to any formal systematization of what was later to be called psychodrama. He did different types of theatre work, from therapeutic theatre with family in *theatre reciproque* to spontaneous experiences on the stage in Vienna, but the real therapeutic value of the technique of psychodrama was slowly emerging.

The publication of *The Theatre of Spontaneity*

This book, *Das Stegreiftheater*, was published in 1924, even though it was in the making for a couple of years. It is a small book of one hundred pages, translated in 1947 as *The Theatre of Spontaneity*. Like *The Words of the Father*, it gives us a profound insight into Moreno's thinking about theatre and therapy. The book is not easy to understand because the plan is not always clear. However, Moreno suggests four forms of revolutionary theatre that are in interaction and interdependence: the theatre of conflict, or theatre critique; the theatre of spontaneity, or immediate theatre; the therapeutic theatre, or *theatre reciproque*; the theatre of the creator.

The first form, theatre of conflict, is illustrated by the play *Thus Spake Zarathustra*. It is what Moreno elsewhere calls axiodrama and is represented in the three protocols referred to as the Godhead trilogy. Here, the audience takes the main role, challenging the *cultural conserves*. The audience is at the core of this form of theatre, forcing actors and everyone else to look at the truth.

The second form, immediate theatre, is based on spontaneity: theatre is what is happening in the here and now, what is being created as life unfolds. It is theatre without spectators, theatre that presents *das Ding an Sich*, the thing in itself. This is the theatre that leads to creativity through use of imagination and spontaneous event. It is total drama: everyone is part of it as an actor and protagonist. It evolved from Moreno's experience with children and his impromptu group. In the United States, Moreno will refer to this kind of theatre as Impromptu Theatre.

The third form, therapeutic theatre, has its base in the individual's own home; the players in it are the inhabitants of the house. The people, the 'community', play their conflict a second time around: this gives them perspective, distance, and often a sense of humour. Here we see Moreno integrating his experiences in therapeutic medical practice, in the House of Encounter, and in cases like that of George and Barbara:

In the therapeutic theatre the persons play before themselves — as they did once out of necessity in the self conscious deceit — the same life again. The place of the conflict and of its theatre is one and the same. Life and fantasy become of the same identity and of the same time. They do not want to overcome reality, they bring it forth. They re-experience it, they are master: not only as fictitious beings, but also of their true existence. How could they otherwise give birth to it once more? Because it is just this which they do. The whole of life is unfolded, with all its mutual complications, in the dimension of time, not one moment, not one instance is extinguished from it; each moment of boredom is retained, each question, every fit of anxiety, every moment of inner withdrawal, comes back to life. It is not only that they come back and re-enact their dialogues, but their bodies, too, come back rejuvenated. Their nerves, their heartbeats, they all play themselves from birth on, as if recalled by a divine memory, like the pre-established plan of a twin, but identical, universal. All their powers, deeds and thoughts appear on the scene in their original context and sequence, replicas of the phases which they have once passed. The whole past is moved out of its coffin and arrives at a moment's call. It does not only emerge in order to heal itself, for relief and catharsis, but it is also the love for its own demons which drives the theatre on to unchain itself. In order that they may be driven out from their cages, they tear up their deepest and most secret wounds, and now they bleed externally before all the eyes of the people.

Spectators of the therapeutic theatre are the entire community. All are invited and all gather before the house. The psychodrama cannot begin unless the last inhabitant of the town is present.

But this mad passion, this unfolding of life in the domain of illusion does not work like a renewal of suffering, rather it confirms the rule: every true second time is the liberation from the first.

(*The Theatre of Spontaneity* 1947: 90–1)

The fourth type of theatre is the most fascinating one. The theatre of the creator is the form of theatre that is the basis of self-actualization in every one of us. The example that Moreno uses is the one of Jesus of Nazareth, who lived his life to the full and is constantly re-created in people's minds. It looks like an illusion, but it is not. The theatre of creation as seen by Moreno is a continuous miracle of 'doing' in the present: the creation is movement, change, existing. It is an ongoing process that involves everyone as a creator. God has a double and is being repeated in each individual through their spontaneity, their creativity. We find here the basis of the theatre of 'I' being materialized in actual encounters with 'thou', the category of self-fulfilment and self-realization as God. Moreno is restating what he wrote earlier, especially in *The Words of the Father*. The theatre of the creator is everyone of us playing his life on the world's stage.[18]

In *The Theatre of Spontaneity*, in addition to proposing the four forms of theatre, Moreno includes interactional diagrams taken from spontaneous plays, giving a very good preview of his skills in observation. From the diagrams we can see how much time each actor uses, the order in which everyone is speaking, the nature of the interactions, and so on. Finally, he also put forward a model of a stage consistent with his view of the theatre.

This book contains most of the ingredients of Moreno's philosophy. It still lacks unity, but the basis of sociometry, group psychotherapy, and psychodrama is there.

Designing a stage and the controversy with Kiesler

Moreno always liked stages. As a child, he played God, standing on the top of a table, in a setting representing heaven. The 'stage' already had a multilevel construction. Later, when he told stories to the children in the park, he described how they would gather in concentric circles, with the sky the limit (see page 38).

We have said that in 1924 Moreno included a diagram of a model of a stage in *The Theatre of Spontaneity*. Moreno conceived that, especially for impromptu theatre, there needed to be an architectural structure that would echo his objective of creating a space in which everybody could be part of the action, in which everybody could be an actor. Even though Moreno suggested that the home should be used for *theatre reciproque*, he came to the conclusion that for spontaneity theatre, or deep emotional disturbance, there was a need for a formal structure to support the therapeutic work. For this purpose he designed a round, multilevel stage, surrounded by smaller 'rosettes' or side stages. Every level represented a different psychological step and level of involvement: the first level, often a side stage, was for warm-up and was a level of conception; the second level was the level of elaboration and growth;

the third level was the level of total involvement, completion and action; the fourth level, often represented later as the 'balcony' level, was reserved for representation of messiahs and heroes. This basic model already operates on the idea that everybody, including the audience, sits on the stage: the 'protagonist' on the centre stage, other members taking places on one or another of the fourteen 'rosettes'. As the protagonist completes his psychodrama, another member of the audience becomes the protagonist, and hence moves to centre stage. It is really a theatre without an audience.[19]

This idea of a theatre without an audience was to be refined during the next few months, following the publication of Moreno's book. Meanwhile, Moreno decided to present his idea of a revolutionary stage at an exhibition of new theatre techniques taking place in Vienna towards the end of 1924. With the help of a friend, the architect Hönigsfelt, he prepared sketches. This new design was slightly different from the one presented in his book, but it still showed a round stage with four 'rosettes'. The number of steps was slightly less, about six, but the central stage was still very much at the top, not easily reached, as if the centre was accessible only to strong personalities or gods. But the idea of a theatre without spectators was there, and the idea of levels to be climbed gradually. The design included a dome to cover the stage as if it were a church or temple. In other words, the stage was the whole theatre.

The design was duly exhibited, but its presentation was somewhat overshadowed by the success of another one by Friedrich Kiesler. Kiesler, who was also the director of the exhibition, succeeded in having his stage actually built, not just presented as a blueprint. It was called 'Raumbühne', or the railway theatre and had two features: the stage was circular and built vertically; the audience sat on chairs that moved around the stage. As we look at the two designs today we can easily see the similarities, but also the differences.

Moreno did not. He was furious and at the official opening of the exhibition publicly accused Kiesler of plagiarism. He created a big commotion and had to go to court to explain his behaviour. It is evident that Kiesler, often referred to as the 'Viennese Bohemian', had met Moreno and many of his friends — he was associated, for example, with Lampl and Rodenberg. He toured the cafés. He took part in the Stegreiftheater. He certainly knew about Moreno's stage project. Did he copy it, or part of it?[20]

A close look at the railway theatre shows us that the project was very different from Moreno's, with the exception of the circular stage; but Moreno did not invent the circular stage. Moreno wanted to bring about

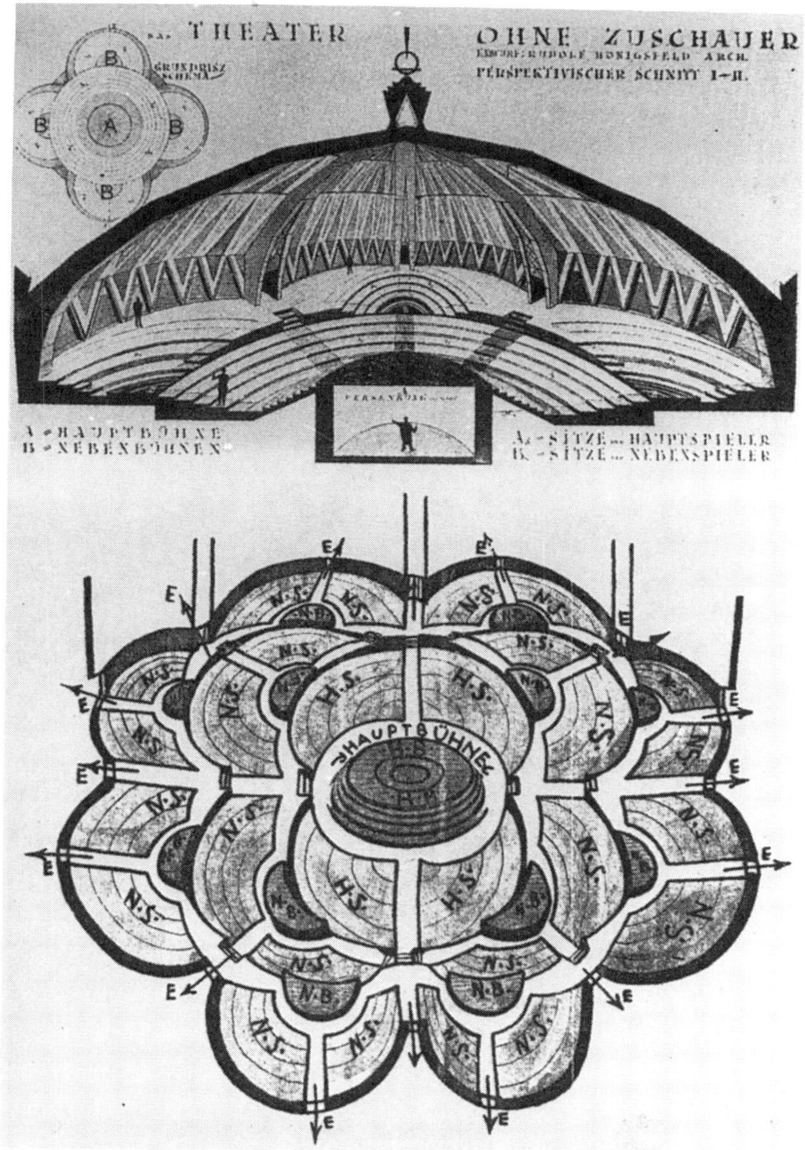

Figure 11 Moreno's design for a stage displayed at The International Exhibition of New Theatre Techniques, Vienna 1924. (In *Stegreiftheater* 1924; *Psychodrama, Volume 1* 1946; and Lesak *Die Kulisse Explodiert* 1988; rephotographed by Claude Demers.)

a total revolution in theatre itself and created a stage accordingly. Kiesler created a stage that did not question the purpose of the performance: he wanted action and movement, with actors still 'running the show'. It is clear that Moreno's real grudge against Kiesler was that he used his position as director of the exhibition to get his design actually built, taking unfair advantage over other exhibitors.

Figure 12 Caricature of the Moreno-Kiesler contest by Ladislaus Tuszynsky which appeared in *Die Götz von Berlichingen* 3 October 1924. (In Lesak *Die Kulisse Explodiert* 1988; rephotographed by Claude Demers.)

Controversy raged and caricaturists had a field-day drawing the two protagonists. Artists and architects took sides, some for Kiesler, others for Moreno. The quarrel certainly had negative effects on both men. It may have been more than coincidence that both emigrated to the United States the following year.

The incident raises two further questions: Where did Moreno draw inspiration for his ideas? What happened to his philosophy of anonymity?

Moreno was an avid, if unsystematic, reader. There is no doubt that he derived many of his ideas for theatre and therapy from his reading. His concept of catharsis owed a lot to Greek drama, but also to Freud and Breuer. Many of the techniques he used in psychodrama can be traced back to Socrates and ancient theatre. It was the same in the development of his stage design: the theatres of ancient Greece and medieval mystery plays were both possible sources of inspiration. At the same time, we have to remember that the whole field of theatre was renewing itself in the early twentieth century, and that people like Adolphe Appia, Konstantin Stanislavski, Max Reinhardt, Luigi Pirandello, and Erwin Piscator were producing plays that were to have revolutionary effects. Moreno knew this, and certainly participated in the movement. Further research could still be done to assess the extent of the cross-fertilization that went on in this period.

One rather surprising outcome from the controversy with Kiesler concerned Moreno's philosophy of anonymity. Earlier Moreno had played several times with ideas concerning names, his own name and anonymity. He had linked the idea of anonymity with the idea of God (see page 19). Even though he published some of his books under the name Jacob Levy, he also published some anonymously. This was true of *The Words of the Father, The Theatre of Spontaneity*, and also in the case of his stage design for the exhibition. Moreno now found himself in the curious position of having to defend a property that was officially anonymous. On being called by the judge to present his case, he delivered the following long speech:

> I have given away my ideas to the community, to all its parts, for free perusal; with this I have given the privilege to all, and have given everyone the right to consider my ideas common property, to take them over to the letter, and to use and distribute them in any manner, in printed form, or by mouth, provided it is accomplished without reference to their names, or any other name. But it was not my idea to leave my contributions to a single individual for the purpose of bringing to that person a proprietary relationship towards my ideas, of linking my contributions to someone's family name for the purpose of enriching him . . .
>
> When a common good is announced publicly as a private good, the return of this good to the community must be

demanded at the site of the theft, and before the same public. Had my work also been signed by a name, then a cheated person would confront a cheating person. Here, however, I acted, not in my own name, but in the name of a cheated community, not as a private person, but as a public person. The public world is the place where the public blunder must be corrected. Democracy has given mankind a terrible blessing, the Ego . . .

The plaintiff belongs to those who have met with me, eaten at my table, and slept in my house. Had he not met me and done as he did, I would not have looked at him. Had he met with me and done the same, but with full anonymity — holding back both my name and his — or had he, at least, printed his name in small letters, I would not have looked up. But the noise which someone can make with himself must have a limit. And, as a work has a certain place in an order of values, exaggerated praise deprives it of its true position . . .

My conflict with the plaintiff developed the moment I read his reports in the newspapers. I asked myself what I should do. I searched for an appropriate form of action. The immediate thing was to be silent. Because I had already long ago transferred my work to the public, it was up to the public to defend itself and not up to me. I remained silent and waited. The second alternative was an accounting under four eyes. A meeting would have been the legitimate form in any private case. But there was no private conflict because I had not suffered any damage, nor was I requested by the public to be lenient. A public conflict cannot be solved privately, particularly after action has been urged by the participation of an indeterminate number of persons, known and unknown. The necessary place of action for a meaningful correction had to have a public character. I saw the need to step out of my privacy. The appropriate transaction of a public conflict requires a particular immediacy, a form that is as real as the meeting and is as general as the printed word. Such conditions were met on the first exhibition day. The dignitaries of the city were present and, in their midst, was the President of the country and the Mayor of the city. To speak there, in the face of the responsible authorities, in the presence of the plaintiff, and of the entire town — a more perfect time and place could not be found. The danger of creating a public nuisance was great, but the danger of perpetuating a nuisance by silence was even greater. . . . I spoke. I am before the judge. The public

> should be here instead. The public is accused. As it is not present I ask to be considered its witness. . . .
>
> As a private person I cannot reproach the plaintiff. He has not taken anything away from me. He has deprived the public of a good in a manner that violates the moral law. It is not in the nature of the law court to contest the right of all in favor of one individual. If the court approves his suit, then the public is condemned. Then I must suffer the fine as its representative. In that event plagiarism is cleared, and anonymity a wish of the devil.
>
> ('Autobiography' 1985: ch. 6: 39–45)

This speech is very instructive and displays a talent for highly sophisticated argument. It tells us a lot about the philosophy behind Moreno's policy of anonymity, and makes it clear that the noisy controversy with Kiesler, however justifiable he may have felt his case to be, also held a deeper meaning for him. This was to be a continuing trend in Moreno's later confrontations with Brill, Lippitt, Slavson and so many others. The Moreno who accuses Kiesler of theft is the same Moreno who 'used' his own father's name and accused himself of stealing his own father's ideas.

The invention of a sound-recording machine

During this period Moreno was working with Marianne's brother, Franz, on a sound-recording device. It all started with a dream that Moreno had, a dream in which he heard recorded messages. This gave him the idea of creating a machine capable of reproducing music and the voice. Moreno himself had no technical ability or knowledge, but Franz Lörnitzo was an engineering genius and after a lot of hard work was successful in producing a machine. The invention made international news and achieved a notice in *The New York Times*. This clearly stated that the invention was a joint effort by an 'Austrian scientist', Jacob Moreno Levy, and the engineer, Franz Lörnitzo. Later on, a controversy broke out between Lörnitzo and Moreno as to who was the real inventor, paralleling the controversy with Kiesler, illustrating once more Moreno's 'paternity syndrome', but it seems appropriate to acknowledge the major part that Franz contributed as a technical expert, even if the popular belief is that 'Moreno invented a recording device'. Moreno himself, in his unpublished autobiography, acknowledges the part Franz played.

Figure 13 Franz Lörnitzo and the sound-recording device. This is the only known picture of the Moreno-Lörnitzo invention, taken at 4 Maithal Street. (Gertrude and Veronika Selb; rephotographed by Peter Selb and Claude Demers.)

The two men were invited to the United States by the General Phonograph Company in Ohio and their invention was also duly patented with the government office in Austria. Probably because many other engineers were working at this time on similar projects, the 'invention' did not 'take off' as they had hoped, but it gave Moreno an immediate reason for emigrating to the United States.[21]

* * *

As this chapter comes to a close, let us summarize the considerable amount of work accomplished by Moreno in the seven years 1918–25. It included two major publications, *The Words of the Father* and *The Theatre of Spontaneity*; medical work in general practice and psychiatry; the founding of a journal, *Daimon*, to publish new works by young and promising writers and artists; the exploration of new avenues in theatre performance; the design of a new stage; a contribution, however small, to the development of a recording device with Marianne's brother, Franz. Along the way he made a few friends, but lost most of them through public confrontations. In 1925, in spite or because of his success, Moreno was becoming more and more isolated. He was not accepted in his own country. He was facing considerable problems in Bad Vöslau. A move was necessary.

Part Two
Action and sharing

Introduction to Part Two

This second part of this biography deals mostly with Moreno's years in the United States, beginning with the actual experience of emigration and the early days when he had to dig deep into his personal resources of creativity and perseverance. Eventually, by about 1931, everything he had done previously became integrated into a broader system. Sociometry, group psychotherapy, and psychodrama all became sides of the same three-dimensional picture: the picture of a person being alive and creative, defined as much by his own 'I' as by his relationships with others, the 'Thou'; a person whose actions, encounters, and spontaneity all express the basic desire for survival. Moreno was to say: 'Everyone who is born is entitled to live and survive.'

Part Two is called 'Action and sharing'. When one looks at the second half of Moreno's life, from 1926 onwards, one is struck by how his talent finally comes alive, how he is at last able to share his knowledge and commitment to the world, first with only a few disciples, but then with a far greater number of people, while still remaining true to his philosophy of action.

The words 'action' and 'sharing' came to be used for the second and third stages of a psychodrama session, following the 'warm-up'. According to Moreno, these three stages are essential to a meaningful psychodrama. It therefore seems only appropriate to apply them to Moreno's own journey. The term 'warm-up' was applied to the European period. As we enter a more mature stage of his life, we use the terms 'action' and 'sharing'.

The reader should note that the second part of this book does not always follow strict chronological order, but, after 1931, is organized by themes, representing Moreno's personal and professional development.

Chapter 5
Emigrating to the United States: a stormy trip

In 1925, the situation Moreno found himself in was difficult. Even though he had gone some way to establishing himself, Austria was never to be a country where he could hope to be completely at ease or enjoy great success. He had reached a difficult point in his relationship with Marianne, and they were continually harassed by young Vöslauers who would follow and threaten them. As a doctor, he was practising less and less; the money he earned was going towards his publishing ventures, and he was accumulating more and more debts. The controversy with Kiesler had not helped his reputation with the artistic and literary world, and the suicide of a patient had left him in some personal disarray. Moreno was becoming isolated.

It was in this context that Moreno took the decision to emigrate to the United States. At first he hesitated about where to go. Many of his friends had gone to Russia because of their political ideology; Moreno, a man of the people, was politically in sympathy with the Russians, but afraid of restraints on his freedom. His brother William, who had helped him a great deal, had already left for New York and he soon decided to follow him.[1]

Moreno left Austria at the same time as his father was dying alone in Bucharest. As the father was ending his long journey in the son's city of birth, the son was crossing the ocean — a dream of his father's — to make a fresh start in New York. The paths of the two men, who understood each other well and who were so much alike in many ways, had never crossed again after Moreno Nissim's separation from Paulina, but deep down Moreno continued to hear his father's call and to fulfil his wishes.

At some point in 1922 Moreno had a dream in which he pictured himself on Fifth Avenue in New York, hearing a recorded message: he set about taking the necessary steps to help the dream materialize and with the help of Franz Lörnitzo, worked for three years on the 'Radio-Film' recording device. In the hope of selling the invention to an American company, and of earning a large sum of money, he embarked on an ocean liner to America with the idea of returning eventually to Austria, or better still maintaining dual residency. He left on 21 December 1925, soon followed by Franz Lörnitzo. He left Marianne behind to take care of the house in Bad Vöslau[2] and arrived in America with very little luggage. However, in his hand he carried his three inventions: the magnetic sound-recording device,[3] the interactional sociogram, and plans for the psychodrama stage. He had great hopes of the future.

Reality was somewhat cruel. No synagogue was waiting for Moreno the prophet, no university offered him a contract as a scientist, and no theatre company was expecting Moreno the revolutionary. He visited the General Phonograph Company in Elyria, Ohio but did not meet with the enthusiasm he had expected. No company records indicate any deal made with him or Franz Lörnitzo. Many inventors were working in the area of sound-recording in the mid-1920s, and better machines were already being developed. If any money did change hands, the amount was small, and passed under the table or was put directly into Moreno's pocket. That was the end of the 'Radio-Film Invention', and the beginning of an argument with the Lörnitzo family. Moreno never revealed to Franz how the invention was sold, or shelved, and it is probable that he had raised such high hopes in the young man's mind that he could not face telling him the truth when the project failed. However, Franz felt cheated and departed in anger. The family in Austria took sides with Franz, but Marianne, although unhappy, remained faithful to Moreno.

Moreno's arrival in the new world was the beginning of an adventure that was in no way easy. Reading through his letters to Marianne, one gets a picture of a man going through depression, anger, and even paranoia. He had left Austria promising everybody that his invention would revolutionize the world of sound-recording, and here he was penniless. His brother William was supporting him, but at the same time was still struggling to establish himself in New York. Moreno's visa situation was unclear: he did not have a permanent visa, and immigration was difficult because of quotas. He was travelling on an Austrian passport, and this was a further problem because of strained political relations between the two countries in the past.

The first five years were a constant struggle. Moreno went to Montreal, in Canada, to obtain a new temporary visa. He hid in different cities and kept his address a secret. He had to do this to avoid immigration officers, but also to hide from Austrian creditors who were eager to find him. He spoke very little English, which made employment difficult. He could not work as a doctor because he had no licence for New York State.

Moreno had faced challenges before, but now found himself up against the wall. He had no sure welcome back in Austria and in any case would have felt humiliated had he returned without succeeding in New York. On the other hand, he had no roots or employment in America. He was compelled to deploy all his strength and assets.

First, he needed a licence to practise medicine. He was fortunate enough to meet Dr Bela Schick, the originator of the Schick test for diphtheria immunity, and to do some work at the children's clinic of Mt Sinai Hospital under his tutelage. Eventually Moreno gave demonstrations of spontaneity work with children and was able to gain the hospital's attention and interest. Meanwhile, he arranged for Marianne to send him all the papers necessary to petition for his medical licence. He prepared for the examination and sat it for the first time in January 1927. The examination was in English, which made performance difficult for a new immigrant who was just starting to learn the language, and it is not surprising that in these circumstances, he failed the gynaecology examination (although one has to remember his previous problems in the field of gynaecology). He took the examination again in May and was awarded his licence in September 1927. This not only gave him the right to open an office but also a stronger position from which to apply for permanent status.

Even though his status was still uncertain, he acquired a temporary visa which was renewed after a year. He travelled to Montreal, contacted the Austrian consulate, and obtained a new passport. He also went to the United States consulate to renew his visa there for another year and had his status cleared. Meanwhile, he met Beatrice Beecher, the granddaughter of Henry Ward Beecher, a famous evangelist in New York. Beatrice was lecturing on child psychology at Mt Sinai Hospital and took an immediate interest in Moreno's spontaneity work. She offered to marry Moreno, as a means of helping him obtain immigrant status, on the understanding that they would divorce as soon as possible afterwards. The marriage took place on 31 May 1928, followed by divorce in 1934, soon after Moreno became an American citizen. Moreno and Beatrice had an intimate and mutually caring relationship that developed into a professional cooperation;[4] later, for example, Beatrice worked on a first translation of *Das Stegreiftheater* and Moreno went to demonstrate his work at the Plymouth Institute in Brooklyn where she was working, and did some follow-up work with children.

While Moreno was gradually establishing himself in New York, he continued to correspond with Marianne, promising that she should soon join him. Meanwhile, she sent him all the newspaper clippings she could find about his work in Austria, and copies of his publications and diplomas. Moreno, in turn, sent money to pay off some of his debts with publishers, libraries, and lawyers. He was still hoping to keep two homes, one in New York, the other in Vöslau. Marianne was working miracles trying to keep the house and furniture from being requisitioned by the city council and accepted some money from her parents so that she could continue living there. Unaware that Moreno was organizing his own life without her, Marianne continued to help the man she loved to establish himself in America. But, Moreno was drifting away from Marianne, meeting other younger women in America; he did not tell her about his marriage of convenience with Beatrice Beecher. When, early in 1930, Marianne could no longer keep the city council from taking over their house in Bad Vöslau and had to leave 4 Maithal Street – the 'castle', the beautiful 'Valley of May', where together they had created *The Words of the Father* – Moreno became irrationally upset and used the opportunity to break off in an angry letter a relationship which had become increasingly inconvenient. Moreno talked very little afterwards about this sad conclusion to a mutually profound experience. He even invented a story in which Marianne chose to become a nun! Just as he was unable to face the fact that he had left his father behind to die in Bucharest, neither could he face the fact that he had abandoned Marianne, and tried to erase the memory of this romantic love affair. Marianne herself, who had left everything to follow Moreno, was devastated; much later, she married, but had no children. She died in 1984, leaving behind her correspondence with Moreno as a testimony of her involvement with the man and his dream. Up to the end she was a defender of her former partner, following from afar the development of his ideas and choosing to remain silent about her own fate.[5]

Towards the end of 1927 prospects had begun to look much better for Moreno, thanks to Beatrice Beecher and William H. Bridge, the future director and manager of the Martha Graham Dance Company. Moreno started to give lectures and demonstrations of spontaneity work in schools, churches, and universities and eventually was able to found The Impromptu Theatre. (The term impromptu was preferable to the term spontaneity, according to Bridge, who was then a teacher of speech and English literature at Hunter College.[6]) The Theatre was based at the Carnegie Hall and here again, as in Vienna, Moreno showed good business sense in choosing a central and significant location for his new venture and in making advantageous connections with leading figures in the theatrical world.

It was at the Impromptu Theatre that Moreno met Helen H. Jennings who was to be a leading force behind the publication of *Who Shall Survive?*

Figure 14 Helen H. Jennings, the driving force behind the development of sociometry and the publication of *Who Shall Survive?* (Zerka Moreno, private collection; rephotographed by Johanne Doyon.)

and Moreno's numerous research projects. She was then a graduate student at Columbia University. She introduced Moreno to her own mentor and supervisor of her doctoral thesis, Professor Gardner Murphy: he was to become a supporter and associate of Moreno, and a significant connection between Moreno and the social psychologists and sociologists. Another member of the Theatre was J.J. Robbins, a poet, playwright, and translator of Stanislavski's *My Life in Art*. Robbins was associated with many artists and intellectuals in New York and was instrumental in giving the new group visibility and recognition.[7]

Moreno already had quite a lot of experience in impromptu theatre from his work in Austria, but because of his lack of fluency in English decided to start off in a small way in New York. His new group worked privately together for some time before giving their first public performance in 1931. Meanwhile, Moreno got involved with the New York Civic Repertory Theatre, at that time under the direction of Eva LaGallienne. He worked with actors and actresses such as Burgess Meredith, Howard da Silva, John Garfield, and Beverly Roberts. In a way, he was repeating in America what he had already done in Vienna: working with children in schools, establishing an impromptu theatre, and training well-established actors and actresses in new methods.

We could consider these five years as the American 'warm-up' for the work to come. They had been difficult years, but with his usual ability to adapt to present circumstances, Moreno successfully set the scene for the most creative years of his life.

Chapter 6
In search of a new muse

The next twenty years were the most productive of Moreno's life. As we shall see, he finally succeeded in synthesizing the various aspects of his philosophy and through hard work achieved a high level of professional success. His total personal commitment to his beliefs meant that there was no separation between his personal and his professional life; the one continually interacted with the other, in keeping with his philosophy that just as we are born in relation to others, so everything we accomplish is rooted in interpersonal behaviour. Nowhere do we see this more clearly than in Moreno's search for a new muse. We have seen the importance of his mother, Pia, Chaim Kellmer, and Marianne at different periods of his life, and it is clear that Moreno could not function effectively without such a relationship. When he came to America, Moreno had left behind the most significant person in his life — Marianne — and by 1930 had broken with her entirely. Now he began to develop other existing and new relationships.

An early important relationship for Moreno in America was the one with his brother, William, who had always been an unconditional supporter. Back in Vienna, William had contributed to the rent of the Stegreiftheater and when Moreno arrived in America, William was already there ready to help financially and emotionally: he opened such doors as he could for his brother and used every possible source of influence to facilitate his immigration. The two brothers were very close. They knew how to use each other's strength to minimize their own weaknesses. William was an admirer of Jacques' boldness, spontaneity, and dedication to a cause. Moreno needed his younger brother's financial ability and constant support, especially in the first lonely days as a new immigrant. Later, in 1941–2, William helped Moreno to establish the Institute of Sociometry in New York, contributing both time and money. In return, Moreno dedicated his book *Psychodrama, Volume 1* to

William.[1] But Moreno needed a woman as a muse, even though he appreciated his brother's company and encouragement.

Soon after his arrival Moreno had sought out relationships with women — he rationalized his behaviour by saying that it was the best way to learn the language — and among those who helped him redirect his energy towards intellectual productivity was Beatrice Beecher whom he married to obtain immigrant status in 1928. Although Moreno thought highly of Beatrice — a name associated with Dante's muse — the relationship was in no way romantic or passionate and, when he became a naturalized American citizen in 1934, they divorced amicably as previously arranged. However, the relationship with Beatrice had been very fruitful and it was thanks to her that Moreno was able to give demonstrations of using psychodrama with children. He also worked with her on some teaching and publishing projects and through her was introduced to other educators and therapists.[2]

Moreno was also very close to Helen H. Jennings who was a constant support in his research and experiments, but apparently he did not wish to become emotionally involved with her, or marry her; rather, he felt a deep respect for a woman he considered to be one of the most talented social scientists he had ever met. In fact, Helen Jennings was a major force behind Moreno, both in the area of sociometry and in the impromptu theatre. Her talent for methodology and statistics was very helpful to him, especially when he carried out his research in Sing Sing prison and at the Hudson School for Girls; it is fair to say that the work would have lacked precision and refinement without her help. Later, when Moreno was well on his way to fame and surrounded by numerous other important figures, she remained a guiding force in many of his projects.[3]

While demonstrating sociometry in Dr Stevens' class at Columbia, Moreno met a young woman who was also doing an internship at the Hudson School as part of her training in social work. Her name was Florence Bridge. Born in 1912, Florence was almost twenty-five years younger than Moreno, a 'pretty woman, small in stature and dark haired'. She had a passionate, sensuous nature, but was also a loner. She had lost her mother when she was very young, and was very devoted to her father. When Florence met Moreno she saw in him someone to replace her father. She was very impressed with the side of Moreno that related to the role of the prophet and identified strongly with the book *The Words of the Father*. The theme of God was to become a major bond in the relationship between them. This bond was so strong that Florence can still, up to this day, forty years after their divorce, quote excerpts from *The Words of the Father* in an accent reminiscent of Moreno himself.

The name Florence had associations for Moreno with the beloved Italian city of Florence where he had met Pia, his first romantic love. He was at this time living by himself on a large piece of property just purchased in Beacon, New York and feeling very lonely, while Florence was unattached and admired him very much. In these circumstances the relationship developed apace and Florence eventually moved to Beacon. They were married in 1938 and had a daughter, Regina, the following year.

Figure 15 J.L. Moreno, Florence Bridge, and Regina Moreno. (Regina Moreno, private collection; rephotographed by Claude Demers.)

Moreno's marriage with Florence was not a happy one for him. It was different for her: she admired him so much that it was enough for her just to live in the 'little house in Beacon' and to take care of their daughter. The two were not living in the same world: Moreno needed more than admiration and adulation. He needed a muse, someone who could inspire him as Marianne had done, who could be a professional partner, a co-creator. He needed another Marianne, but one who could function within the American system. In fact, he needed a relationship which would be an inspiration to the better side of himself, while curbing the more difficult aspects of her personality.

In Florence Bridge he found someone who 'fused' with him: she would literally engage in God-like dialogues with Moreno. She did not seem to be aware of the 'as if' level of thought and utterance which allowed him to speak in the name of God as a way of speaking about himself, rather than the God of the Bible, and Moreno grew less and less at ease with the difficulty that Florence had in treating him as an ordinary human being. In the past, he had been more tolerant of this sort of adulation, when he lived among the poets and the writers of Vienna, but in America, in 1936, he was the director of a sanatorium, with a new image to maintain. Gradually, as Moreno moved away from Florence, she identified even more with the godhead aspect of him and, soon this became an embarrassment.

Florence had little contact with the patients of the sanatorium that Moreno had opened in 1936. She lived with Moreno in the little house away from the hospital, looking after her daughter Regina, a devoted wife and mother. Professionally, even though she contributed articles in the field of sociometry and did some pioneer work, she never really captured the imagination of her husband. She was married to Moreno for ten years and lived a life that anyone else would have found intolerable. A certain naïveté, coupled with a blind admiration for Moreno, allowed her to weather many storms. Meanwhile, Moreno had found his real muse and the situation finally became too difficult to accommodate. The couple were divorced in 1948.[4]

In 1941 Moreno had met another woman who was to fulfil all his expectations, and more. Celine Zerka Toeman came to his office at the Beacon sanatorium when she brought her psychotic sister to the hospital for treatment. She was again much younger than Moreno, but shared with him a European and Jewish heritage. Born in the Netherlands, she had lived in England for a while; she could think like a European, but had an appreciation of English culture, an important asset in a city like New York. She was to be a meaningful link between Moreno's European and Jewish past and his future life and work in America. Moreno knew nothing of her past before he met her, but as with Marianne more than twenty years earlier, he felt love at first sight. He trusted his feelings, his intuition, his 'tele'. He felt that he had found the *integrated partner* he had been looking for. It was clear that she felt the same about him.

Zerka was a very talented fashion student. She had never thought of getting involved in the psychological arena, even though by nature she was concerned about others and their well-being. However, her experience with her psychotic sister had given her some insight into the sort of work Moreno did and she rapidly became very involved in his projects. He asked her to read the proofs of the English translation of *The Words of the Father* and when she had done so she told him that she felt as if she had written the book herself. Her immediate understanding of the book and his philosophy cemented the relationship and gave Moreno a great sense of security in finding a partner ready to share his ideas. From this point on Zerka entered his life as no one before or afterwards. She became his constant associate and companion.

In 1941 Moreno was still married to Florence and it took many years before he was ready to divorce her. Meanwhile, he developed an all-inclusive and fruitful relationship with Zerka. First, he asked her to take charge of his office in New York. This was the office of the Institute of Sociometry and the Theatre of Psychodrama that he had opened in New York City with the financial backing of his brother William. William took care of daily operations and soon Zerka became a partner in the project too. Gradually, she became involved in the sanatorium in Beacon and rapidly became Moreno's *alter ego*, inspiration, co-therapist, co-researcher, and above all his true love. In 1941, after meeting her, Moreno wrote Zerka this poem:

I wish
That I had been born with you
As one being,
But then I thank God
That I was born apart from you,
So that I could meet you
As a separate being.

But helas
O God: O my God,
Now that I have met you
And have become one with you,
I wish
That I would die with you,
As one being.

(Original: Zerka T. Moreno; copy in Harvard archives)

The strength of Moreno's attachment to Zerka is clear. As we look at the poem more than fifty years later, we can see that in many ways he did become one with her: each integrated the other into their own 'journey', but they also remained two separate beings, each contributing to science in their own way. Moreno did not completely avoid other women after he met Zerka, but nobody was a threat to her, for nobody contributed as much to the development of Moreno's ideas as she did, and her own input, though difficult to differentiate from his, has a secure place in the history of science.

Moreno and Zerka married in 1949 and had a son, Jonathan, in 1952. Both Jonathan and Regina, the older daughter, also contributed in their own way to the development of sociometry and psychotherapy, since Moreno incorporated the knowledge that he gained from parenthood in his work. At the same time, Moreno also applied his theories to the upbringing of his children. In the 1950s, for example, he engaged an *au pair* from Europe, Gretel Leutz, to be a companion to Regina during the difficult period when the family was readjusting to the divorce and the birth of Jonathan. By providing Regina with an older 'sister', Moreno and Zerka were able to redirect destructive energy in more positive ways and apply a 'sociometric' solution to a family problem. Gretel Leutz returned to Germany to become a doctor and group psychotherapist and became a spiritual daughter to Moreno.[5] Regina herself later became a frequent guest and protagonist at the Beacon Theatre.

The Morenos educated Jonathan by using psychodramatic techniques and role playing. For example, role reversal would be used to give everyone a better understanding of each other's needs and feelings. Here again, Moreno showed his preoccupation with action in the practical application of therapeutic principles. In fact, he used his family as a living laboratory: many articles and a book were published as a result of his experience of child-rearing and family development.[6]

Zerka, in addition to having the responsibility for overseeing the household, was a constant help and partner to Moreno. He called her his 'right hand' and it is difficult to imagine him accomplishing much without her, but in 1958, as a result of a malignant tumour in her shoulder, she had to have her right arm completely amputated. There was a period of agony, helplessness, and distress in the family. Zerka showed great strength in recuperating and was to totally resume her work after the amputation, but the process was not easy and gave Moreno a lesson in humility about the limits of medicine. Here again, the whole family used psychodrama techniques to explore their thoughts and feelings, and to support each other. The story of Zerka's misfortune takes us back to the 'Psychodrama of the Fallen God' which Moreno played when he was four years old, when he himself broke his right arm and learned to question his own strength. Because of her faith, her openness

Figure 16 Zerka Moreno at Beacon in the early 1940s. (Zerka Moreno, private collection; rephotographed by Claude Demers.)

about the difficulties of the ordeal, and her skill in using her left arm in order to remain the right arm of the developing Morenean movement, Zerka's influence and reputation grew even greater. During this period Moreno was travelling a lot abroad, lecturing about his work around the world. He was almost seventy years of age, while Zerka was not yet forty: her presence was essential for the movement to continue to expand.

From 1942, when Zerka and Moreno together published their first small brochure called *The Group Approach in Psychodrama*, and up to Moreno's death in 1974, Zerka was his partner in all his publications, conferences, workshops, and many other ventures. There is no doubt that she was not only his inspiration, but also full-time administrator, organizer, co-trainer and co-therapist. However, perhaps her most important and unrecognized role in Moreno's life was that of peacemaker in the years when he was fighting to establish himself and his ideas in a new country: as in Vienna, this often led to confrontation and controversy.

It is difficult to imagine Moreno's life without the constant presence of his muse Zerka. She was so much part of his undertakings that only a detailed analysis of Moreno's works could give us the exact nature and scope of her influence. In his own way, Moreno acknowledged this in an interview with Walt Anderson published in 1974:

> When I was gathering information for this short biographical outline, I asked Dr Moreno what he considered to be the single most important event in his creative life. He replied that it was his partnership with Zerka Toeman, who began to work with him in 1941 and became his wife in 1949. I also asked him if there was anything in his career he would like to change, or that he wished might have been different. The only thing he could think of was that he wished he had met her fifteen years earlier.[7]
>
> (Greenberg 1974: 211)

Chapter 7
The development of group psychotherapy and sociometry

Moreno's basic philosophy and its relation to *The Words of the Father*

Moreno considered *The Words of the Father* to be his most important book. He says this in his autobiography and it is confirmed by the way the two most significant women in his life became involved with the book. Marianne was his partner in writing it, Zerka read the proof of the English translation and was immediately in sympathy with its ideas. It was a book that laid the foundations of what Zerka calls Moreno's 'theory of life'.[1]

It is a book that has fascinated everybody and can be interpreted in different ways; Moreno cannot be understood without reference to it, for it contains the core of his teaching about spontaneity and creativity. The 'God' vocabulary has often taken on too strict a theological meaning and has been seen as an expression of his megalomanic tendencies. I do not wish to minimize either aspect, but it is also interesting to read Moreno as an author who is putting forward a person-centred, existential philosophy. This philosophy is evident throughout *The Words of the Father* and revolves around the dyad I/Thou, creator/co-creator. Its territory, or psychological geography, is the family, the group, the world, the universe — the place where the person is expressing himself at any given moment.

The basis of Moreno's philosophy was always the importance for every individual of expressing themselves through their own spontaneous and creative means in a world where everyone is part of a group or social entity. From this perspective, everyone has to learn to carry on a meaningful dialogue with themselves and the world, the I and Thou dialogue, giving rise to the concept of 'self and encounter' with its implication of social responsibility. It is a philosophy that assumes that I am God, and that we are all Gods:

> The idea of God became a revolutionary category, removed from the beginning of time into the present, into the self, into every I. 'He', God of the genesis, may have to prove his existence. It is the 'Thou' God of the Christian gospel who may need proof of meeting, but the 'I' God of the Self was self-evident. The new 'I' could not imagine being born without being his own creator. He could not imagine anyone being born without being his own creator. Too, he could not imagine any future of the world ever to have emerged without having been its creator. He could not imagine any future of the world to emerge without being personally responsible for its production.
>
> (*The Future of Man's World*, 1947: 13)

Being God, being creator also means being in tune with the universe which is 'infinite creativity'. In order to follow Moreno's thinking one has to do away with preconceptions: the preconceptions of theologians who cannot accept the pantheism of Moreno's position; the preconceptions of psychiatrists who look at Moreno's personality from a 'psychopathological' point of view; the preconceptions of sociologists who refuse to associate a transpersonal approach to psychology with science; the preconceptions of the theatre people where God is seen just as another actor being represented on stage. Moreno's philosophy of life simply states that all human beings are infinite creativity and that a new order could be established in the universe accordingly. Ultimately, we are all creators and co-creators living in a world of interpersonal relationships, interdependent on each other. In the beginning was the action. In the beginning was the group.[2]

In reality the synthesis of Moreno's ideas, his 'philosophy', came about slowly and gradually. He acted intuitively most of the time, but always placed the emphasis on development of the individual in and through the group. Children in the Augarten, prostitutes in the Prater, and refugees in Mitterndorf were all members of groups looking to fulfil themselves; so were Moreno's patients in Vöslau and the 'protagonists' in the theatre. I talk about Moreno's 'philosophy' here because in 1941 he translated *The Words of the Father* into English, giving sociometry and psychodrama the basis that had so far been missing for his American students. He published the book anonymously again, writing a preface this time, but not integrating the work into his complete system of thought. This was to cause problems, because people did not know what to make of the book. However, in order to make sense of Moreno's work, we have to remember that the basic themes of the *Words of the Father* are continuously present in his views of sociometry, group psychotherapy, and psychodrama.

When he came to America, Moreno developed his ideas in two directions, sociometry and psychodrama, leaving the God hypothesis somewhat in abeyance. In fact, for many years, Moreno played down his notion of godhead, probably recognizing that this sort of vocabulary would be unacceptable to sociologists and psychiatrists alike. He chose to stress different aspects of his theories depending on which audience he was addressing. He developed sociometry within the sciences of sociology, anthropology, and social psychiatry, whereas the techniques of psychodrama were developed for mental health practitioners.[3]

A third direction in which Moreno developed his ideas was that of group psychotherapy. One could devote a whole chapter to developments in this field, but it is not appropriate here. In Moreno's professional development, group psychotherapy was used mostly in association with either sociometry or psychodrama, to which it is closely related.

From an epistemological standpoint the concept of group psychotherapy is vast and ill-defined. From it, Moreno attempted to create a new science, *sociatry*, to deal with the 'prophylaxis, diagnosis and treatment of groups and intergroup relations' and this would have been a new and fascinating area of research. It was a concept that included both prevention and therapy and would have had a larger scope than group psychotherapy. Sociatry surfaces, disappears, and resurfaces in Moreno's writings. I mention it here as an example of one of his ideas that may still need clarification. It could have been a legitimate alternative to the over-used group psychotherapy concept and become the necessary metaconcept lacking in Moreno's writings.[4]

In this chapter I will focus on the development of group psychotherapy and sociometry and in the next on group psychotherapy and psychodrama. However, this division is somewhat arbitrary and we will return for a while to chronological order. In Moreno's professional life, the year 1931 was marked by three major events: his involvement in sociometric research, the public inauguration of the Impromptu Theatre, and his controversy with Abraham Brill and psychoanalysis. In the rest of this chapter I will discuss the development of sociometry, addressing the last two events in the next chapter.

Developing the tools of sociometry

Back in Vienna, Moreno had given some thought to the measurement of interpersonal relationships and the spontaneous involvement of people in theatre improvisation. He had presented some very interesting interactional diagrams, for example, in the *Das Stegreiftheater* book. While he was trying to develop his career and expertise in America, he had found a way to use these primitive sociometric tools in work carried out with schoolchildren with the help of Beatrice Beecher. Later, at a luncheon of the American Psychiatric Association in Toronto in 1931, he discussed and volunteered to study the feasibility of group psychotherapy within the penal system along similar lines. Following his comments on the necessity to classify people according to certain sociometric principles, he was asked to carry out a research project at Sing Sing prison. He was greatly encouraged in this by Dr William Allison White, one of the most respected psychiatrists in the United States, who at that time was working at St Elizabeths Hospital in Washington where he was also the protector of another innovator in the field of interpersonal relationships, Harry S. Sullivan.

With the help of Helen H. Jennings and the support of E. Stagg Whitin, a well-known criminologist and chairman of the National Committee on Prison and Prison labour, Moreno completed a qualitative and quantitative study of individual relationships with a group of prisoners at Sing Sing and presented the results at a round table conference at the Annual Meeting of the American Psychiatric Association, held in Philadelphia in 1932. This event is generally considered to be the formal start of group psychotherapy for which Moreno is credited: the year 1932 was a landmark both in Moreno's career and in the history of group psychotherapy. After the report of his sociometric study at Sing Sing was published, he started some further major sociometric research at the Hudson School for Girls in New York. Let us look more closely at these two events.[5]

Research at Sing Sing prison and at the Hudson School for Girls

Moreno had developed a profound interest in group work. It was very clear that individuals were essentially part of a group, and his keen sense of observation made him realize that it was by exploring individual situations within the group that one could find answers to psychological problems. At Sing Sing, he proceeded to work on a classification of prisoners which would enhance the rehabilitation process. Using interviews and questionnaires, Moreno touched on about thirty variables for each prisoner and made an analysis of their answers. Then, he proceeded to compare the answers of every prisoner with answers from every other individual prisoner. In this way, every prisoner was 'matched' on a variety of factors with everyone else. For example, prisoner M1 was compared to prisoner M2 for age, sex, race, nationality, immigration history, family background, neighbourhood experiences, language, religion, education, vocational choice, occupation, behaviour, social habits, mental age, reaction type, etc. This comparison yielded a number of similarities, contrasts, and complementaries. A score was then made up and derived from a ratio of positive factors divided by negative factors. From this score it was possible to predict how two individuals might or might not profit from each other's presence in the same group. The comparison was repeated for every individual, and in pairs. From this analysis Moreno derived a social quotient, and ultimately recommended a new classification of prisoners aimed at transforming the prison into a better social community. This long process of analysis and synthesis of data broke new grounds in institutions where classification was a major concern. Moreno had just used 'applied sociometry'.

The year 1932, when Moreno presented his results at Sing Sing to the American Psychiatric Association, is generally given as the date when the term 'group psychotherapy' was used for the first time in the history of social sciences; in fact, Dr W.A. White traced it back to the Toronto luncheon meeting of 1931. But as an experiment, Sing Sing represented much more than the development of a new term, it also introduced a new method, sociometry, as a group therapeutic tool.

Moreno was now in very good standing with White, Whitin, and Jennings. When he presented his report in Philadelphia, the best known American criminologists and psychiatrists working in the penal system were present. His research was well received and was considered to break new ground in the field of diagnosis and therapy for prisoners. About seventy-five professionals took part in the discussion, including Dr Franz Alexander, a well-known psychoanalyst, and Mrs Fannie French Morse, Superintendent of the New York State Training School for Girls in Hudson. Moreno made an impression on both, and this was the start of a long-lasting cooperation, especially with Mrs Morse.[6]

From the Sing Sing experience Moreno went on to add formal therapy to the classification process in work carried out at Hudson. Mrs Morse had herself pioneered a more human approach to delinquency and was attempting to apply new educational principles in her school. After hearing Moreno talk about his sociometric experiment in Sing Sing, she invited him to conduct research at Hudson. The two of them were very much on the same wave length. Moreno was appointed as Director of Research at the New York State Training School for Girls and held the position from 1932–4.

It was here that the principles of spontaneity in interpersonal relationships, so often talked about by Moreno, were put into practical application for the first time. With the help of Helen H. Jennings, Moreno designed tests to study the girls' preferences in roommates, playmates, and leaders and developed *sociograms* depicting different types of interaction between them. In addition to studying the outcomes for the community of pairing girls in different ways, Moreno also involved the girls themselves in the process of choosing their groups and group leaders, according to different variables. At the same time, group leaders were asked to choose the girls they felt they would work better with. Very rapidly Moreno was able to draw up maps, or sociograms, to describe desirable social interactions and more workable units. In 1933, he presented these 'maps' at a medical convention in New York.

But Moreno went much further than sociometry at Hudson; he started to use role-playing and psychodrama to change the girls' attitudes and behaviour. He asked them to play real or imaginary situations, giving each other feedback, and then used analysis of what he saw to help them reflect back on what happened. Often, he would get the girls to play the same situation again so that they could measure their own progress. He was really *training*, or *retraining*, the girls, using techniques based on the level of trust among them and a willingness on their part to play their *true* selves. This created a revolution that soon permeated other institutions and fields. Role-play training was born, but so was the systematic use of psychodrama and group therapy. Moreno's experience with the girls at Hudson can be considered as one of the most important moments in the history of group psychotherapy. It carried a step further the original intent of the 'encounter group' with the prostitutes of Vienna by clearly stating the therapeutic aim, by developing tools to predict behaviour, and creating instruments to help change behaviour. Moreno made 16 mm films at Hudson to illustrate group psychotherapy and the use of role retraining: it was to be regarded world-wide as a major breakthrough in training methods. Moreno wrote extensively on this subject long before the contemporary fashion for 'communication techniques'.[7]

Moreno was again helped in this research by Helen H. Jennings who carried out very thorough data analysis and synthesis of the research results. Graduate students at Hudson also became involved in the girls' retraining programme, taking on assumed roles to help the girls gain insight into their maladjusted and self-punishing behaviour. One of these students was Florence Bridge who, as we have seen, was later to become Moreno's second wife.

It was during this period that Moreno began to become better known and respected. He invited colleagues to the Hudson school, and visitors included Gardner Murphy, a well-known psychologist from Columbia, who was to become Moreno's friend and very involved in his work. He had a great influence and following in academic circles and with his support Moreno began to climb the academic ladder.[8]

Who Shall Survive?[9]

In 1934 Moreno published *Who Shall Survive?* This book was, and still is, a monument to the science of sociometry, but it also presents Moreno philosophy concerning the place of creativity and spontaneity in life. Moreno's thesis is: 'who can create will ultimately survive.' Moreno insisted on the fact that science and religion need not to be in opposition. On the contrary, the future of science lies in its integration with a philosophy of God, and, as we have already seen, every human being, for Moreno, is God, when being creator and co-creator. In fact, in *Who Shall Survive?* Moreno repeats the message of *The Words of the Father*, within the framework of a scientific project.

The bulk of the book presents research findings in relation to the science of group measurement and community regrouping, drawn mainly from research material gathered at Hudson, but also from some other research projects. It also contains material from past European publications, especially in the field of creativity and spontaneity, but it is first and foremost an attempt to consolidate a young science, 'sociometry', whose aim is the mathematical study of the psychological properties of a population by quantitative and qualitative analysis.

The first edition was dedicated to Mrs Fannie French Morse as a testimony to her work at Hudson, and in acknowledgement of the support she gave Moreno. It is a dificult book to read, but very rich in ideas and findings. It soon became a reference book for the student of microsociology.

The foreword to the book, written by Dr White for the first edition, pays general tribute to the wisdom of Moreno's philosophy. After presenting the book, White concludes:

> Dr Moreno comes back to the position in which the environment seems to have greater significance, but he comes back to that aspect of the problem not on the same level as it existed originally but at a higher level; and the interesting thing is that while

> he does come back to a consideration of the environment, that consideration includes the subjective aspect which has been almost exclusively emphasized in the development of child analysis. So we have here one of those typical advances which swings from one point of view to another, but in doing so includes that other . . . And think, further, if you have no objections to flights of the imagination, of what possibly it may offer to an understanding of the problem of democracy as they occur in a country like the United States made up of races from all the four quarters of the globe.
>
> (*Who Shall Survive?* 1934: iii–iv)

Who Shall Survive? is seen, and was possibly conceived by Moreno, as the bible of sociometry. Moreno was particularly proud of the sociometric diagrams that illustrate the interactions between people and show, for example, zones of affinity and repulsion between individuals. These very mathematical models were easily readable and interpretable. It became the standard of the new science, against which other researchers would be judged. The book received generally good reviews. It brought sociologists into the psychological arena and helped to launch the *Sociometric Review* in 1936 and the journal *Sociometry* in 1937. It also helped Moreno to develop a university course in sociometry and in 1937 he was invited to teach in this subject at the New School of Social Research in New York.

Who Shall Survive? was much more popular with sociologists and social psychologists than with psychiatrists. In some ways, Moreno's influence followed a similar path to that of Freud, who also won support from the public, the literary world, and educationalists before convincing psychiatrists of the value of his work. (This trend was particularly evident in the case of *The Interpretation of Dreams*.) Moreno, however, was to take another route to persuade psychiatrists, by meeting them on their own ground and opening a sanatorium. We will talk about this in the next chapter.

Finally, we should note that in 1953 Moreno wrote a second, expanded edition of *Who Shall Survive?* dedicated to his third wife, Zerka. This later edition contains new material, including the autobiographical 'Preludes to the Sociometric Movement' which sheds some light on Moreno's own intellectual heritage and his 'paternity syndrome'. The 'Preludes' is a book by itself, and its inclusion in the new edition of *Who Shall Survive?* was probably a bad decision. Moreno is so confrontational in this text, so eager to show himself as the creator of almost any new idea, that its publication caused a lot of ill feeling. Many readers never get past the 'Preludes' and overlook the main purpose of the book. However, the new edition was a better quality production than the first and its organization is more coherent, even though the reader still needs to work quite hard to extract the essence of the text.

Now let us turn briefly to another anecdote about Moreno which shows yet again his talent as a diagnostician and his ability to apply sociometric principles in a very practical way.

Predicting boxing matches

In 1933 Moreno became acquainted with Howard Blakeslee, a journalist from the Associated Press. By means of this contact he was able to publish articles about sociometry and psychodrama in newspapers that reached a very large audience.

As he got to know Moreno, Howard Blakeslee convinced him that he should get involved in sports psychology. The long-awaited fight for the heavyweight championship in the boxing world was scheduled between Max Baer and Joe Louis for September 1935 and Moreno, who had never been particularly interested in sports, took up the challenge of predicting the winner, using sociometric principles. He went to visit the two boxers in training and made a thorough study of the number of punches delivered by each boxer per minute, the number of punches landed directly, and the strength of these 'killing' blows. (The technique was reminiscent of one he had already used in Vienna in 1924 to study the impromptu process, in the Stegreiftheater, where he had measured the 'spontaneity quotient' of actors and actresses by counting the number, length, and direction of dialogues.) In this case, Moreno also studied what he came to call the *social atom*, or the immediate and meaningful environment, of each boxer: his relationship to his parents, spouse, siblings, friends, and trainers. He studied the style and state of mind of the two protagonists. In the process he had to do a lot of role reversal, imagining, for example, what it meant for Baer to prepare for a fight while he was still on honeymoon. This is reminiscent of his techniques when predicting the outcome of trials in Vienna and also of those he used at Sing Sing and Hudson.

From all this information Moreno determined the ongoing physical and psychological process of Max Baer and Joe Louis. He even went so far as to publish a chart of the greatest influences in Baer's life, with lines representing positive and negative relationships. This chart is clearly a forerunner of representations of the social atom and family genograms.

Moreno drew different hypotheses from his observations, with levels of probability for each of them; each probability level was explained by the research. Ultimately, Moreno predicted a win for Joe Louis and was quite accurate as to how and when. He repeated this kind of study in 1948 for a fight between Joe Louis and Joe Walcott, and in 1954 for the bout between Rocky Marciano and Ezzard Charles.

This type of work exemplifies the extent to which sociometry can practically be applied in many different areas of social life. It also shows how accurate an observer of human behaviour Moreno could be: from his detailed observations, he was able to derive a 'spontaneity quotient' from which he would in turn make predictions about the outcome of the fight. It is possible to see how this process could be applied to numerous other areas and all types of activity.

Moreno made some interesting findings while doing this research. One was the importance of observing the body and not hesitating to touch it:

> A number of the younger, eclectic psychotherapists, such as Fritz Perls and William Schultz, are using these body methods. For a long time, we stood alone. It was assumed by others that all this bodily involvement was harmful for the patient, especially as it changed his relationship to his therapist, from an objective to a highly subjective one. They appreciated and understood. Moreno stuck to his guns. The only concern, he preached, is whether all this is done for the welfare of the patient. It is never intended to fill needs of the therapist. After all, how could a dentist, a surgeon, a gynaecologist or obstetrician, or a dermatologist, practice his skills without 'touching'? Is the psyche more, or less, sacrosanct than the body? Where does one begin and the other end?
>
> (*Psychodrama, Volume 3* 1969: 257)

Another observation had to do with the similarities between what he observed in the training camps and the therapeutic arena:

> I made a fascinating series of discoveries while doing all this, not the least of which being that trainers intuitively chose sparring partners who represented the fighting style of the opponent he was training to encounter. I designated the sparring

> partners — naturally — as auxiliary egos, stand-ins for the real person and the real event, very much in the way the psychodramatic chief therapist proceeds to prepare his patients by means of auxiliary egos for his eventual return to his own real life partners and the inevitable encounter with them.
>
> (*Psychodrama, Volume 3* 1969: 257)

If there is a negative side to the story, it is the difficulty that Moreno had in refusing this kind of challenge which put him in the limelight. However, he shows here again his strength as a diagnostician, and his originality in thinking.

The founding of journals and the development of sociometry

Moreno was very much a founder. There is probably no other place where his talent was put to better use than in founding professional journals, associations, and institutes. For example, in 1931, he founded a little journal, *Impromptu*, which was published only twice, but created a lot of interest in spontaneous theatre. However, shortly afterwards Moreno was to abandon the realm of theatre almost completely to focus more on sociometry and psychodrama. In spite of his heroic efforts to bring about a revolution through theatre, he inevitably failed: actors needed to perform and resisted the call to free themselves; theatre was not the real world, and Moreno wanted to invest in a world where he could free souls imprisoned by the social and *cultural conserves*; he wanted to help people searching for inner and outer freedom.

In order to achieve these aims, Moreno needed a vehicle to carry his ideas to a wider public. In 1936, he had again created a journal, the *Sociometric Review* in which he presented ideas and methods that had not found a place in *Who Shall Survive?* His main collaborator was again Helen H. Jennings. But Moreno knew that he had to broaden his base and his audience, so, in 1937, he created *Sociometry: A Journal of Interpersonal Relations*. This new venture was important in many ways and introduced yet another new term, 'interpersonal relations', to the academic world. The journal rapidly reached a much bigger audience than the *Sociometric Review*, helped by the creation of a board of editors, for which Moreno was able to secure well-known names in sociology, anthropology, psychology and social psychology. The first editor of the journal was Gardner Murphy, then at Columbia University, followed by George A. Lundberg from the University of Washington. Respected academics such as Margaret Mead (American Museum of Natural History), Gordon Allport (Harvard University), Charles P. Loomis (Michigan State College), Hadley Cantril (Princeton University) agreed to contribute.

The creation of *Sociometry* gave Moreno a distinct advantage in publishing his own research and theories. He was also able to give his close collaborators an opportunity to express themselves. The selection of papers was no doubt conducted on very fair principles, but one could argue that it removed the need for Moreno to risk rejection by other competitive journals. *Sociometry* was an opportunity for him to publish papers on the development of spontaneity tests and training, on sociometric studies and on the history of the sociometric movement.

The journal was published by the Morenos until 1955, when it was transferred to the American Sociological Society. It is interesting to note that the transfer coincided with the creation by Moreno, of the *International Journal of Sociometry and Sociatry*. By this time Moreno had been touring America for more than twenty years lecturing about his ideas and demonstrating his methods. He felt that the time had come to expand his activities. By the mid-1950s, sociometry had developed in many countries outside the United States. From now on Moreno was to leave more and more of his work in America to be carried out by his friends and colleagues in the American Sociological Association, while he himself carried the message further afield.

The development of sociometric studies was accelerated by the war. The army needed quick and reliable answers in different areas. Sociometry proved useful, and Moreno was often called in as consultant. His biggest breakthrough was at the St Elizabeths Hospital in Washington where his methods were widely tested and approved, but he was also involved indirectly with the selection and training of officers of the British Army through Major G. Fitzpatrick and Lt.-Col. J.D. Sutherland, who visited the Sociometric Institute in New York for a month and applied sociometric methods upon his return to England. During the war, Moreno was very active in training programmes for the American army as well: sociometry and group therapy were highly regarded as a means of selecting personnel and boosting morale.[11]

It was also during this period that Moreno became associated with Pitirim A. Sorokin from Harvard, a man who Moreno considered to be 'one of the greatest social scientists of our time'. Through discussion and critique, Sorokin was instrumental in helping Moreno clarify many of his concepts. According to Moreno, the two men agreed on a lot of things, but disagreed on one vital issue, that of their perception of science:

> It became clear to me that much of Sorokin's work had been done behind a desk. Although he was a gifted social scientist, our main point of difference was that I was out in the world trying to live out my philosophy, testing it every day in my life and in the lives of my students and patients, whereas he was confined to his desk, his laboratory, and his classroom . . . I was an experimenter and experimenters like Jesus, Buddha, St Francis often look inadequate even pathological, but they are trying to live a life of truth and prefer an imperfect existence to a perfect theory.
>
> ('Autobiography' 1985: ch. 11: 24)

Moreno had many other colleagues with whom he discussed and developed sociometric tools. In addition to his association with Columbia, Harvard, New York University, and the New School of Research, he was soon invited to lecture at universities throughout the United States, including Denver, Ohio, Stanford, Chicago, and Los Angeles. His teaching was another way of forcing him to clarify his position and refine his techniques. At times, he may have spent too much energy in this way, performing countless demonstrations of his work rather than focusing on his writings.[12]

Moreno's main contribution to sociometry remained his basic research at Sing Sing and Hudson. He never pushed further, even though he continued to be active in the field. In 1951 he published *Sociometry, Experimental Method and the Science of Society* and in, 1956, *Sociometry and the Science of Man*. But all this was old wine. Basically, Moreno did not have the patience to be a full-time researcher. He was more attracted by the practical world and a certain glamour associated with it. This might explain why psychodrama gradually became his favourite tool.

The developments in the field of sociometry were accompanied by their share of controversy. Moreno had an obsession with 'fatherhood'. In the mid 1930s he had some contact with Kurt Lewin, author of *Topological Psychology* and leader of the group dynamics movement. Moreno was quick to claim that Lewin, and in particular Lewin's students, were greatly influenced by his own theory. Moreno certainly had a case, in that many of Lewin's followers were also students of the Institute of Sociometry and contributed articles to the journal *Sociometry*. Moreno was unable to stay away from controversy when it was related to the 'paternity of his own contribution'.[13]

Eventually the field of sociometry and small group research boomed:

Moreno's influence could be felt everywhere, even though his name gradually started to be forgotten. Very few young students of sociology or social psychology today would ever have suspected the impact that Moreno had on this field of research and practice more than fifty years ago. One reason is that Moreno really did very limited research in this area, with the exception of the projects at Sing Sing and Hudson. Another is that he left the arena to other outstanding researchers, maintaining for a while the 'official' leadership role, with no real power. There were also controversies and struggles with and between associates and students.

However, more might be learned from Moreno, for rooted as he was in the present, he tried to preserve our future, our survival:

> Man must take his own fate and the fate of the universe in hand, on the level of creativity, as a creator. It is not sufficient if he tries to meet the situation by technical control — defense weapons — nor by political controls — world government — he should face himself and his society in *statu nascendi* and learn how to control the robot not after it is delivered, but before it is conceived (creatocracy) . . . The future of man depends upon counterweapons developed by sociometry and sociatry.
>
> (*The Future of Man's World* 1947: 21)

Chapter 8
Group psychotherapy and psychodrama

Moreno recognized that in modern society the ideal of a completely spontaneous and creative life is difficult to achieve and designed the techniques of Impromptu theatre, and eventually the method of psychodrama, to overcome this. After 1931, the development of both techniques took place, as with sociometry, in the general context of group psychotherapy. The philosophical base was still in the relationship I-God, as creator, and in meaningful encounter.

Why did Moreno choose expressive methods to promote individual or group fulfilment? The answer lies in Moreno's own personality. It is as if we were to ask the same question about Freud. Psychoanalysis was created by someone at ease with dream analysis, and curious about the meaning of his own unconscious. Moreno was to create a theatre and later a therapeutic method to justify his personal desire to play God. He was even to say that thanks to psychodrama he was able to master his own megalomania. Reference to his own experience led him to believe that everyone enjoys a 'normal' desire to be centre stage and that in order to attain full psychological development, to be creative, everyone has to find a way to perform spontaneously in front of an audience. Moreno's own life exemplifies his search for a stage: he entertained children in the park and in the theatre: he did it in a reciprocal way having children play a major role in their own story while retaining the leadership. His own experience as a charismatic doctor led him to *theatre reciproque*, a form of community psychotherapy with a cathartic approach and religious overtones. His work with prostitutes made him realize that everyone can play the role of co-therapist for someone else. But Moreno needed a 'real' stage and his experience with the Stegreiftheater gave him the chance to experiment.

In order to understand the development of psychodrama, one has to look closely at the different roles played by Moreno. He wanted to do away with *cultural conserves* and to bring about 'spontaneous man'. In order to do this, he first needed to act his own spontaneous being, then to bring about his revolution; he also felt that he needed to teach how to rid of the stiffness of modern man. To achieve this he himself became an *actor*, an *author*, and a *preacher*. We saw how Moreno played all these roles before writing about them. He was to repeat them in the development of psychodrama, becoming in turn role model, director, and analyst.

Psychodrama as we now know it evolved gradually. We saw how Moreno brought his stage to the United States, the stage which was conceived as a place of total involvement for people in the theatre of their own lives. Moreno failed to make progress with this idea in Vienna: his actors there were professionals who ultimately derived their pleasure from moving the emotions of spectators; they did not see themselves as 'patients' needing help to recapture their own spontaneity. If they did profit from their experience in Moreno's theatre, they later left and resumed their professional careers as actors. Moreno was disappointed, failing to understand that he might have succeeded in releasing in actors such as Peter Lorre, Elisabeth Bergner, and Anna Höllering the potential for enhanced professional performance. What he wanted was to replace traditional plays by spontaneous scripts, involving everyone.

On moving to the United States, Moreno had hoped to find a more receptive theatre environment in which to implement his revolutionary ideas. He repeated his experiment of the Stegreiftheater and rented space at the Carnegie Hall to resume his work with a new group of artists ready to carry out his ideas. He also worked at the New York Civic Repertory directed by Eva LaGallienne. In 1931, the same year that he started his sociometric research at Sing Sing and became involved in a controversy with the psychoanalyst Abraham Brill, he opened his impromptu theatre.

The impromptu theatre

The official opening took place at the Guild Theatre on 5 April 1931. Ten years after his failure at the Komödienhaus in Vienna, Moreno went public again. But this time, it was not April Fools Day, and Moreno was not alone on the stage; neither did he have Franz Werfel and his group to applaud the performance, no matter what the quality or content.

From the official programme we get a sense of the type of work that Moreno was doing during this period. There were some impromptu plays by the group and some post-analysis by him. Moreno would 'comment' on performances and act in the role of analyst or 'explain' them in the role of teacher, living up to the meaning of his Hebraic name, 'Morenu'. Also included in the programme was a small classical orchestra which improvised on stage. This latter experiment was not very successful and was soon discontinued, but it did allow Moreno to understand the limits of spontaneous performance in classical music and the conditions necessary to enhance it. He saw the difference between improvisation for musicians and actors.

By 1931 Moreno had recaptured all the energy that he had shown in Vienna. He now found a place to experiment with his *psychodrama stage*. The work at the Impromptu Theatre had started informally in 1929 continued to take place at Carnegie Hall for some time and focused mainly on spontaneity training, the 'living newspaper' technique, and impromptu theatre performances based on conflicts presented by members of the audience. It took some time before Moreno resumed his therapeutic work on stage, possibly because of the memory of the unforeseen suicide in Vienna.

Ultimately the impromptu theatre was no more successful, in Moreno's view, than the one in Vienna. It was appreciated by the audience, but for Moreno it fell short of the fundamental revolution he had hoped to achieve. As in Vienna, the audience hesitated at getting involved in the way Moreno wanted them to, and the actors, with a few exceptions, used the stage as a place to recapture their spontaneous ability and to warm-up to traditional plays. In fact, Moreno was doing just what Stanislavski was doing, simply training better actors.

In 1931, as we have already seen, Moreno produced and published two issues of a magazine called *Impromptu*. It reproduced many of the texts that he had already published in Vienna, but also included articles by J.J. Robbins, Theodore Appia, and Helen H. Jennings. Even though the magazine was short-lived, it did allow Moreno to present his views and to take some sort of leadership again.[1]

However, by this time, Moreno had already decided to take up psychiatry as a result of his work at Mt Sinaî Hospital in New York and his therapeutic work with schoolchildren in association with his first wife, Beatrice Beecher: this gave him yet another stage on which to perform. He attended the annual meeting of the American Psychiatric Association for the first time in 1931, and as a new member was very active during the convention. Not only did he take part in discussion groups on prison reform, a turning point that eventually gave birth to sociometry, but he was also involved in another event, of a more controversial nature.

Moreno, Abraham A. Brill, and psychoanalysis

Dr Abraham A. Brill was a highly respected psychoanalyst in the United States at that time, and an orthodox Freudian. At the APA convention Moreno was asked to be a discussant for Dr Brill's paper, 'Lincoln as a humorist', which presented a very unflattering picture of the past American president. Moreno not only attacked the content of the paper, challenging Brill's analysis of Lincoln on the grounds that it was impossible, if not unfair, to interpret the personality of a dead person, but also delivered some harsh personal criticism of Brill himself. By 'role reversing' with Lincoln, Moreno managed to present an equally unflattering picture of Brill. Here are some of Moreno's comments, which appeared in newspapers all around the world the following day:

> Mr President, Ladies and Gentlemen: I have listened carefully but I am not sure whether Dr Brill's paper was a paper on Lincoln or on psychoanalysis. The title of his paper is 'Abraham Lincoln as a Humorist'. It might just as well have been called 'Dr Brill as a Humorist'. It is not fair to psychoanalyse the personality of a man now dead, as you have to do it without his consent. One must have therefore a special reason. Dr Brill's conclusions are based on the statements of friends and contemporaries who may have had all kinds of motives to relate all kinds of stories about Lincoln. Had a contemporary psychiatrist made a study of Lincoln, Dr Brill would have been justified to some extent in accepting the findings. But as no scientific study of the great American emancipator has been made during his life-time there was no justification for any attempt to analyse his personality from what is related about him by laymen.
>
> It is difficult to understand how the dead Lincoln could have made a 'transference' to the living Brill. It is obvious, however, that Brill has developed an extraordinary transference to Lincoln. The unconscious psychodynamics which become 'available in the course of analysis' are those of Brill, only they are 'here and now'.
>
> Brill has attempted to prove that Lincoln's coarse and vulgar humor was unconsciously determined, a form of libidinal sublimation. My opinions have developed by means of a different method — the psychodrama. They are based on the study of persons placed in improvised situations. Those persons respond

> spontaneously to a new situation much as an actor or actress on the stage of life, and cultivate a personality such as is deemed by them to be the most suitable for the circumstances and which best will meet the purpose they are endeavouring to serve. In a man of Lincoln's genius an enormous amount of creativity must have gone into the reorganisation of the psychic material emerging from the private person. The more unusual the character and the circumstances, the more dangerous it is to apply an 'accepted formula'. The psychoanalytic method has not developed sufficiently to the point where it could attempt an analysis of Lincoln. Not only has no expert in psychiatry first hand knowledge of Lincoln when he was alive but a genius of his type was capable of playing roles and saying many things which could be explained in a multitude of ways.
>
> (*Who Shall Survive?* 1953: xliv–xlv)[2]

In addition to these comments, Moreno also answered four questions that give us some insight into his own capacity to analyse psychological material and to use his opponent's weapon to fight him on his own ground.

> First, why did Brill pick on a dead person instead of a living one? Second, why did he pick on an illustrious, outstanding character and particularly an American? Third, why did he pick on Abraham Lincoln? Fourth, why did he choose me to discuss his hypothesis?
>
> (*Who Shall Survive?* 1953: xlvii)

Moreno's answers to these questions are particularly interesting because of his 'psychoanalysis' of Brill, and because they also shed further light on his conflict with Freud:

> The first question is comparatively easy to answer. It is easier to analyse a dead man, that is, easier for the analyst. He is not exposed to any 'counter spontaneity'. . .
>
> This brings us to the answer to the second question. It *had* to be an illustrious, outstanding character, because the paper was apparently intended to give psychoanalysis great publicity, to document before the world that psychoanalysis has the intellectual power of coping with creative geniuses and the most outstanding individuals of history and put them in their proper place. But why did it have to be an American? Obviously Brill

picked on an American because he was personally involved with the American people. Very possibly America was the country he had set out to conquer for psychoanalysis and for himself. . .

This brings us to the third question. It is more difficult to answer. I may be able, if you will permit me, to psychoanalyse Dr Brill himself. . . He was building himself up to appear before the world, the American public, in a great role, the role of the psychoanalytic emancipator and liberator. Seeing him in action, I could not help comparing him with Lincoln, the object of his analysis. He is little more than five feet tall. Lincoln was a giant, way above six feet. Both have a beard and both have the first name, Abe. . . Brill had waited patiently for a chance to measure up to that other Abe and today, in this hall, before all of us, he had this opportunity — the President of the American Psychoanalytic Society versus the President of the United States. . .

Last but not least, the question must be answered: Why did he choose me to discuss his paper? It was, to say the least, an irrational choice, irrational, in a psychoanalytic, but not in a sociometric sense. Brill and I were, as we sociometrists call it, in the 'networks', although strangers, closely related. We had many emotional acquaintances in common, psychoanalysts, psychiatrists and others, with numerous links between them. These links are channels of influence and communication preparing the individual target for important decisions. These 'tele' factors work on an individual although he is hardly conscious of the complex network which it forms around him. Why did he choose as a discussant one of the opponents of psychoanalysis? Why did he choose an immigrant like himself?. . . I was already in Vienna a blunt critic of psychoanalysis. Brill must have known of my radical theories about the group and the therapeutic theatre. I was dangerous, not so much because I knew its limitations but because I had developed methods which the future will, as I claimed, prove to be superior. My answer as to why Brill slipped is: he was not quite sure that psychoanalysis is able to analyse geniuses of the calibre of Abraham Lincoln; he was not quite sure that he, as an individual — an immigrant — was the one to deliver the blow to American autism; and he was not quite sure that the American people would accept him, Abraham Brill, the deliverer, as an idol instead of Lincoln. He feared that he was playing a losing game. He felt guilty, Freud was not around to help him, and in a masochistic mood, with a brazen gesture, he called upon the very man whose ways of production and presentation should have been as mysterious to him as those of Abraham Lincoln. He called upon myself. Like the dying Hamlet he called Fortinbras to take over.

It would be only fair for me to tell you also why I accepted Brill's invitation. I had two reasons. The one was that Brill represented psychoanalysis which I esteemed highly but considered as my natural opposition. The second reason was my profound sympathy for Abraham Lincoln. I felt as if I took his place, like an auxiliary ego in a psychodramatic session. As I spoke, I felt as though, in a way, Lincoln spoke through me. He, the defenseless dead, defended himself. He appealed to me as a psychodramatic character in real life, a producer of ideas and actions. The psychodrama of his own life and the sociodrama of the American continent were merging on that morning of June 5th, at the Hotel Royal York, into one great, indissoluble event. The history of the last twenty years had made the Brill-Lincoln incident symbolic.

(*Who Shall Survive?* 1953: xlvii–l

I would like to take up a few points here. The first concerns Moreno's knowledge of psychoanalysis. Because of his opposition to psychoanalysis, people sometimes get the impression that he did not know much about it. However, his discussion of Brill's paper indicates clearly that he knew the concepts that Brill was using, and that he could use them himself to his own advantage. From his personal library, we can see that he read Freud with some attention, making many comments in the margins of his own copies of Freud's works.

On a further reading of the account of the 'incident' with Brill, it becomes clear that through Brill, Moreno wanted to strike at Freud. He had made the same negative comments about Freud's analysis of Moses as he made about Brill's analysis of Lincoln, and his real target here was undoubtedly Freud, the father of psychoanalysis. In 1931, Moreno was attacking psychoanalysis just as he did in his encounter with Freud almost twenty years before. He had probably not wished or expected to find psychoanalysis so firmly established in the country to which he had come to make a fresh start. As evidence of Moreno's real motive in attacking Brill, one can refer to the psychodrama monograph, no. 42 (1967): its title is 'The Psychodrama of Sigmund

Freud', but the content essentially deals with the Brill story.

Another point to be noticed is the opportunism shown by Moreno. Here was a new immigrant to the United States defending a much loved American president. His identification with Lincoln was doubtless authentic and he probably also wanted in some way to free psychology from psychoanalysis, but he did show a sense of *à propos* and timing that were just right. The controversy brought immediate fame: the account of Brill's analysis and Moreno's response to it was in most American and international newspapers the next day. But this instant fame was not without a price and most psychoanalysts turned against Moreno.

There are many other aspects that could be analysed in this 'incident': Moreno's personal identification with Lincoln; the 'repetitive' side of this confrontation; the double standard that he used in publishing this account in 1953, a few years after Brill's death; the actual consequences in psychiatric circles of Moreno's intervention at the Toronto conference.

Moreno's confrontations with psychoanalysis were to continue throughout his career. He never met Freud in person again after the encounter of 1912 or 1914, but wrote so much about and against him that it is clear that he profoundly envied this other founder and father. At the end of his life Moreno became somewhat less aggressive towards other analysts, but before this he was to have many other battles, especially with S.R. Slavson the proponent of psychoanalytic group therapy in the USA. Both were giants in the field of group therapy and were to fight directly and indirectly through their associates and students for almost three decades in ways reminiscent, at times, of child rivalry. It is impossible to assess responsibility in a conflict that led the two protagonists to create separate associations and professional journals, competing for national, and later world, leadership, but is clear that no real benefit came from these constant fights between the Moreno and Slavson factions.[3]

These controversies put Moreno on his mettle: it was not enough to criticize, he felt he had to present alternatives. He not only succeeded in doing so, but put them forward in his opponents' own field, psychiatry. Moreno would always be a performer, and at best in adversity. However, one often wonders how much better he would have fared without these constant fights which drained so much energy and put the focus of attention on the man rather than on his theories. As he himself said, 'I was the controversy.'

Beacon: the birth of a dream

By 1936 Moreno was well on his way to having a secure and meaningful life. He had opened two offices in New York from which he practised medicine, one in a poor area where he would see people without charging, the other in a wealthy area where he could earn himself a living. He was doing research at Hudson, teaching at the university, and experimenting with impromptu theatre, but he still needed somewhere were he could be in complete control, commanding the centre of the stage. The idea of owning his own hospital and training facilities came to him gradually. He was commuting by train every week from New York to Hudson, and developing an increasing appreciation of the countryside and landscape. He was also becoming more involved in psychiatry, and growing rapidly dissatisfied with the theatre experiment.

At one point he was called in by a wealthy family to treat one of its members who was psychotic and who thought he was Jesus Christ. Moreno employed the techniques of psychodrama to treat the young man, using auxiliary egos to play parts in the hallucinatory world of the patient and entering his delusion system. The treatment was successful partly because it took place outside a conventional institution. In a traditional setting Moreno could not have entered into his patient's fantasy in this way, especially as it concerned nudity, without upsetting the institution's rules and regulations. This experience underlined for Moreno the importance to him of the freedom to use unorthodox treatment which in this case proved very beneficial to the patient.

Because of his ability to enter the imaginary world of other people, Moreno was particularly successful with psychotics. But these were just the patients who were most restrained in traditional mental institutions. This was the decisive factor, coupled with his desire to own his own hospital, that led him to buy an estate in Beacon, a small town on the Hudson River, about sixty miles north of New York City, for transformation into a hospital.

From a historical perspective, 1936 could be considered the most important date in Moreno's life. He was at a crossroads: he could either continue to practise psychotherapy within the mainstream of existing institutions, or create a new centre from which to disseminate his ideas to the rest of the world. He chose the second alternative. An old school, a fact highly symbolic in itself, was transformed into a small psychiatric hospital. In turn, this hospital was to become a 'training school' and a centre for the diffusion of Moreno's ideas: the Beacon Press was to be located on the premises. In the long run, Beacon was everything that

Moreno needed: a place in which to carry out therapy, to again become actor, preacher, author.

Figure 17 Beacon Sanatorium. (Zerka Moreno, private collection; rephotographed by Johanne Doyon.)

In 1936 Moreno was granted a licence to open the Beacon Hill Sanatorium, which was to be renamed the Moreno Sanatorium in 1951. This small hospital soon became the laboratory for all Moreno's ideas and hypotheses. At first, it was a hospital without patients and Moreno was beginning to wonder how he would pay for his investment, but his luck soon changed after a meeting with Mrs Gertrude Franchot Tone, who suffered from alcoholism, but was also extremely wealthy. She met with Moreno a few times to discuss his ideas, read *Who Shall Survive?*, and soon became a resident of the newly created hospital. She also offered money to build the first theatre of psychodrama, a stage dedicated to the exploration of therapeutic issues among the patients. At last, twelve years after the publication of his plan for a theatre at the International Exhibition of New Theatre Techniques in Vienna, Moreno could build a stage in keeping with his own ideas about therapy and psychodrama. The stage differed quite a bit from his original idea, but it still included the main elements of his first design: everybody in the theatre was a participant and the stage had different levels, including a balcony. Moreno dedicated this theatre to Mrs Franchot Tone and it soon became world famous.

Figure 18 A typical scene taking place on the psychodrama stage at Beacon, Moreno directing. (Zerka Moreno, private collection; rephotographed by Johanne Doyon.)

After this the hospital received many patients, most of them very difficult cases rejected by other psychiatrists, and began to function as a therapeutic community reminiscent of the group founded by Moreno and his student friends in Vienna, the 'House of Encounter'. Moreno himself lived on the premises with his wife Florence in 1938, and later with Zerka.

Soon the stage was used by people other than patients as a place to explore conflicts. The actor Franchot Tone, Gertrude's son, used it to explore some of his marital problems with his wife, Joan Crawford; young students of psychodrama came from Hudson, and through other colleges and universities. Eventually Beacon became an institution and the stage designed by Moreno was imitated in the United States and throughout the world.

The Beacon stage retained some of the characteristics of the Viennese design, but in order to understand Moreno's vision in its entirety, we have to consider not only the stage itself, but the theatre, and the whole Beacon estate as a therapeutic means. The Beacon sanatorium was as we have said, a therapeutic community: both staff and patients lived on the premises; they met regularly, and were very open with each other. People could circulate quite freely and discuss their life at the sanatorium; their families could be integrated in both the therapeutic process and life at the hospital. The sanatorium became like a vast church, incorporating every meaningful person, real or imaginary, patient or not, in a new philosopy of interpersonal relationship.

In the theatre patients were encouraged to act out their past and present lives, and fantasies about the future. It was the place where the whole community met to explore each other's ideas and ideals about living. There were no spectators since everybody was involved in one way or another.

The stage, with its different levels and balcony, was the place for immediate psychological exploration. The warm-up process took place in the audience, or on the first level of the stage, but action took place on the upper levels, through catharsis and analysis. A conflict was experienced or re-experienced using all the tools of psychodrama: mirroring, role reversal, doubling, chorus, soliloquy, and so on. When people entered the theatre or went on stage, they knew that the rules of reality were changed: they were in the world of 'as if', and could allow themselves to explore their life from different and new perspectives. Time was taken later for sharing experiences.

The Beacon theatre, because it was inside the walls of a sanatorium, served a different purpose to the one in the Carnegie Hall or the Stegreiftheater in Vienna. Spontaneity, creativity, and encounter were still the key words, but every enactment was in the interest of the patient: Moreno was practising psychotherapy, and more precisely group psychotherapy. There was no ambiguity about the goal. Every psychodrama was an act of therapy in the narrow sense of the term. The Beacon theatre was the place where psychodrama began to take on a life of its own with a systematic use of auxiliary egos and a director servicing the 'protagonist'. Psychodrama became a way for people to explore their lives, or as Moreno put it, their 'truth'.

The Beacon sanatorium was more than a treatment centre. Of course, Moreno was dedicated to the welfare of his patients, but he also used the Centre as a laboratory to test his hypotheses about mental health, his theory of the dyad creativity/encounter, the numerous techniques of psychodrama, and the limits of group psychotherapy. Gradually, the term psychodrama came into general use, the role of the director, the auxiliary egos, and the protagonist were clarified, and techniques were refined: it was at Beacon that the birth of psychodrama really took place.

Beacon sanatorium became a new utopia for Moreno. He had already had a taste of such a concept in Austria: his little house in Bad Vöslau and his involvement in the community there had been in a sense a warm-up for the more integrated ideas of Beacon. In Bad Vöslau, Moreno had been a doctor, a writer, an actor, and the 'Valley of May' was the prefiguration of Beacon.

In concept and in reality, Beacon was a prototype: it was seen by Moreno as a hospital responding to an *intraverted* model, a place where patients could experience inner freedom through exploration of their feelings, even though these might be confused and incoherent at first. It was a prototype for psychotherapy using psychodrama as its main tool, a training school for psychiatrists, psychologists, nurses, social workers and educators, who would develop a full range of necessary expertise in diagnosis, treatment method, epistemology, and ethics. Beacon was to provide an all-encompassing environment for the promotion of individual and social mental health. The psychodrama stage was the symbolic representation of the therapeutic liberation to come, and was reproduced all over the world. It was a prototype of individual and family life, a psychodramatic model, put to the test by the leading actors, the Morenos themselves.

Beacon was also a utopia, a very seductive reality, and a model that worked for many years. This model needed constant readjustment, but was very helpful to patients, stimulating for students, and rewarding to its creator and co-creators. Here, Moreno could be doctor, psychodrama leader, sociometrist, author, religious leader, and creator. While working at Beacon, he did not lost contact with the rest of the world because he continued to teach and practise in New York City, but Beacon was the place which gave him the freedom to excel. Of the birth of this project he said:

> Having my own hospital was a sort of liberation from the establishment. It was, on another level, a parallel to my earliest Godplaying venture at the age of four. Then I decided to play God and to be on the top of the game. I had the bright idea of going back to the fantasies of my childhood. Then I wanted to teach children how to play God. Now I wanted to start with adults, with the mentally sickest, to cure them through psychodrama. There I was, God, using psychodrama as a cosmic remedy.
>
> ('Autobiography' 1985: ch. 8: 46)

As Moreno developed the idea of a cure through psychodrama, Beacon became more and more important and eventually known world-wide. Beacon was to the history of psychodrama and institutional group psychotherapy, what Freud's consulting rooms on the Berggasse were to psychoanalysts: a place of birth, a very fertile ground for the development of sociatry, the theatre replacing the couch, the community extending the boundaries of the therapeutic dyad.

Unfortunately Beacon was to disappear.[4] At the height of its success, Moreno continued to be active in New York City and maintained two offices, just as in the 1920s he had worked in both Bad Vöslau and Vienna; he needed a small laboratory, while continuing to teach the world at large. In 1942 he opened the Sociometric and Psychodramatic Institutes in New York where he was to give public demonstrations and do some formal teaching. Already, even though he may not have realized it, he was diluting his efforts. Soon he accepted invitations to teach in various settings in the United States and, after 1950, around the world. Moreno had chosen to conquer a larger territory, true to his philosophy and inclination. In 1967, he closed the hospital, retaining only his training and publishing interests. As Moreno himself became less able to carry out a demanding schedule, Zerka took a more prominent role in the training programme and, in the late 1960s and early 1970s, she really took over the leadership, becoming an established figure in the world of group psychotherapy and psychodrama. Beacon, as a training centre, survived Moreno and even developed further under Zerka's direction. The place was sold in 1982 to an organization, Horsham. It did not survive, even though its spirit can still be felt in the work and dedication of Zerka and Moreno's many students and disciples. The idea of Beacon was imitated by many. Could it have been saved in reality? It is difficult to say. How can such a place survive? How can a 'dynasty' be transmitted?

Moreno's children were to develop their personal and professional lives in different directions and there was no obvious spiritual heir to a movement which had needed dedication, wisdom, favourable conditions, faith, and indestructible perseverance to be born. The Morenos — Zerka as much as Jacob — had brought to fruition an exciting experiment which had brought tangible and positive benefits to the world, but a close look at the Beacon experience reveals the conditions that such a utopia needs in order to develop and survive: it must remain a small venture, resisting both internal and external pressure to grow too big, and above all, there must be an unshakeable conviction that the small experiment will be ultimately successful as it is gradually reproduced elsewhere by well-trained students. The fact that Beacon eventually closed might be seen as a failure, but as an expression of an alternative to traditional therapeutic and training models it has survived. Many different models have succeeded it, with more or less success, and with a variable life span. They have mostly been offspring of the original Beacon idea, and from that point of view, Beacon can be seen as a success.

For almost forty years the Morenos directed the Beacon sanatorium, and later the Moreno Institute, and its greatest interest, and limitation, might have been that in that time it remained a 'family' operation. Very few modern 'centres' could claim such a long life span and the diversity of services that Beacon once offered.

The development of psychodrama

Psychodrama as a therapeutic method was developed by Moreno from his earlier experiences in spontaneous theatre and community therapy. Its development was gradual, but gathered momentum at Beacon, and later at the Sociometric Institute in New York. By 1942, when Moreno published his first paper on the subject with Zerka, the principles of a psychodrama session were pretty much set. There were three parts, the warm-up process, the action, and the sharing; the group included protagonist, auxiliary egos, director, and audience; the main techniques were role reversal, doubling, and mirroring: finally, processes such as tele and co-unconscious were evident during a session that often dealt with the exploration of a patient's social atom. In the next few years the method was greatly expanded and refined. Moreno developed the techniques mainly through impromptu theatre, but learned to apply and adapt them in a therapeutic setting. His staff learned to become auxiliary egos, and soon interns, mainly nurses and social workers, came to learn how to practise psychodrama. Beacon, because of its small size and the community atmosphere, was an environment particularly conducive to learning. The New York Institute drew people from different fields and was another exceptional laboratory: people like Fritz Perls, S.H. Foulkes and Eric Berne, to name just a few who became known in their own right, participated in Friday-night sessions. For years Beacon and New York were the training grounds for hundreds of future psychodramatists and a gathering place for curiosity seekers.[5]

As we have seen, Moreno had succeeded in interesting Dr William Alanson White from St Elizabeths Hospital, Washington DC, in sociometry and psychodrama. In the autumn of 1939, a group of professionals from the hospital came to Beacon to watch a demonstration and to get acquainted with the basic techniques; they were sent by Dr Winfred Overholser, the new Superintendent of the hospital, and included, among others, the clinical director, Dr Roscoe W. Hall and Miss Margaret Hagan: they were both to be instrumental in the development of psychodrama in mental institutions. On 8 June 1941, a theatre of psychodrama was officially opened at St Elizabeths, the first public hospital to have such a theatre built. This development was helped by the large population of army people who had to be treated and the numbers of Red Cross personnel who needed training. In 1942 the hospital created an official position for a psychodramatist and from then on took a leading role in pioneering the use of psychodrama as a group therapy technique and in training other psychodramatists. The first director was Miss Frances Herriott, former stage manager with The Theatre Guild and director of the west coast production of 'Porgy and Bess': it is interesting to note that the first 'official' psychodramatist was from the theatre world for it facilitated the use of music, dance and drama within the therapeutic setting of the hospital.[6]

It did not take long, especially because there were so many war victims in need of treatment, for psychodrama to become implemented in hospitals and universities throughout the United States. Soon psychodrama stages became a necessary part of most psychiatry departments in hospitals and psychology faculties. Henry H. Murray, one of the originators of the Thematic Apperception Test was eventually to build a stage at Harvard.[7] In the late 1940s psychodrama was well on its way to being recognized as a specific form of therapy requiring a certified therapist. All this created new needs for other things: a more integrated book on the topic of psychodrama, an association to regroup psychodramatists and group psychotherapists, and a training programme. Moreno addressed them all.

Writing about psychodrama

Now that Moreno had a place, Beacon, from which he could spread his message, he became more seriously and systematically involved in writing and publishing. He knew that his projects always worked best when they were completely under his own control and for this reason decided to run his own publishing venture. He had already had some experience of publishing and setting up journals in Austria and was to repeat the experiment on a much larger scale in America. We have already seen how he promoted sociometry through books and journals, now let us look at how he came to disseminate his ideas about psychodrama and group psychotherapy. In 1943 he published two series of small books, the 'sociometry monographs' and the 'psychodrama and group psychotherapy monographs'. Many of them contain papers already published by Moreno in his professional journals, but they also give a very good idea of the wide range of topics he covered, which included history, theory, training, ethics, and case studies.[8]

In addition to the *Sociometry* journal founded in 1937, in 1947 Moreno published a new journal: *Sociatry, Journal of Group and Inter-Group Therapy*. This was the official organ of the American Society of Group Psychotherapy and Psychodrama, founded by Moreno in 1942. The journal became *Group Psychotherapy: Journal of Sociopsychopathology and Sociatry* in 1950, then *Group Psychotherapy and Psychodrama* in 1970, and finally *Journal of Group Psychotherapy, Psychodrama and Sociometry* in 1976. Moreno was the main force behind the journal and its leading contributor. The nature and level of his articles varied: some were very challenging and thoughtful papers on psychotherapy or psychodrama; some were repeats of previous publications; some, unfortunately, were justifications of the value of his own work and attacks on other prominent therapists.

However, in the field of psychodrama, the most significant publication was his book *Psychodrama, Volume 1*, which appeared in 1946. This book is dedicated to Moreno's brother, William, and begins with the now famous poem about creation and encounter, first published in *Invitation to an Encounter, Part 2* in 1915. It is reproduced in full on pages 47–8 in Part One of this book and declares: 'More important than procreation is the child. More important than evolution of creation is the evolution of the creator.'

On the following page of *Psychodrama, Volume 1*, Moreno wrote: *'God is spontaneity. Hence, the commandment is: Be spontaneous!'*

This book contains many sections dealing with the history of psychodrama, the nature of therapeutic theatre, the basis of creative revolution, the principles of spontaneity, and role theory. It also contains a major section on psychodrama itself, followed by three sections dealing with psychomusic, sociodrama, and therapeutic motion pictures. It is a book full of material relevant to the student of group therapy and psychodrama. Unfortunately, like most of Moreno's written work, it lacks unity and clarity: it is difficult to see the wood for the trees. Every aspect of the subject is amply covered, but the student has to work hard, skipping sections here and there, working backwards at times, to get an integrated picture.

Here again we see Moreno's all-encompassing genius, making a case for the use of music and recording in psychotherapy, and creating a whole new vocabulary to describe his concepts. Words like tele, surplus-reality, auxiliary ego, director, protagonist, soliloquy, warm-up process, sharing, sociatry, and social atom are familiar today to many psychotherapists, but in 1946, they were new and surprising. It is a tremendous *tour de force* to have one or two new words accepted in the fields of psychology, psychiatry, or sociology: Moreno not only had dozens to suggest, but many survived him and came into common use on a wider basis, while their author fell into oblivion.

In spite of its limitations *Psychodrama, Volume 1* was a landmark in Moreno's development and represents his first attempt to synthesize a completely new approach to psychotherapy. It was followed in 1959 by *Psychodrama, Volume 2* written in collaboration with Zerka. This book is fascinating both in content and form. It presents a series of topics, put forward by Moreno in a 'discussion' format. Among the thirty-five discussants, we find the names of Nathan W. Ackerman (Columbia University), Franz Alexander (University of California), Gordon W. Allport (Harvard University), Robert R. Blake (University of Texas), Medard Boss (University of Zurich), Serge Lebovici (Hôpitaux de Paris), Jules H. Masserman (Northwestern University), and Pitirim A. Sorokin (Harvard University). The topics are: transference, countertransference and tele; interpersonal therapy, group psychotherapy and the function of the unconscious; the significance of the therapeutic format and the place of acting out in psychotherapy; the discovery of the spontaneous man with special emphasis upon the technique of role reversal; the psychodrama of Adolf Hitler; existentialism, *Daseinsanalyse* and psychodrama; psychodrama and psychoanalysis. The book remains a classic for people interested in the epistemological basis of Moreno's works.

Finally, *Psychodrama, Volume 3*, deals with questions of theory and technique, both in overview and for specific topics such as psychodrama with children and adolescents, and psychodrama and psychopathology. With this third volume, Moreno had more or less completed his writings on psychodrama, which included numerous journal articles as well as the books.

Of the other books and articles dealing with specific aspects of group psychotherapy or psychodrama, a good example is *Group Psychotherapy: A Symposium*, which contains articles on ethics, history, and concepts. Moreno also took the leadership in the publication of five consecutive volumes of *Progress in Psychotherapy*, first with F. Fromm-Reichmann, and then with Jules Masserman, from 1956 to 1960,[9] and edited *The International Handbook of Group Psychotherapy* with A. Friedemann, R. Battegay, and Zerka T. Moreno in 1966. Finally, there was the very personal account of the use of psychodrama in Moreno's own family, *The First Psychodramatic family*, published in 1964, written with his wife Zerka and their son Jonathan.

Moreno's work was above all original. He created a new science and innovative methods for which he invented a new vocabulary. He did it more or less alone, in partnership with Zerka, who by 1946 was making a significant contribution. It had been a very exhausting and demanding task. Moreno was involved with so many projects at this time and his output was so great that it is understandable if at times the quality of his writing suffered.

Creating associations and training programmes

Since the early 1940s Moreno had understood the importance of creating new organizations to act as a forum for professionals interested in his work, but also recognized the need to work within existing organizations.

To develop the sociometry movement, he chose to establish a sociometry section within the American Sociological Society. This decision was in many ways a natural and easy choice: the sociometry movement had created a very strong following amongst sociologists, anthropologists, and social psychologists, and Moreno enjoyed the support of such people as George A. Lundberg, Leonard S. Cottrell, Margaret Mead, and Bruno Solby. A division within the larger association ensured the recognition of sociometry and facilitated access to a larger audience. In 1955 the journal *Sociometry* came under the umbrella of the American Sociological Association.

It may be that Moreno's decision to let go of sociometry was indicative of a relative lack of interest in this aspect of his work. In any event, sociometry was eventually to have a life of its own, and Moreno's role in developing it was to be forgotten by the third generation of practitioners. His contribution to the field, directly and indirectly, is far from recognized, but the bibliographies of sociometry and small group research still bear testimony to his influence and pioneering work.

For psychodrama, Moreno used a different strategy. He had encountered a lot of opposition from psychiatrists to group psychotherapy, and to the psychodrama method in particular. This probably played a part in his decision to create a separate association. In addition, Moreno was much more protective of psychodrama, the offspring of his twin interests, theatre and therapy. However, the decision may have contributed later to his difficulty in presenting a coherent picture of the relationship between sociometry, group psychotherapy, and psychodrama. As we have seen, the three aspects of his philosophy were presented separately by Moreno, and were not integrated by an overarching concept. Sociatry might have been the concept that could have best served this purpose, but it never became accepted outside Moreno's immediate circle.

In the case of psychodrama Moreno chose, for personal and professional reasons, to create his own association dedicated to its development and advancement. Following a meeting and discussion with colleagues, he created in 1942 the Society of Psychodrama and Group Psychotherapy. The name was important because a society implies a less formal grouping than an association. That the word psychodrama appears first, before group psychotherapy, is indicative of Moreno's preference for this therapeutic method. But in 1950 the Society was incorporated as the American Society of Group Psychotherapy and Psychodrama, 'reversing' its name to reflect the association's wish to act as an 'umbrella' for group therapy in general, and psychodrama, in particular.

The society was like a child to Moreno and Zerka and they both devoted much time and energy to promoting its future. It became the main forum for Morenean-oriented psychotherapists, and especially psychodramatists. The Society started to hold an annual conference in 1943 and set the standards for trainees. It was the necessary institutional arm of a new science and field of practice. But what was this new science or and what was its field? It was here that some confusion and difficulty arose. If it was *group* psychotherapy did it include analytical group therapy? Where was the place of sociometry in the organization? What was the place of other approaches in group therapy using a different vocabulary, methodology and techniques to psychodrama? What was the exact relationship of group psychotherapy to psychodrama? These and many other questions were raised and discussed, helping Moreno to clarify important issues. It was also an opportunity for Moreno to get embroiled in further clashes with the proponent of psychoanalysis and group dynamics. A rival organization and journal was started by S.R. Slavson, and the confrontation between the two men somewhat tarnished the professional image of group psychotherapy. Here again, Moreno felt that his role as founder was not sufficiently acknowledged and his 'paternity syndrome' resurfaced. Both groups went their own ways and later rapprochements were rather superficial.

In 1942 the Society was created as a 'family' group, a first psychodramatic society. People who were trained by Moreno and knew each other both professionally and personally met in New York each year for the annual meeting. They shared in the excitement and pain of the birth and development of a new 'society'. Society members related to the father figure of Moreno and, to a lesser degree in these first years to Zerka.

The Society remained a place where psychodrama in particular was explored as a new therapeutic method. Even though the Morenos were the leaders, students would contribute their energy, ideas, and new techniques. New ways were set up for groups to meet: not just to talk, but to experiment with psychodrama in action. Moreno was a pioneer in this respect, organizing the first professional meetings with an 'experiential' base. A tradition was established of using the Society and its annual meeting as an opportunity to update techniques, to explore personal issues with experienced leaders, and to get to know each other in a spontaneous way. This meeting soon became an essential personal link between Morenean psychotherapists, but research, theoretical discussion, and business were not excluded. In fact, the Society was instrumental in allowing and forcing debates on training issues within the Morenean orthodoxy, on ethical considerations in group psychotherapy, and on the 'licensing' of psychodramatists. These debates reveal the problems involved in setting up a new group based on a new school of thought. Moreno had to face issues and challenges on a daily basis. Freud, Jung, and Adler had all encountered much the same problems before him. There were particularly resounding debates around the late 1940s and early 1950s when some people were 'forced out', and others left the society in disenchantment. The confrontations were almost exclusively with men; Moreno appeared to have a magical ability to deal on much smoother terms with female colleagues and students.

Gradually the Society became more formal, losing some of its 'family' atmosphere of the 1940s, and gaining in transgenerational dynamics and scope. It became more institutionalized, but its founder was still its effective leader. Chapters were created within the United States.

Formal training in psychodrama was carried out by 'Institutes', later called 'academies of psychodrama and group psychotherapy'. The first institute was set up in Beacon in 1941, preceding the founding of the Society by more than a year. Among the first students were S. Chase, Dr Ernest Fantel, Joseph Sargent, Frances Herriott, Anita Uhl, Denton Morford, Dr Bruno Solby, and M. Treudly. Then came a second training programme, (it would today be called a one-day workshop) that included F. Stuart Chapin, Leonard Cottrell, George Lundberg, Margaret Hagan, Paul Lazarsfeld, Margaret Mead, Helen H. Jennings, George P. Murdock, Samuel Stouffer, Adolf Meyer, Theodore M. Newcomb, Werner Wolf, S. Bernard Wortis, and Eugene Hartley. The training, carried out under Moreno, rapidly evolved into a more elaborate curriculum and spread over a longer period. The first formal Moreno Institute developed in two training centres, Beacon and New York. A third institute was recognized at St Elizabeths Hospital, Washington, under the direction of Frances Herriott, and later James Enneis. Most first-generation graduates came from these three centres. The Moreno Insitute continued to operate separately from the Society, but close ties existed between the two. The Institute set standards for accreditation and certification of psychodramatists and group psychotherapists. It was recognized by New York State University and awarded two diplomas, 'Auxiliary Ego', and 'Director'.

In 1957, Moreno created the Academy of Psychodrama and Group Psychotherapy for postgraduate training under the auspices of the Moreno Academy and, in 1961, the World Academy of Psychodrama and Group Psychotherapy, to integrate and accredit institutes abroad. He also created a World Centre for Psychodrama, Group Psychotherapy and Sociometry in order to facilitate training in different parts of the globe. At this international level, new problems arose that were never to be solved. The main issues revolved around the question of certification. It proved impossible to give an international official status to the Moreno Institute or the Moreno Academy of Psychodrama and Group Psychotherapy; it also proved impossible to regulate the use of terms such as psychodrama or group psychotherapy, in which there was no copyright. Following tradition, Moreno claimed a moral right to control their use and emphasized ethical considerations, but individual countries insisted on having the final say.

Undeterred, Moreno spent considerable effort in developing an adequate curriculum, selection procedures, and standards of certification for his own organization. The man who had opposed *cultural conserves* in the past found himself creating standards, committees, examinations. . .

Had he refused to do so, there was the risk that others would do it for him, inevitably deforming his ideas. It meant a constant struggle to establish norms and rules, and Moreno spent considerable time managing the training and dissemination of his methods, at the expense of his writing. By the early 1950s he had gained the expertise that would have allowed him to synthesize his work and express his ideas in a more definitive form. Instead, he chose to create associations and to travel the world. Moreno remained a man of action.

Chapter 9
The pilgrim

One of Moreno's role models was Jesus. He had visited people in their homes, walked from one village to the next, from one province to another, in order to transmit the Word: Moreno saw himself in the same role. In the early 1940s he had travelled every week from Beacon to New York City to demonstrate psychodrama and to carry out training; he did not wait for trainees to come to him, but went out to meet them in their own environment. With the professionalization of psychodrama, he continued to teach in this way, offering workshops, lectures, and demonstrations in people's places of work. Perhaps he was identifying not only with Jesus, but also with a more earthly model, his father, a constant traveller.

In any event, Moreno travelled extensively, especially during the Second World War. He visited Washington, Boston, Denver, San Francisco, and Los Angeles and toured most of the important American universities: Duke, Stanford, St Louis, Johns Hopkins, Buffalo, Oklahoma, Columbia, Harvard. . . By 1950 there were very few states, hospitals, or universities that he had not visited. Everywhere he went he gave demonstrations and lectures, particularly enjoying the renewed opportunity to deal with unexpected situations and let spontaneity take over.[1]

The year 1950 had a special connotation for Moreno, but first came a disappointment when he stood unsuccessfully for the presidency of the American Psychiatric Association. Moreno claimed that this was because most people were still opposed to group psychotherapy and were frightened of himself and his ideas. This might well have been true. Even though he had become more open and flexible to other approaches, he was still intolerant of many psychiatrists. On the other hand, during the Association's annual meeting, a petition signed by more than 1,500 members was successful in organizing an annual symposium on 'group psychotherapy theory and practice', and a 'round table' on group psychotherapy and psychodrama was also established. In 1931 Dr William A. White had predicted: 'First you will get the sociologists, then the social psychologists, then the general practitioners, then the common people, but you will never live to see the day when psychiatrists will accept group psychotherapy.' He had been proved wrong: the idea of group psychotherapy had slowly gained ground, even among psychiatrists, and Moreno could take credit for this.[2]

This fact, among others, signalled to Moreno that the time was ripe to extend his territory. He wired a telegram to Paris, to the organizers of the first world congress of psychiatry, simply stating: 'Two papers. Psychodrama. Sociometry. Signed: Moreno.' This was received in Paris with some amusement: Moreno's reputation had already crossed the Atlantic. However, it was no accident that Moreno chose Paris as the place for his first international intervention: he considered himself French in spirit and had been brought up by a mother who was very influenced by French culture. A few years later, at the opening of the first international congress of psychodrama, he was to say: 'If this congress takes place in Paris, it is because both France and psychodrama mean for me: freedom, equality, and fraternity.'

His first return to Europe was a very moving experience for Moreno. He was able to establish long-lasting contacts with group psychotherapists in France and even to build bridges with psychoanalysts. Professor Juliette Favez-Boutonier was instrumental in this, introducing him to many of the leading figures, and in 1955, with the help of Anne Ancelin Schützenberger, she presided over the creation of the Groupe Français d'Etudes de Sociométrie, Dynamique des Groupes et Psychodrame. Moreno also made contact with other analysts and psychiatrists such as Leon Michaux and Serge Lebovici, and included them in the International Committee of Group Psychotherapy in 1951. He established a friendship with George Gurvitch who developed sociometry in Europe, editing *Sociometry in France and in the United States* in 1950 and contributing to *Sociometry and the Science of Man* in 1956.

Moreno went back many times to France and was involved in different projects, including a film, 'Psychodrama of a Marriage', made by the Centre d'Etudes de Radio et Télévision in 1964. In 1954, he conducted a psychodrama session at the Salpétrière Hospital, proud to follow in the footsteps of Philippe Pinel, who brought about the first psychiatric revolution in 1793, and of Freud, who is credited with the second revolution; Moreno claimed that he himself had brought about the third, with the introduction of group psychotherapy.[3] Moreno's ties with France were to be kept alive through the unceasing work of Anne Ancelin Schützenberger, a pioneer in the European development of Moreno's ideas. As Moreno's reputation expanded abroad, he opened up new opportunities for American psychotherapists to train people in other countries: indeed, many of his 'core' faculty went to France, including James Enneis, Leon Fine, Hannah Weiner, Antony Brunse, and Dean Elefthery. This trend was to continue in other countries and finally reach all continents.

From 1950 on, Moreno travelled extensively throughout the world. In 1951 he went to England and gave demonstrations at the Royal Medical Society, the Maudsley Hospital, and Bedford College for Women. He had made his first contacts with British therapists in the early 1940s through J. Sutherland and George Fitzpatrick who were at that time employed by the British army. Moreno established links with the Tavistock Clinic and was to cooperate closely on the international scene with S.H. Foulkes who had visited him at the New York Institute in the 1940s.[4]

Another memorable occasion was his trip to Russia in 1959, important to Moreno for various reasons. On the point of leaving Vienna in 1925, he had hesitated whether to go to Russia like some of his friends; it was a country where his methods could be easily implemented because of its strong theatre tradition and its communist ideology. He had also become increasingly preoccupied with world affairs and peace and was looking for a way to get involved at international level.

Moreno visited the Psychological Institute and the Academy of Medical Science in Moscow, and the Bechterev and Pavlov Institutes in Leningrad. He met with Professors Smirnov, Luria, Bykov, and Guilyarovky. He also found that one of his books, *Sociometry, Experimental Methods and the Science of Society* had been translated into Russian and published a few months earlier, and was able to receive his royalties in person. While in Moscow, he suggested that for the advancement of peace, the Russian and American leaders, Khrushchev and Eisenhower, should reverse roles. Moreno made this suggestion on many other occasions: his students in Beacon remember the night he tried to get in touch with the Chinese leader, Mao Tse-tung, to offer his services in discussing frontier problems with Russia. During the Vietnam War, he also offered his help to President Lyndon Johnson. He was convinced that role reversal by world leaders would increase the likelihood of peace. He was also to try this approach on other occasions such as the mock trial of Eichmann in 1961, and the trial of Oswald and Ruby after Kennedy's assassination. As he grew older,

Moreno was looking for a solution to universal problems and gave more importance to sociodrama. He believed that through role reversal people could gain a perspective that would bring about understanding and peace and that by re-enacting social or political conflicts, it would be possible to bring about a new social order.

Moreno wanted to build bridges between east and west. After his trip to the Soviet Union, he wrote:

> We psychiatrists should be the first to open our arms wide and start on the road of international scientific cooperation. International scientific cooperation means the exchange of the best ideas and methods developed East or West, as much as possible free from ideological bias and national persuasions, in the spirit of genuine mutual appreciation. Through personal acquaintance with each other we should share our experiences and learn the basic elements of each other's language. We should try to understand and respect the similarities as well as the differences in the foundations of American and Soviet psychiatry. . . If I take my journey as a symbolic encounter between American and Soviet psychiatry, then the sincerity, the warmth, the cordiality, and the dignity with which we were treated is an invitation to every American psychiatrist to visit the U.S.S.R.
> ('Psychiatric Encounter in Soviet Russia' in *International Journal of Sociometry and Sociatry*, 2, 1960)

It is interesting to reread this statement in the context of east-west relations in the late 1980s. Moreno had many encounters with people from the eastern bloc, visiting both Prague, and Belgrade. He found himself in trouble at times, being impatient for reforms and individual freedom, but his trips were a direct challenge to the existing political order and served as a reminder of the necessity to keep open the channels of communication.[5]

Moreno also revisited Austria. In 1954 he went back to the neuropsychiatric clinic in Vienna with his friend Dr Hans Hoff, who had replaced Dr Pötzl as head of the clinic. Moreno and Zerka did some demonstrations of psychodrama and Dr Hoff was so impressed that he had a stage built in the garden of the hospital. But Moreno's most emotional moment was without a doubt his return to the University on 14 May 1969 to receive a honorary diploma and his return to Bad Vöslau for the unveiling of a plaque the day after. It is of interest to note that Moreno, receiving the diploma from the hands of Professor Mainex, the

Dean of Medicine, paid tribute to other giants, such as 'Freud and Adler who never received such an honor from their Alma Mater'. It gives an indication of how much he had mellowed with age. Dr Raoul Schindler, initiator and leader of group therapy and psychodrama in Austria, was present at the ceremony and a number of European colleagues such as Professor Ramon Sarro from Spain and Professor Anne Ancelin Schützenberger from France.

The next day the group met in Bad Vöslau and a plaque was unveiled at 4 Maithal Street in honour of Jacob Levy Moreno, founder of sociometry, group psychotherapy, and psychodrama. This historic moment took Moreno back fifty years to when he had accepted the position of health officer for the town and doctor for the textile factory. His sobbing at the ceremony was an indication of the overwhelming feelings that he felt on this day when speakers acknowledged the importance of this little place in Austria, the cradle of *The Words of the Father* and *The Theatre of Spontaneity*. As Moreno was reminiscing with local people about his memories and involvement in Bad Vöslau, we now know that Marianne, still alive, had chosen to stay away out of respect for Moreno's wife Zerka, who was present. As the interior of the old house was not accessible, the romance that had taken place there in earlier years, and Marianne's energy that had supported Moreno for years were kept intact. But it is certain that feelings were running high on 15 May 1969 in Bad Vöslau.[6]

One year earlier Moreno had received another recognition, this time from Spain. The University of Barcelona awarded him a honoris causa doctorate. The honour had a personal, but also a political meaning: Moreno had done so much for science that the honour was clearly warranted, but Professor Ramon Sarro, Chairman of the Department of Medicine at the University of Barcelona, also stressed the fact that Moreno, as a Sephardic Jew, had Spanish roots. His parents spoke the language that was kept alive through centuries of separation from their original land. Honouring Moreno was a way of making up for the suffering endured by thousands of Jews and symbolically reconnecting the exiles with their beloved land. The ceremony that took place at the University of Barcelona in 1968 was a moving and emotional occasion. At the end of his life Moreno received many honours and citations from America and abroad. The therapeutic and scientific communities were finally recognizing his contributions.[7]

The last twenty years of Moreno's life were years of expansion and consolidation and this was the purpose of his travels. During this period he was working to establish two important associations: the International

Association of Group Psychotherapy and the International Association of Psychodrama.

Moreno had set up an International Committee on Group Psychotherapy in the course of his trip to Paris and London in 1951. It included, among others, leading representatives from England and France, Drs Joshua Bierer, Juliette Favez-Boutonier, Jean Delay, S.H. Foulkes, George Heuyer, and Serge Lebovici. In America, after many discussions, Moreno brought about a rapprochement with his rival, S.R. Slavson. The first International Congress of Group Psychotherapy took place in Toronto in 1954, where Moreno had first used the word group psychotherapy in 1931. This committee became an umbrella for national federations of group psychotherapy and eventually created the International Association of Group Psychotherapy. The next meetings were held in Zurich, Milan, and Vienna. The interesting aspect of this association from the standpoint of Moreno's biography was his decision, at last, to open up to other groups and consider them equal partners. Moreno was the first president of the association, with S.H. Foulkes and Serge Lebovici as vice-presidents. Moreno himself actively maintained the leadership role, appointing as immediate collaborators people who did not represent a threat to him.[8]

As psychodrama became increasingly popular, a need arose at the international level for people to meet more formally. In 1961 Moreno created the World Academy of Psychodrama and Group Psychotherapy. He himself was its first president. This association had the mandate to integrate and accredit institutes outside the United States and to coordinate international congresses. The first international congress of psychodrama was held in Paris in 1964 and drew over 1,000 participants from thirty-five countries. As stated in the announcement leaflet, the aim of the meeting was 'to bring together training specialists and practitioners from every part of the globe, so that they can share their experiences and stimulate research'. The organization of the congress in Paris was handled by Anne Ancelin Schützenberger, while Zerka Moreno looked after the practical organization in America.[9]

Since this first congress, psychodramatists have met regularly for international meetings: Barcelona in 1966; Baden (instead of Prague) in 1968, where the First International Congress of Sociometry also took place; Buenos Aires in 1969; Sao Paulo in 1970; Amsterdam in 1971; Tokyo in 1972; and Zurich in 1974. During his lifetime Moreno witnessed the development of his ideas and methods in every continent.

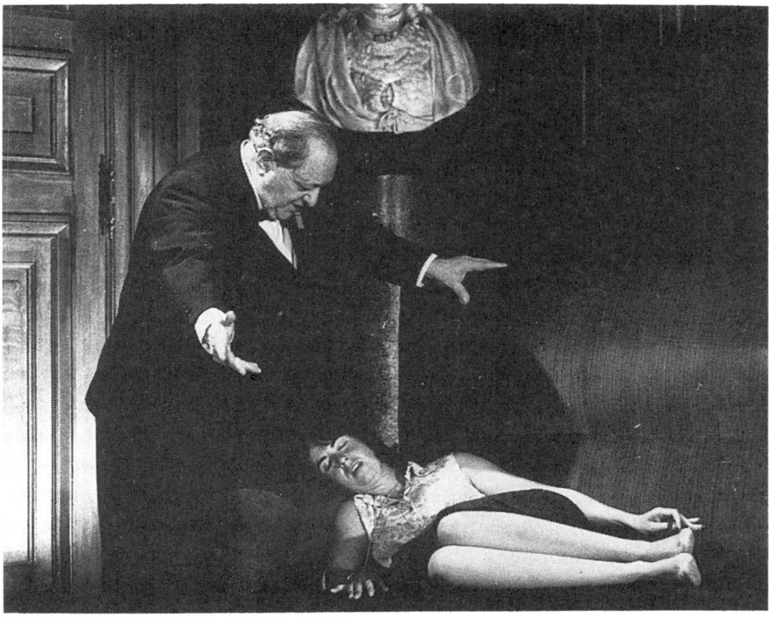

Figure 19 First International Congress of Psychodrama, Paris 1964. (Anne Ancelin Schützenberger, private collection; rephotographed by Claude Demers.)

It would be possible to spend more time on the years when Moreno was travelling so much — we could talk about his trip to Israel, or his encounter with Fritz Perls at the annual meeting of the American Psychological Association in San Francisco, or the moving celebration that was held on his eightieth birthday — but there is no space. Right up to the end of his journey Moreno was active, dedicated, and unpredictable. Nobody knew what he would do or say, for he did not know himself; spontaneity and creativity remained the keynotes.[10]

Chapter 10
Death and legacy

Moreno's last intellectual project was the writing of his autobiography. After the international psychodrama conference in Amsterdam in 1971, he started the monumental task of putting his memory to work for one last time. He had already published a 'Prelude to the Sociometric Movement' in the 1953 edition of *Who shall survive?* and, under a separate cover, *Preludes to my Autobiography* in 1955, but his life had been so eventful that it was a worthwhile undertaking for him to leave students and historians something of his memoirs. He worked for months on this project, writing most about events that took place in the early years. The book, unfinished and unpublished, is written in true Morenean style, a tale to be told sitting under a tree in a garden. It is a collage of stories, thoughts, and anecdotes, but above all it is a compelling testimony of Moreno's productive and active life.[1]

Moreno became gradually less active and more depressed as he saw his physical strength diminish and did not have the energy to complete the autobiography which ends in the period of the early 1950s. In 1974 he had a series of small strokes that left him partially paralyzed and determined to put an end to his own journey, in the knowledge that he would never be totally creative again. From then on, he refused to eat and drank only water.

This was his last public psychodrama. Word got around that Moreno was dying, and people came from all over the world to meet him for the last time: Gretel Leutz, his spiritual daughter, came from Germany and read from the *The Words of the Father*; Anne Ancelin Schützenberger, another 'daughter', was there to remind him of his connections with the French Revolution and encounters in Russia; Ada Abraham, a Roumanian psychodramatist now living in Israel, was asked by him to sing Eminescu's lullaby 'Ce te Legeni'. Meanwhile, his partner and muse Zerka, while sharing her deep affection with him, continued to train promising young psychodramatists in the nearby Beacon theatre. For three weeks family and students took turns at vigils. Moreno took time to say goodbye to his biological and his psychodramatic family. He took three weeks to warm-up to his final moment.

He had travelled a long way since the old gypsy prophecy made to his mother in Bucharest: 'The day will come when he will be a great man. People from all over the world will come to see him.' Now the prophecy had been fulfilled. Not only had Moreno left behind the image of himself as a creator, but he could take comfort in the knowledge that his ideas were spreading all around the globe: training institutes were being developed[2] — and psychodrama was being practised in Europe, South America, Australia, New Zealand, and Japan; countries in the eastern bloc were also opening up to Morenean theories. Bridges were being built between opposing factions and Moreno lived to see rapprochement between psychoanalysis and psychodrama. 'Moreno', the 'teacher', even though in a way he had become anonymous, had succeeded in spreading his message. His books had been translated into more than twenty different languages.

On 14 May 1974, Jacob Levy Moreno died; with him in the room was one of his students, John Nolte, and his nurse, Ann Quinn. He died quietly, gently.[3]

* * *

Moreno often made reference to the year 2,000, claiming that although his ideas might be premature for the twentieth century, the next century would belong to him. Moreno's legacy to the world was significant in its day and may become even more important in the future: sociometry, group psychotherapy, and psychodrama have all developed as independent sciences, practitioners of his methods can be found everywhere, and research in small and large groups has made significant breakthroughs. Moreno's students have kept the faith and the flame alive, with the continuing support of Zerka T. Moreno, his beloved partner.

The future of Morenean ideas will be enhanced by the rediscovery of Moreno 'as a whole', as a philosopher who rooted his philosophy in the concrete existence of every human being. The big challenge ahead, it seems to me, is an epistemological one: to build and rebuild on Moreno's foundations in a coherent, systematic, and all-encompassing way. However, it is still difficult to grasp all the facets and contradictions of the man himself, especially his ability to get close to people while remaining essentially self-centred. In fact, Moreno may have been his

Figure 20 J.L. Moreno and Zerka T. Moreno (1972). (Zerka Moreno, private collection.)

own most severe critic. At one point he admitted to Pierre Weil, a French psychodramatist living in Brazil, that he had failed in his quest to transform the world.[4] If he failed, it was in the same way that every human being fails, by discovering his limits and this aspect of his story may be the most precious part of his legacy. Moreno was not a superman, a super-God, he was a human being, a god whose challenge was to be and remain a creator, leaving to the rest of us the responsibility to be co-creators of the universe.

Glossary of Morenean terms

The main sources for the definitions or explanations are: Anne Ancelin-Schützenberger: *Précis de psychodrame*; Adam Blatner: *Psychodrama*; René F. Marineau: *Ainsi parle Jacob Levy Moreno*; J.L. Moreno: *Psychodrama, Volume 3.*

Action or *Enactment:* the part of psychodrama when a situation or conflict is actually represented on *stage*, after discussion. People are encouraged to portray their life situations in dramatic form, to physically enact encounters and conflicts that exist only in their memories or fantasies. Thus the person whose situation is the focus of the group, the *protagonist*, is helped to experience the working out and working through of the attitudes and feelings involved, whether they be in the past, the present, or the future. The enactment takes place only after an appropriate *warm-up* and is followed by a post-action or *sharing* period. For Moreno, reliving a situation, the loss of a loved one, for example, allows not only for insight, but gives a proper distance to an event that can be looked at in a less dramatic or pathetic way when experienced a second time around.

Auxiliary ego or *Ego auxiliary*: a person from the group, either a co-therapist or a participant, who plays a role in someone's else *psychodrama*; this person contributes to the *enactment* of a scene by playing an active role. For example, in a scene where the mother of a protagonist is needed, someone, under the direction of the *protagonist* and the *director*, will play her role. The auxiliary ego has to follow the indications of the director, since their role is 'servicing' the therapeutic needs of the protagonist. The phenomenon of *tele* often plays an important role in the choice by a protagonist of an auxiliary ego.

Axiodrama: drama that is based on exploration of social ethical values, and developed by Moreno as a way to do away with *cultural conserves*. Moreno published axiodramatic protocols to illustrate this concept: the best known is the one where a spectator in a theatre confronts an actor playing the role of Zarathustra. The ultimate aim of this axiodrama is to force everyone, the actor, the director, the writer, and even the spectator, to let out his true 'self', rather than hide behind a mask or a role. Another axiodramatic protocol describes a confrontation with a priest who is forced to deliver his sermon on the street, rather than in church. Moreno saw axiodrama as the first stage in the development of *sociodrama* and *psychodrama*.

Chorus: the audience or a sub-group of auxiliaries are instructed to repeat certain phrases or amplify certain feelings as if they were the modern equivalent of the ancient Greek chorus. Repeating the haunting reproaches, doubts, or other anxiety-provoking words or lines, can deepen the *protagonist*'s experience. Confronting or supportive statements may be used depending on the actual psychological state or process, or the protagonist's therapeutic needs.

Co-unconscious: see *tele*

Cultural conserve: the finished product of a creative effort. For example: a book, a play, a symphony. Moreno devoted a lot of effort to doing away with cultural conserves, especially in the field of theatre. He saw cultural conserves as a barrier to creativity and hoped to substitute a new, spontaneous way of behaving.

Director: in *psychodrama* or *sociodrama*, the leader or therapist is referred to as the director. In developing psychodrama technique, Moreno used theatre vocabulary. It gives some indication of the role or function of the person who creates and guarantees the group a safe place to explore a life situation. The director takes charge of the group, leads the psychotherapeutic session according to the rules and techniques of psychodrama, and has the responsibility of ensuring proper follow-up. The director has a more active and directive role than in psychoanalysis, for example, while minimizing the transference process.

Double: a person who plays the role, or an aspect of the role, of the *protagonist*. The protagonist sometimes needs a person who stands in for him or her, who plays him or her, who '*doubles*' for him or her. This person, an *auxiliary ego*, can either be a trained therapist or a participant from the group. An example of the use of a double would be the following: an inhibited adolescent cannot let out his aggressivity, following a humiliating scene with his father; a 'double', in touch with the repressed aggressivity, is called to stand in for the adolescent. As the double plays the part, the adolescent, warmed-up to his anger, joins in, hence the need for the 'double' becomes superfluous.

Enactment: see *Action.*

'in situ': Moreno suggested that *psychodrama* should be applied in the very situation and place where the conflict might be occurring, 'on the spot' so to speak. This might be in the home, on the school yard, at work, or on the street. The idea of doing family therapy in the family's home is one example of this idea, though Moreno would probably have the family use the kitchen and bedrooms to enact scenes as well as the living room. Moreno felt that Freud saw his patients in an 'artificial setting'. In psychodrama, even though the action takes place on the stage, a good deal of time is taken for the *protagonist* to recapture the concrete elements of the setting, and he or she is invited to describe them in detail to allow the director to come as close as possible to re-playing the exact details of a scene, as if 'in situ'.

Mirror: the *protagonist* may be unable to represent himself, or the *director* may want the protagonist to gain some distance or insight: in such a case, the director could use the mirror technique: essentially, the protagonist is asked to remain seated and watch an *auxiliary ego* representing him in words and action. The auxiliary ego re-enacts the protagonist, copying his behaviour and trying to express his feelings in words and movement, showing the protagonist 'as if in a mirror'. The auxiliary ego aims at as close a representation of the protagonist as possible, a type of 'video playback'. However, there might be situations when the mirror is consciously exaggerated, employing the technique of deliberate distortion in order to arouse the protagonist, so that he or she changes from a passive spectator into an active participant, an actor, correcting the enactment and interpretation.

Protagonist: the person whose life, or aspects of it, is being explored through a *psychodrama* session. This person is then playing the principal role in an enactment from the psychotherapeutic point of view, even though the role played by the person may be secondary to that of other participants in the scene. The protagonist is often selected during, and as part of, the *warm-up* in the actual psychodrama session.

Psychodrama: a therapeutic method developed by Moreno consisting of exploring life situations and conflicts by enacting them rather than talking about them. Psychodrama aims at uncovering the 'truth' of each person's life in relation to other people and the environment.
A psychodrama 'session' is divided into three parts: *warm-up, action* or *enactment*, and *sharing*, and calls for the use of numerous techniques, including *doubling, role reversal, mirroring, chorus, soliloquy*. Different types of psychodrama were developed by Moreno, including the spontaneous psychodrama, the planned psychodrama and the rehearsed psychodrama. Even though psychodrama is usually done within a group of participants, individual psychodrama has also been developed, especially in cases of severe mental illness.

Role reversal: a participant in a *psychodrama* or *sociodrama*, especially the protagonist, changes role with someone else in order to gain perspective and look at a situation from the other's point of view. The protagonist, a son for example, in an interpersonal situation with his mother, 'steps into his mother's shoes' while the mother steps into those of her son. The mother may be the real mother, as is done in psychodrama '*in situ*', or may be represented by an *auxiliary ego*. In role reversal, the son is now enacting the mother, the mother enacting the son. Distortions of interpersonal perception can be brought to the surface, explored, and corrected in action. The son, who is still himself, must now warm-up to how his mother may be feeling and perceiving himself; the mother, now the son, goes through the same process.
Role reversal was for Moreno the single most important technique of psychodrama and sociodrama, the one that allows everyone to understand everyone else's inner world. It requires a capacity for empathy, but goes one step further by enacting the other person's world.

Sharing: the third part of a *psychodrama* or *sociodrama* session when everyone, from the *protagonist* to members of the audience, is invited to share their experience of the just-finished *enactment*. What is shared is everyone's feelings and thoughts, not interpretations and explanations. Through the sharing, people can become aware of their identification with certain roles and other people in the group. It often leads to insight or to the enactment of another member's own psychodrama. The sharing on the part of the *auxiliary egos* is especially important because they have been cast sometimes in good, warm, and supporting roles, and sometimes as the villains of the scene. The phenomenon of *tele* is an important factor in the process of choosing someone for a role and needs to be acknowledged.

Social atom: the representation or configuration of all the meaningful relationships in one person's life. For example, a person's social atom could include a spouse, family, friends, co-workers, possibly even a pet or a deceased relative who still carries meaning for him. The social atom can be represented in graphic terms, identifying significant relationships, past or present, in terms of intensity and/or distance. The development of the genogram was greatly influenced by Moreno's concept of the social atom.

Sociodrama: a psychodramatic treatment of social problems developed by Moreno and subdivided in the same way as *psychodrama* into spontaneous, planned, and rehearsed categories. It is different from a 'social drama', the product of an individual playwright only vaguely or indirectly related to the audience and the playwright himself. 'West Side Story' is a good example of a representation of a social drama. The difference between psychodrama and sociodrama is one of structure and objective. Psychodrama deals with a problem in which a single individual or a group of individuals (family psychodrama) are *privately* involved. Sociodrama deals with problems in which the collective aspect of the problem is put in the foreground, the private relation in the background. A good example of sociodrama is the exploration with a group of black and white people of racial problems. In sociodrama, subgroups are 'protagonists'; the session includes *warm-up*, *action* and *sharing*.

Sociometry: a scientific method whose purpose is the measure of interpersonal relationships in a group. It involves the study of psychological properties of populations through the use of experimental methods and the representation of results by way of mathematical formulae and/or graphs. By this means the rules and laws of interpersonal relationships in a particular situation can be deduced.

Soliloquy: a *protagonist* shares thoughts or feelings that he or she normally keeps inside or suppresses, as an aside. For example, the *director* may suggest to a protagonist about to meet his dying mother in the course of a psychodrama: 'Before we enter the room, lets take a little walk, and tell me what is going on inside as you are about to enter your mother's room.' The protagonist then says aloud what he or she thinks and feels. This may give the protagonist or the director new insights, may be useful as a warm-up for a future real meeting between the protagonist and his dying mother, etc.

Spontaneity: the capacity of an individual to give an adequate response to a new situation, or a new response to an old situation. In other words, the response of the individual is based on what is required *now*, and not on what he learned in the past, applied almost blindly in every situation, all the time. Moreno links the capacity for a person to be creative to the capacity to maintain or regain a spontaneous state. Children, 'unspoiled' by conventions, *cultural conserves*, or stereotypes are Moreno's models of spontaneity.

Stage: a place designed and reserved for psychodrama sessions. Since everyone is a participant in a session, being a member of the audience or the *protagonist*, the stage could be seen, as in Moreno's first model, as the whole theatre. In a more restricted sense, the stage is that portion of the theatre where the protagonist stands and enacts a particular situation. There have been different models for stages, but the ones used by Moreno usually had different levels, representing various degrees of involvement, and a balcony. In a psychodrama 'in situ' the real place of action becomes the stage.

Surplus-reality: that realm of dramatic action in which the ideas of the mind can find a proper expression. Thus, events of science fiction, fantasy, and the emotional happening that we fear or yearn for, can be vividly experienced in an imaginative realm created as a space for their manifestation. In other words, surplus-reality is reality modified, amplified, or minimized by one's imagination. In psychodrama, as in reality, people are invited to add to life, to make it better or 'larger' since this process may help them to change their perspective on reality. This 'supplement' to reality can be used in 'real life' insofar as it does not create or represent a loss of contact with reality.

Tele: according to Moreno, tele is the factor responsible for the degree of reality of social configurations as they deviate from chance. Gordon Allport defines tele as insight into, appreciation of and feeling for the actual make-up of another person. In operational terms, tele could be seen as immediate, non-verbal communication (for example, the unspoken factors that draw two strangers together in a crowd); or unconscious ties of a reciprocal nature (for example, in psychodrama a man would choose another participant to play the role of his mother and she would 'know' that he was going to chose her). Tele is an essential factor in group work for ultimately it allows people to become aware of their identification and transference dynamics.

Chronology

YEAR	ARTS, MEDICAL AND SOCIAL SCIENCES	MORENO
1801	*Traité sur l'aliénation*, P. Pinel (1745–1801) founder of the first psychiatric revolution	
1824	Ninth Symphony, L. Beethoven (1770–1827)	
1825	Birth of Jean Martin Charcot (d. 1893) known for his research on hysteria	
1856	Birth of Sigmund Freud (d. 1939) founder of psychoanalysis and second psychiatric revolution	Birth of Moreno's father, Nissim Moreno Levy
1859	Birth of Edmund Husserl (d. 1938) known for his work in phenomenology	
1870	Birth of Alfred Adler (d. 1937) founder of Individual Psychology	
1873	Birth of Sandor Ferenczi (d. 1933) disciple of Freud	Birth of Moreno's mother, born Paulina Iancu (Volf, Wolf, or Stern)
1875	Birth of Carl Gustav Jung (d. 1956) founder of Analytical Psychology	
1876	*The Origin of Species*, Charles Darwin (1809–82)	

1877	Birth of Karl Abraham (d. 1925) disciple of Freud	
1878	Birth of Isadora Duncan (d. 1927) creator of Modern Dance; met Moreno in Stegreiftheater in Vienna	
1879	W. Wundt (1832–1920) first laboratory of experimental psychology in Heidelberg	
	Birth of Ernest Jones (d. 1958) founder of British Psychoanalytical Association	
	Birth of Alma Schindler, later known as Alma Mahler (d. 1964); future wife of Franz Werfel; close to *Daimon* circle	
1881	Birth of Ludwig Biswanger (d. 1956) leading figure in existential psychoanalysis	
1882	Birth of Melanie Klein (d. 1964) renowned child psychoanalyst and founder of Kleinian school of analysis	
1883	*Thus Spake Zarathustra*, F. Nietzsche (1844–1900)	
1884	Birth of Otto Rank (d. 1939) disciple of Freud, known for development of concept of birth trauma	
1885	Birth of Karen Horney (d. 1952) psychoanalyst associated with the 'Cultural' school of analysis	
1888		Marriage of Moreno's parents
1889	Birth of Martin Heidegger (d. 1976) philosopher	Birth of Jacov Levy (Moreno) in Bucharest, Roumania
	L'automatisme psychologique, Pierre Janet (1859–1947)	
1890	Birth of Kurt Lewin (d. 1947) psychologist associated with Gestalt school	Birth of sister Victoria

	and the movement of 'group dynamics'	
	Birth of the architect Friedrich Kiesler (d. 1956) author of the 'Railway Theatre'	
	Birth of Fritz Perls (d. 1970) associated with the Gestalt therapy movement	
	Birth of the expressionist painter Egon Schiele (d. 1918)	
	Principles of Psychology, William James (1842–1910)	
1892		Birth of brother William
1893		Birth of sister Charlotte
1895	*Studies on Hysteria*, J. Breuer and S. Freud	(?) Moreno's family moves to Vienna
	Birth of Anna Freud (d. 1985) psychoanalyst associated with child psychoanalysis	
1896	Freud introduces the term 'psychoanalysis'	
1897	Creation of the Secession movement in Vienna by painter Gustav Klimt (1862–1918) and his friends	
	Birth of Wilhelm Reich (d. 1957) unorthodox psychoanalyst associated with body therapy, sexual revolution, and 'orgone' research	
1898	K.S. Stanislavski (1863–1938) creates the Arts Theatre in Moscow and brings about a revolution in acting	Birth of sister Clara
	Birth of S.H. Foulkes (d. 1976) founder of the Institute of Group Analysis, London	
1899		Birth of brother Norbert
1900	*The Interpretation of Dreams*, S. Freud	
1901	Birth of Jacques Lacan	

	(d. 1981) French psychoanalyst, founder of l'Ecole freudienne de Paris	
	First use of 'conditioned reflex' by Ivan Pavlov (1849–1936)	
1904		(?) Moreno's family moves to Berlin
1905	*Three Essays on the Sexual Theory*, S. Freud	(?) Moreno's family moves to Chemnitz
1907	S. Freud meets with C.G. Jung and L. Biswanger	
1908	'The Dreaming Children' painted by Oskar Kokoschka (1886–1980)	
1909	Freud visits USA with C.G. Jung and S. Ferenczi	Moreno enters University of Vienna, first as a student of philosophy, then of medicine
1912	*Pierrot Lunaire* composed by Arnold Schoenberg (1874–1951) who developed theory and practice of twelve-tone music	(?) Moreno meets Freud (or in 1914?)
1913	*Psychology as the Behaviorist Views It*, J.B. Watson (1878–1958)	
1914		*Einladung zu einer Begegnung* (*Invitation to an Encounter*)
1917	*Metapsychology*, S. Freud	Receives M.D. degree, 5 February
		Birth of Celine Zerka Toeman
1918		Publishes *Daimon*, a journal associated with the expressionist movement
1919		Moves to Bad Vöslau and lives with Marianne Lörnitzo
1920		*Das Testament des Vaters*
1921	*Six Characters in Search of an Author*, L. Pirandello (1867–1936) Italian playwright	
	Basic Principles of Psychoanalysis, A.A. Brill	

	(1884–1948)	
1923	*I and Thou*, Martin Buber (1878–1958) Jewish philosopher and theologian	
1924		*Das Stegreiftheater* (*The Theatre of Spontaneity*)
1925	*Mentality of Apes*, W. Köhler (1887–1967) founder of the Berlin School of Gestalt psychology	Emigrates to the United States
	Der Prozess (The Trial) Franz Kafka (1883–1924) author, close to Max Brod and *Daimon* circle	
1926		Patents 'Radio-Film' with Franz Lörnitzo in Vienna
1927	*The Social Basis of Consciousness*, T. Burrow (1875–1951) first to use the term 'group analysis'	Licensed to practise medicine in the State of New York
1928		Marries Beatrice Beecher
1931		Inaugurates Impromptu Theatre and magazine *Impromptu*
		Sociometric research at Sing Sing Prison
		First participation in meeting of American Psychiatric Association
1932		*Application of the Group Method to Classification* Director of Research at Hudson School for Girls
1933	*Character Analysis*, W. Reich	
1934		*Who Shall Survive?*
1935	*A Dynamic Theory of Personality*, Lewin	Creates Therapeutic Motion Pictures
1936		Starts Beacon Hill Sanatorium and opens psychodrama theatre
1937		Founds *Sociometry*

1938	*Psychiatry: Introduction to the Study of Interpersonal Relations*, Harry S. Sullivan (1886–1949)	Marries Florence Bridge
1939	*The Organism*, Kurt Goldstein (1870–1958)	Birth of daughter Regina
1941	*Das Lied von Bernadette (The song of Bernadette)*, Franz Werfel (1890–1945) author, friend of Moreno, husband of Alma Mahler-Werfel	Translates *The Words of the Father*
		Meets C. Zerka Toeman
1942	*Counseling and Psychotherapy*, Carl R. Rogers (1903–1986)	Creates Sociometric Institute and Theatre of Psychodrama in New York
	Studies Psychology of Sex, Havelock Ellis (1859–1939)	Sets up Society of Psychodrama and Group Psychotherapy, renamed American Society of Group Psychotherapy and Psychodrama in 1951
1943	*An Introduction to Group Therapy*, S.R. Slavson (1890–1919)	
1945	*Productive Thinking* Max Wertheimer, (1886–1943) co-founder of the Gestalt School of Berlin	Sets up the American Sociometry Association
	K. Lewin creates Research Center for Group Dynamics, Massachusetts Institute of Technology	
1946		Fellow, American Psychiatric Association
		Psychodrama, Volume 1
1947	*Play Therapy*, V. Axline	Creates *Sociatry: Journal of Group and Inter-Group Therapy* renamed three times and now *Journal of Group Psychotherapy, Psychodrama and Sociometry*

		Translates *The Theatre of Spontaneity*
1948	*Introduction to Group-Analytic Psychotherapy*, S.H. Foulkes	
	Sexual Behavior in the Human Male (and in 1953: *in the Human Female*), Alfred C. Kinsey *et al.*	
	Therapeutic Social Clubs, J. Bierer	
	Cybernetics, N. Wiener (1894–1964)	
1949		Marries C. Zerka Toeman
		Dedicates Theatre of Psychodrama, Harvard
1950	*The Meaning of Anxiety*, Rollo May (b. 1909)	Participates in First World Congress of Psychiatry, Paris
1951	*Gestalt Therapy*, Fritz Perls *et al.*	Organizes First International Committee of Group Psychotherapy
	Psychoanalysis, Man and Society, Paul Schilder (1886–1940)	*Sociometry, Experimental Method and the Science of Society*
1952	Creation of Mental Research Institute, Palo Alto, California by Gregory Bateson and Don Jackson (1920–1968)	Birth of son Jonathan
1953	Therapeutic Community, Maxwell Jones	
	Science and Human Behavior, B.F. Skinner (b. 1904)	
1954	*Motivation and Personality*, Abraham Maslow (1908–1970)	First International Congress of Group Psychotherapy, Toronto, Canada
1955	*Becoming*, Gordon Allport (1897–1967)	
1956	*Le psychodrame analytique chez l'enfant*, Didier Anzieu (b. 1923–)	Creates *International Journal of Sociometry and Sociatry*
		Sociometry and the Science of Man

1957		Participates in creation of International Council of Group Psychotherapy: first president, with S.H. Foulkes and S. Lebovici as vice-presidents.
		Founds Academy of Psychodrama and Group Psychotherapy
1959	*The Divided Self*, R.D. Laing (b. 1927–)	Lectures in Moscow and Leningrad
	Experiences in Groups, W.R. Bion (1897–1979)	*Psychodrama, Volume 2*
1961	*Asylums*, E. Goofman	
	Transactional Analysis in Psychotherapy, Eric Berne (1910–20)	
1964	*Sanity, Madness and the Family*, R.D. Laing and A. Esterson	First International Congress of Psychodrama in Paris
	The Transparent Self, Sidney Jourard	*The First Psychodramatic Family*
	Conjoint Family Therapy, Virginia Satir	
1965	*Reality Therapy*, William Glasser	
1966		Edits *The International Handbook of Group Psychotherapy* in association with A. Friedemann, R. Battegay and Zerka T. Moreno
1968	*General System Theory*, Ludwig von Bertalanffy	Doctor Honoris Causa, Barcelona University
1969	*In and Out of the Garbage Pail*, Fritz Perls	*Psychodrama, Volume 3*
		Golden Doctorate, Vienna University
		Commemorative Plaque, Bad Vöslau, Austria
1970	*The Manufacture of Madness*, Thomas S. Szasz	

	The Primal Scream, Arthur Janov	
1973		Among founders of International Association of Group Psychotherapy
1974		Dies at home, Beacon, New York, 14 May
1985		Copyright in the 'Autobiography' is registered in the names of Zerka T. Moreno and Jonathan D. Moreno

Further reading

Blatner, H.A. (1973) *Acting-in: Practical Applications of Psychodramatic Methods*, New York: Springer.

Blatner, H.A. (1988) *Foundations of Psychodrama*, New York: Springer.

Corsini, Raymond J. (1967) *Role Playing in Psychotherapy*, Chicago: Aldine Press.

Fox, Jonathan (ed.) (1987) *The Essential Moreno: Writings on Psychodrama, Group Method, and Spontaneity by J.L. Moreno, M.D.*, New York: Springer.

Goldman, Elaine E. and Morrisson, Delcy S. (1984) *Psychodrama: Experience and Process*, Dubuque, Iowa: Kendall/Hunt.

Greenberg, Ira A. (ed.) (1974) *Psychodrama: Theory and Therapy*, New York, Behavioral Publications.

Hale, Ann (1985) *Conducting Clinical Sociometric Explorations* (rev. ed.) Roanoke, Va: Royal.

Haskell, Martin (1975) *Socioanalysis: Self-Direction through Sociometry and Psychodrama*, Long Beach, CA: Role Training Associates.

Jennings, Helen H. (1943) *Leadership and Isolation: A Study of Personality in Interpersonal Relations*, New York: Longmans Green.

Kahn, Samuel (1964) *Psychodrama Explained*, New York: Philosophical Library.

Kipper, David A. (1986) *Psychotherapy Through Clinical Role Playing*, New York: Brunner/Mazel.

Naar, Ray (1982) *A Primer of Group Psychotherapy*, New York: Human Sciences Press.

Northway, Mary L. (1952) *A Primer of Sociometry*, Toronto: University of Toronto Press.

Yablonski, Lewis (1976) *Psychodrama: Resolving Emotional Problems Through Role-Playing*, New York: Basic Books.

Notes*

Chapter 1 Ancestors and family

1 See Alfredo Gomez (1987) 'Spain to Give Sephardic Jews Special Place in Columbus Rites' in *Los Angeles Times*, Part II, 25 July 1987. It is interesting to note also how in 1982 the Sephardic community of Bucharest commemorated the expulsion of Jews and Columbus's discovery of America. The teaching of the Rabbi Bejarano was very explicit on this subject and traces of his influence can still be found today, almost one hundred years later, in the Sephardic community of Bucharest. The significance for Moreno of the date 1892 and its relationship to Spain was highlighted when he received, with considerable emotion, an honorary degree from the University of Barcelona in 1968 (archival material).

For further reading on the history of the Jews at this time see: William L. Langer (1948) *An Encyclopedia of World History*, Boston: Houghton Mifflin Company, esp. 'The Expulsion of Jews', 282, and 'The First Voyage of Columbus', 366; Jacob R. Marcus (1938) *The Jew in the Medieval World: a Source Book 1315–1781*, New York: Atheneum, esp. 'The expulsion from Spain', 51–5; Max L. Margolis and Alexander Marx (1927) *A History of the Jewish People*, New York: Atheneum, esp. 'The Expulsion from Spain and Portugal', 470–76.

2 J.L. Moreno (1985) 'The Autobiography of J.L. Moreno, M.D.', Boston: Harvard University Archives, The Francis A. Countway Library of Medicine, ch. 1: 27–31.

Moreno's 'Autobiography', to which I often refer, is the version that was prepared, after Moreno's death, by Zerka and Jonathan Moreno (© 1985) and presented for publication to American publishing houses. Part of this autobiography is to be published in *Group Psychotherapy, Psychodrama and Sociometry* for the 1989 centennial. The final text contains fragments written by Moreno in the last few months before his death and other written material dating as far back as the 1920s and put together in

* In these notes major works by Moreno, frequently quoted in the text, are referred to by title and date only; the complete reference will be found in the Select Bibliography which follows.

a chronological order. The text was rewritten many times, with changes here and there (changes of names to protect confidentiality, and some rewriting for style and content). The autobiography has to be used with special care; the different versions have to be compared and cross-confirmation made with other archive materials and witnesses. I have tried to verify every story from the 'Autobiography', with considerable success. However, researchers should note that it still contains mythological aspects and a subjective representation of its author's role in world history.

3 The name of the grandfather appears on the death certificate of his son Moreno Nissim Levy (Registry of Deaths 1925, Municipal Office of Bucharest). The information about Plevna can be found at the Israelitische KultusGemeinde in Vienna under the declaration of birth for Clara and Norbert Levy, in Geburtsbuch-Turken B II, entries 74 and 101.

4 The name and age of Moreno Nissim Levy is to be found on his son Jacob's birth certificate, no. 2464, in the Bucharest Register of Births for 1889. This certificate was retrieved by Professor George Bratescu in 1975. It has not been possible, so far, to obtain Moreno Nissim Levy's own birth certificate, but all supporting evidence confirms 1856 as the year, and Plevna as the place of birth. Nissim is sometimes written Nisim, and Moreno, Morenu. Morenu means 'teacher' in Hebraic language. Sigmund Freud was born on 6 May 1856. (For the acquisition of Roumanian citizenship by Jewish people, see Max L. Margolis and Alexander Marx, *op. cit.* 683–90.)

5 The true name and age of Paulina Iancu are difficult to ascertain. On the birth certificate of her son Jacob, in 1889, she says that her name is Paulina Iancu, age eighteen; on the birth certificates of her succeeding children she describes herself differently each time: for Rahel-Vittoria (1891), she becomes Paulina Volf, age twenty; for Volf-Valerian-William (1892), she is Paulina Stern, age twenty-four; for Scharloti (1893), she is again Paulina Volf, age twenty-three; for Clara (1898) she is Paulina Wolf, age twenty-five; for Norbert (1899) she is again Paulina Wolf, age twenty-six. Her own declaration, which I was unable to confirm, lacking her certificate of birth, was that she was born on 14 November 1873. Numerous changes of name were not uncommon for Jewish people, who often had to lie in order to be accepted as immigrants or refugees. In this case, the picture is complicated in that the births seem often to have been registered by friends of the family, or by the father. The name Volf/Wolf appears often, indicating that this might have been the family name before 'Iancu'. As for her age, she makes herself older for the birth of her first children, but reverts to her real age later. Jacob Moreno often said that his mother was really fifteen when he was born; he seems to have been right, if one takes the year 1873 as the year of her birth. See Bucharest municipal archives, Register of Births, 1889, no. 2464; 1891, no. 2017; 1892, no. 6266; 1893, no. 6777; Wien Israelitische KultusGemeinde, Geburtsbuch-Turken B II, entries 74 and 101.

6 It has been impossible so far to obtain confirmation of the date of marriage. Neither is it clear where the couple married: Bucharest, Calarasi, or Cacomeanca. In the last two places, most of the Jewish archives were destroyed during the war. The remaining archives are not easily available.

7 The different addresses can be found on the birth certificates of the different children. See note 4, above.

8 The original birth certificate is in Bucharest in the municipal archives, Register of Births, 1889, no. 2464. The translation is as follows:

Registration Office for Births

Mos. (aic) Rum. (anian)	
JACOV	No. 2464
MORENO	The year one thousand eight
LEVY	hundred and eighty-nine, May
Trader	6th, 11.30 a.m.

> Record of birth of the child Jacob, sex masculine, born the sixth of the current month at 4.0 p.m., in Bucharest in his parents' house, 50 Strada Serban Voda, son of Moreno Levi, aged 32, tradesman, and of Paulina, born Iancu, aged 18, housewife, declared by Avram Mitran, aged 38, clerk, living in the same street, who presented the child to us. The witnesses were Solomon Alseh, aged 48, 22 Strada Leon Voda, an acquaintance of the parents, and Solomon Athias, aged 52, tradesman, 10 Strada Labirint, an acquaintance of the parents, who signed this record after it had been read to them, together with us and the declarant. Confirmed according to the law by Nicolae Hagi Stoica jr., counsellor of the commune of Bucharest, and registrar.

There follow the signatures of the declarant, witnesses, and registrar. Contrary to the custom, the child's birth was not declared by his father, but by an acquaintance, the clerk Avram Mitram, who, together with the two witnesses, was a respected member of the Sephardic community of Bucharest. Solomon Athias signed his name in Hebraic characters.

One must assume that Moreno Levi, father of the child, was not at that time in Bucharest. It is probable that he was in Vienna at the headquarters of the company whom he represented as a travelling salesman. The certificate states that he was of Jewish religion and a Roumanian citizen.

On the certificate the spelling of the family name fluctuates — sometimes Levy, sometimes Levi.

The date of birth is 6 May (on the old calendar — 18 May on the new calendar) 1889; for those interested in horoscopes, the birth took place at 4.0 p.m.

From research in the archives of the Museum of History in Bucharest and a comparison of the topographical maps for 1900–11, it appears that the house in which Moreno was born was demolished not long after his birth.

9 Moreno's use of the truth was for him the basis of psychodrama and psychotherapy. But it is important to understand what he means by truth: it is evident that Moreno became more interested in the subjective interpretation of reality, including beautifying reality, than in plain reality. Moreno developed a new concept, *surplus-reality*, to account for this supplement that one can add to life to make it better, more acceptable to oneself. This *surplus-reality* involves the proper use of imagination, spontaneity, and creativity. As for his use of psychodramatic and poetic truth versus historical truth, one can only acknowledge that Moreno made the distinction very clear in his explanatory note to *The First Psychodramatic Family* (1964) before using it. The surprising thing is that nobody challenged him on the historical facts.

10 See I. Semo (1944) *Bejarano*, Bucharest: Institutul de Arte Grafice.
11 Professor George Bratescu, who personally knew Moreno's sister Charlotte in Bucharest was alerted by her to the fact that her brother could not have been born in 1892. When after much searching he uncovered the birth certificate, he published a very interesting article in *Group Psychotherapy and Psychodrama* (1975) 28: 2–3. Soon students and historians became aware of the discrepancies between the date and place claimed by Moreno, and the facts presented by Bratescu. Many people could not understand why Moreno 'lied', while others did not see any reason to make a problem of it.

Chapter 2 A brave child and a rebellious adolescent

1 See 'Autobiography' (1985) ch. 1: 9, 21, 22.
2 See 'Autobiography' (1985) ch. 1: 7, 8.
3 See 'Autobiography' (1985) ch. 1: 24, 40.
4 See 'Autobiography' (1985) ch. 1: 10.
5 The religious influences on Moreno can better be understood if one refers to the biography of the Rabbi Bejarano: this man had considerable influence during his life in Bucharest, and in the Balkan countries in general. See I. Semo (1944) *Bejarano*, Bucharest: Institutul de Arte Grafice and 'Autobiography' (1985) ch. 1: 13–14. For the influence of Jesus, see in particular 'Autobiography' (1985) ch. 1: 1–7.
6 For the repetitive aspect of God playing, see 'Autobiography' (1985) ch. 1: 14–16. This information was also confirmed to the author in a personal interview with Ada Alistar in Bucharest, daughter of Moreno's sister Charlotte.
7 See 'Autobiography' (1985) ch. 5: 13.
8 There are, in fact two complementary ways to look at the influences on Moreno's early childhood. On a more 'secular' level, one is struck by the immediate identification with the father, identification that is so primary that Jacob is not 'like his father', but becomes 'the father'. His father's absence when he was born, and his later absences, Jacob's own special relationship with his mother and siblings, all certainly helped in supporting the role of creator of a new dynasty, including later the change of the family name Levy for the name of his father, Moreno. One could also say that Moreno filled the void created by the absence of his father by becoming the father himself, symbolically. On a 'religious' level, the young Moreno had many examples to copy: in particular, Yahve himself, the story of Jesus and Mary, and the story of Buddha. See 'Autobiography' (1985) ch. 1: 4, 39.
9 G. Bratescu, personal communication.
10 See 'Autobiography' (1985) ch. 1: 37. This story was confirmed to the author in a personal interview with Ada Alistar.
11 See 'Autobiography' (1985) ch. 1: 19–20.
12 See 'Autobiography' (1985) ch. 1: 27–31, confirmed in a personal interview, by Ada Alistar. In no other place, is Jacob's identification with his father so clearly expressed and evident than during these two trips: we can see the young adolescent discovering the world through the eyes of his experienced father, and being totally impressed by the older man.

13 See 'Autobiography' (1985) ch. 1: 40, confirmed in a personal interview by Ada Alistar. The precise date of the move to Berlin remains difficult to pinpoint. However, one has to remember that Jacob Moreno wrote his autobiography as though he were born in 1892. In many ways, everything needs to be pushed back three years. Since we do know from another source that Charlotte went to the gymnasium in Berlin, it makes it highly probable that the family moved to Berlin around 1905 and to Chemnitz around 1906.

14 See 'Autobiography' (1985) ch. 1: 31–4. Later the role of muse was taken by Marianne Lörnitzo and then by Zerka Toeman Moreno. Moreno needed this kind of relationship with women to help him produce intellectually. He was very impressed with the role of women as muses in Plutarch and Dante's lives. Also of interest, is the aesthetic experience that Moreno had with the city of Florence mixed with his platonic love for Pia: later in the United States, he was to marry a 'Florence' in the person of Florence Bridge.

15 See Giovanni Boria (1983) *Tele, Manuale di Psichidramma Classico*, Milan: Franco Angelo Editore.

16 See 'Autobiography' (1985) ch. 2: 1–6.

17 We can see the influence of Nietzsche here. In 'of three metamorphoses' in Ainsi: *Parlait Zarathustra* (1971), Paris: Gallimard, 37 Nietzsche says: 'Innocence of the child, a forgiveness, a new beginning, a play, a free-moving wheel, a first movement, a saintly Yes. Yes, to create requires a saintly Yes. . . . ' In the 'Autobiography' (1985) ch. 2: 22–3, Moreno says: 'When I look at a child I see ''yes, yes, yes, yes''. They do not have to learn to say yes. Being born is yes. You see spontaneity in its living form. It is written all over the child, in his act-hunger, as he looks at things, as he listens to things, as he rushes into time, as he moves into space, as he grabs for objects, as he smiles and cries. . . . '

This story was presented in different ways including a more direct 'encounter' with Jesus through a 'movement' of the statue. The vision probably occurred when Jacob was sixteen or seventeen years of age. Moreno was really fascinated by the person of Jesus, to the point of identification with Him, and, at certain times, even 'personified' the messiah: the episodes of appearing naked in the street or jumping from a tree might well have been a test of the hypothesis for Moreno that he was in fact Jesus. These episodes make one wonder about the mental state of Moreno at times. It seems clear that he could have been 'borderline' in certain situations, but also that these episodes were more in the realms of 'as if' and finally were accompanied by a psychological distancing and a sense of humour. Moreno was eventually able to find an audience before whom he could act out his 'megalomania'. 'Autobiography' (1985) ch. 2:3, 19–22; ch. 3: 8–10 and 'Preludes to the Sociometric Movement' in *Who shall survive?* (1953) Beacon: Beacon House, xix.

Chapter 3 The university years

1 See 'Autobiography' (1985) ch. 2: 9.

2 See 'Autobiography' (1985) ch. 2: 1.

3 See 'Autobiography' (1985) ch. 2: 1. It is interesting to compare Swedenborg's vision with that of Moreno; both 'scientists' became 'instruments of God'.

4 See Jacob L. Moreno (1987) *Psychothérapie de groupe et psychodrame*, Paris: Presses Universitaires de France, 25.

5 Many groups did advocate anonymity during this period. For example, a research group in mathematics at the University of Vienna shared in work leading to the discovery of new mathematical formulae without ever using their names: they thought, as Moreno did, that no-one should have a claim on knowledge — discovery should be nameless. Andras Petö, Moreno's associate, and later to become famous for his technique of 'conductive education' with severely handicapped children at the clinic he founded in Budapest, at that time worked either anonymously or under a pseudonym. Conductive education functions in many ways on the same principles as psychodrama. (Private interview with Maria Hari in Budapest; she was a pupil and close associate of Petö from 1945 to 1967).

6 Chaim Kellmer was born in 1887 and was a student of philosophy. Contrary to Moreno's claim, Kellmer did not complete his studies in philosophy and did not obtain his doctorate. He died 16 May 1916 apparently while working as a male nurse in the army. See Registration of Death, Israelitische KultusGemeinde Wien.

7 See 'Autobiography' (1985) ch. 5: 1–12; archival material, Institut; für Geschichte der Medizin der Universität Wien.

8 See 'Autobiography' (1985) ch. 5: 2–10. Moreno's relationship with Wagner von Jauregg is very interesting when compared to his encounter with Freud. In spite of his dislike for von Jauregg, Moreno never confronted him. He maintained a polite attitude and a safe distance. He must have felt some ambivalence towards a man who was also so opposed to psychoanalysis. As for Pötzl, there is no evidence from his own file of his work with Moreno. While numerous contributors appear in his list of almost two hundred publications, in none of these, so far, can the name of Moreno be found. This fact does not mean that Moreno made up the story of his association with Pötzl, but that no co-publication can be found in the long list of Pötzl's bibliography. Pötzl may have acknowledged verbally the work of his students and assistants. (Private correspondence between the author with Pötzl's son, Hans Pötzl.)

9 See also 'Autobiography' (1985) ch. 5: 12–15.

10 The questions of telepathic dreams and thought transference were puzzling for Freud. He was very uneasy with the subject. We know that his daughter Anna and Sandor Ferenczi carried out 'personal' research into the subject. Freud himself wrote a paper on it in 1922 and commented on the topic in his 'New Introductory Lectures'. See S. Freud (1922) *Dreams and Telepathy*, in the Standard Edition 18, 197; *New Introductory Lectures on Psychoanalysis* (1933) in the Standard Edition 22, 3. See also Peter Gay (1988) *A Life for our Time*, New York: Norton Press; Paul Roazen (1984) *Freud and his Followers*, New York: New York University Press.

11 Moreno and Theodor Reik were introduced to each other by a mutual friend, Hans Brauchbar (a member of the group of the House of Encounter). Reik was going out with Brauchbar's sister. During the period 1922–25, Reik would sometimes go to the Stegreiftheater. After Moreno published his book *The Theatre of Spontaneity* in 1924, Reik showed it to Freud. According to Moreno, Reik did not remember Freud's comments because Freud did

not have any good comments to make about Reik's own book published at the same time. In reality, Freud's comments about Reik's book were rather laudatory: 'I have read your thoughtful and extremely important book with great interest. . . . Although, through my custom, I am avoiding pronouncing final judgement on a work I have just read, still I hazard the impression that here you have produced something especially valuable. Now dispose of the manuscript.' 13 January 1925, quoted in Theodor Reik (1956) *The Search Within*, New York: Farrar, 643. Here too, there may be a case of brothers' rivalry. See also 'Autobiography' (1985) ch. 6: 34.

12 In 1918 Alfred Adler became a member of the editorial committee of *Daimon*, the literary journal created by Moreno; he was instrumental in finding its publishers. However, this relationship too was ambivalent and Moreno eventually found Adler too much of an analyst for his liking. See 'Autobiography' (1985) ch. 6: 34, and personal archival material.

13 See note 5.

14 For Elisabeth Bergner's point of view, see Eloesser (1927) *Elisabeth Bergner*, Berlin: William and Co. Verlag, 23–5; Elisabeth Bergner (1978) *Bewundert Viel und Viel Gescholten*, München: Bertelsmann Verlag, partially translated by Zerka Moreno, in 'Escape me never' in *Group Psychotherapy, Psychodrama and Sociometry* (1979) xxxii: 5–11. For an account of Elisabeth Bergner's talent see Joseph Sachs (1937) *Beauty and the Jew*, London: Goldston, especially the chapter 'The Jew on the Stage', 200: 'Elisabeth Bergner's personality breathes a sublimation of the instinct, a refinement and spiritualisation of the passions, that is new on a stage accustomed to make more capital out of sex than aesthetic purification — that doubtful katharsis of the dramatic legacy. Her child-like being precludes grossness, but the puck-like grace and humour add charm to her elusive womanhood. Her St Joan will disarm the sceptics and the cynics, who have plied their trade since Voltaire. She lends reality to the myth, by the ethereal purity of her own sylph-like being. It would be erroneous to suppose that this fairy-like grace and freedom from encumbering matter, is sheer nature, rather it is the result of a consummate art, the art that conceals art. Child-like as Elisabeth Bergner appears, she is extremely intellectual, her art is under constant subjection to the critical faculty, and it is subtly analytical, even though it appears lightheartedly naive.'

15 For Elisabeth Bergner's relationships with Adler and Freud, see Bergner (1978), *op. cit.*, 143, 146; also confirmed in a personal interview with Elisabeth Bergner.

16 See *Who Shall Survive?* (1953) xix and 'Autobiography' (1985) ch. 2: 2–35.

17 Moreno published *Der Königsroman* (1923) anonymously, a book containing examples of the games he played with the children. See also 'Autobiography' (1985) ch. 2: 25–34.

18 Doubts have been raised about the accuracy of the story concerning Moreno's children's theatre. Was it a real theatre, or just an occasional improvisation group in the parks? It seems that at times, at least, there was a small acting group. Elisabeth Bergner refers to playing the role of Toinette for Moreno, and even Henry A. Phillips refers to Bergner's first experience on stage in Vienna at the age of eleven. Moreno himself says that at one point the group met in the same building that was rented by Trotsky for

meetings, lent by him for the children theatre. Moreno later published some of the plays they performed, including *Thus Spake Zarathustra*. See Elisabeth Bergner (1978), *op. cit.*, 15; Henry Albert Phillips, 'Greater than Bernhardt?' in *The Stage* (1935), reprinted in Elisabeth Bergner (1978), *op. cit.*, 286. For the reference to Trotsky, see the 'Autobiography' (1985) ch. 4: 4.

19 Moreno got into trouble quite often during his life. It might well be that he got into trouble with the police for the role that he played in the parks, encouraging children to resist their parents and their schoolteachers. It might be that the real reason for 'leaving the children's realm' was pressure from the police. See the 'Autobiography' (1985) ch. 2: 34.

20 A. Alistar, personal communication.

21 This story is presented again in different places. This version is from *Who shall survive?* (1953) xxviii–xxx; but it also appears in the 'Autobiography' (1985) ch. 4: 7–11.

22 Even though there is no doubt that Moreno actually worked in these camps, it is difficult to trace the evidence. Because of the changes in boundaries and political status of Austria after the First World War, the archives of the Ministry of the Interior are scattered in different places. Some of the material referring to refugee camps is also in the army archives. The details given here about Moreno's experience in the refugee camps, are taken from the 'Autobiography' (1985) ch. 5: 17–37. It is difficult to ascertain for certain the exact status of Moreno in these camps. He might even have been drafted in the medical corps. However, it seems more probable that he volunteered for the work. (Zerka T. Moreno, personal communication.)

23 See *Who shall survive?* (1953) xxvi. Moreno indicates that he first developed axiodrama (1918), then sociodrama (1921), and then psychodrama. Psychodrama can be traced back to his work with Barbara and George in the spontaneous theatre group in the period 1922–4.

24 The protocol 'Godhead as Orator or Preacher' is related to the philosophy of the here and now and the existential movement. See *Who Shall Survive?* (1953) xxii–xxiii. It is also related to Kierkegaard, see the 'Autobiography' (1985) ch. 4: 22.

25 For the influence of Socrates, see the 'Autobiography'(1985) ch. 4:19–23.

26 For Moreno's encounter with Freud, see *Who Shall Survive?* (1953) xxvii and the 'Autobiography' (1985) ch. 5: 12–16.

27 Moreno finds Bergson's position centred on the final product, the creation. He claims that the *élan vital* ought to be seen through the *evolution of the creator*. See *Who Shall Survive?* (1953) 8.

28 The similarities between Moreno and Buber could be the subject of a whole book. For example, Buber's concept of encounter. 'The primary word I-Thou establishes the world of relation' is echoed by Moreno when he says: 'meeting' means more than a vague interpersonal relation. It means that two or more actors meet, not only to face one another, but to live and experience each other, as actors each in his own right.' See Will Herberg (1956) *The Writings of Martin Buber*, New York: Meridian Books, 45 and *Who Shall Survive?* (1953) 65; Paul E. Johnson, 'Interpersonal Psychology and Religion: Moreno and Buber' in *Group Psychotherapy*, September 1959 (3) 211–17; also, Maurice Friedman (1988) *Martin Buber's Life and Work*, Detroit: Wayne State University Press.

Chapter 4 Marianne, Bad Vöslau, and the first promises

1 There are many books dealing with Vienna from 1880 to 1938. A short list of recommended reading might include: Jean Clair (1986) *Vienne 1880–1938, L'apocalypse Joyeuse*, Paris: Editions du Centre Pompidou; Françoise Giroud (1988) *Alma Mahler ou l'art d'etre aimée*, Paris: Laffont; William M. Johnston (1972) *The Austrian Mind*, Berkeley: The Regents of the University of California; Yves Kobry *et al.* (1985), 'Vienne 1880–1938' in *Revue D'Esthétique*, (9); Malcolm MacDonald (1987) *Schoenberg*, London: J.M. Dent & Sons Ltd; Alma Mahler (1985) *Ma Vie*, Paris: Hachette; Michael Pollak (1984) *Vienne 1900*, Paris: Editions Gallimard/Juillard; Arthur Schnitzler (1987), *Une jeunesse viennoise*, Paris: Hachette; Carl E. Schorske (1985) *Fin-de-Siècle Vienna*, Cambridge: Cambridge University Press; Klaus Wagenbach (1968), *Kafka*, Paris: Seuil; Stefan Zweig (1964) *The World of Yesterday*, London: University of Nebraska Press.

2 For the situation of the Jews in Vienna, see: Marsha L. Rosenblit (1983) *The Jews of Vienna 1867–1914*, Albany: State University of New York Press.

3 See in particular Carl E. Schorske, *op. cit.* 212 *et seq.*

4 See Wolf-Dieter Dube (1972) *The Expressionists*, London: Thames and Hudson.

5 For Moreno's relation to psychiatry, see the 'Autobiography' (1985) ch. 5: 2–9. Comments in this section also come from Franz G. Alexander (1966), *The History of Psychiatry*, New York: Harper and Row.

6 For the creation of the *Daimon, Der Neue Daimon*, and *Die Gefährten*, see Murray Hall (1985) *Österreichische Verlagsgeschichte 1918–1938*, Vienna: Böhlau, 2 volumes. As for the writers in these journals, most of them are recorded in Paul Raabe (1985) *Die Autoren und Bücher des literarischen Expressionismus*, Stuttgart: J.B. Metzlersche Verlagsbuchhandlung.

7 See 'Autobiography' (1985).

8 See 'Autobiography' (1985) ch. 7: 9.

9 The story about the confrontation with the preacher is difficult to place in a logical sequence. In *Who shall survive?*, Moreno says that the incident took place in 1911. In 1919 it was published in *Der Neue Daimon* and Moreno then placed it in Bad Voslau where he stayed from 1919 to 1925. He may have repeated it in different places, or it may have been first written, and then tried out. I believe that the story has a historical basis, regardless of the time when it took place. See *Who shall survive?* (1953) xxiv, *Der Neue Daimon* (1919) January, (1–2); 'Autobiography' (1985) ch. 7: 39–43.

10 See 'Autobiography' (1985) ch. 7 : 45–9.

11 See *Time* magazine, 24 October 1988, 19.

12 See 'Autobiography' (1985) ch. 6: 22–3.

13 See 'Autobiography' (1985) ch. 7: 28 on charisma and ch. 7: 23 on the rumour-mongering.

14 People in the town were curious about the man who had visitors like Elisabeth Bergner or Peter Altenberg, visitors who behaved and dressed with some originality. It might well have been Altenberg who defined the difference between psychoanalysis and psychodrama as follows: 'Moreno, I agree with you, if I have to die I would rather die of diarrhoea than of constipation.

As I see it, this is the difference between you and Freud', from *Who shall survive?* (1953) xxviii.

15 See *Who shall survive?* (1953) xxvi, 87–9 and the 'Autobiography' (1985) ch. 6: 10–12.

16 The two men involved here are Geroge (Georg Kulka) and Robert (Robert Müller). Kulka was born in 1897 and died in 1929; Müller was born in 1887 and died in 1924. Moreno talks about George's 'sensitive and fragile personality'. As for Robert Müller, Moreno admits he was 'completely taken by surprise'. In both cases, it is interesting to observe that Moreno used the woman as protagonist most of the time, overlooking possibly, the personality of the two men. See the 'Autobiography' (1985) ch. 6: 30–1, 33. The two men were relatively well-known to Moreno since they both wrote in the *Daimon*, and George Kulka was working with Moreno's publisher, Kiepenheuer. George Kulka got in a controversy about plagiarism with Karl Kraus and it also seems that he had a personality that was not easy to handle. Anna Höllering (Barbara) might have had very good reasons for leaving him, reasons that a 'too much involved' Moreno might have overlooked. (From a personal interview with Anna Höllering's sister, Lana Sutton.) See Brigitte Marschal (1988) *Ich bin der Mythe*, Vienna: Böhlau, 49.

17 On catharsis, see in particular *Psychodrama, Volume 1* (1946) 12–20. It is interesting to compare Moreno's definition of catharsis with that of Freud and Breuer: 'For we found, to our great surprise at first, that each individual hysterical symptom immediately and permanently disappeared when we had succeeded in bringing clearly to light the memory of the event by which it was provoked and in arousing its accompanying affect, and when the patient had described that event in the greatest possible detail and had put the affect into words. Recollection without affect almost invariably produces no result. The psychical process which originally took place must be repeated as vividly as possible; it must be brought back to its status nascendi and then given verbal utterance.' From Sigmund Freud and Joseph Breuer (1983) *Studies in Hysteria*, New York: Penguin Books, 57. This is very close to what Moreno will discover on his own. Freud was to abandon the catharsis approach, while Moreno was to use it as *action method*, as the basis for psychodrama.

18 See *The Theatre of Spontaneity* (1947) 96 and also 'The philosophy of the Creator' in *The Words of the Father* (1971), 163.

19 See *Das Stegreiftheater* (1924) Table 1 and also *Psychodrama, Volume 1* (1946), photographs of stage.

20 See *The First Psychodramatic Family* (1964) 11. For the Kiesler controversy, see Barbara Lesak (1988) *Die Kulisse explodiert: Friedrich Kiesler Theater-experimente und Architekturprojekte 1923–25*, Vienna: Löcker.

21 See 'Autobiography' (1985) ch. 8 : 1–5. Also confirmed in a personal interview with Gertrude and Veronika Selb, sister and niece respectively of Marianne and Franz Lörnitzo.

Chapter 5 Emigrating to the United States: A stormy trip

1 See 'Autobiography' (1985) ch. 6: 45; ch. 9: 1; also *Who shall survive?*

(1953) Beacon: Beacon House, xxxix.

2 According to the Lörnitzo family, Moreno and Franz left on two different ocean liners, the *Aquitania* and the *Bremen*, Moreno on 21 December 1925 and Franz a few months later. Franz was 'invited' to the USA because he was the only one able to use the 'Radio-Film' properly. Moreno's memory was of arriving in New York in October 1925 on board the *Mauretania*, the ship of his dream, but also at the time of his father's death. See 'Autobiography' (1985) ch. 8: 1–3. In my personal file, I have a copy of the letters written by Moreno to Marianne and a personal correspondence with Marianne's sister and niece, Gertrude and Veronika Selb. They also generously provided me with other archive material, including photographs of Marianne, Franz, and Moreno around 1922–5.

3 The name of the invention on the Austrian patent is *Selbsttätige magnet-elektrische Lautsprechvorrichtung* and explains the basic processes used in the device. The English name, 'Radio-film', given to the invention by Moreno, refers to his dream. I researched the claim made by Moreno that the General Phonograph company employed Franz and him in Elyria and produced the 'Radio-Film' on an industrial basis. Moreno told this story in a letter to Marianne (28 January 1926). Here is an excerpt from a letter that I received from the Vice President of the Company, in reply 'Dear Professor Marineau: With reference to your letter of January 19th and our earlier phone conversation, I have personally researched our employment records which go back to 1904 and I also have a detailed summary of all patent numbers issued to our company from January 31, 1911 thru December 20, 1932. No where in these records can I find the names J.L. Moreno, Levy, nor Lörnitzo. I can assure you that they were not regularly employed by our company, which does not preclude the possibility of a special temporary arrangement . . . ' (Letter to the author, 11 February 1988, from J.M. Callihan, The General Industries Company, formerly General Phonograph). According to Mr Callihan, it is most likely that the 'Radio-Film' was never patented in the USA; in order to 'discourage' the 'competition', sometimes a small amount of money was given to inventors in return for a promise to forego their involvement in a project.

4 See 'Autobiography' (1985) ch. 8: 6. The marriage licence between Beatrice B. Beecher and J.L. Moreno is to be found at the New York State Department of Health, Albany, New York, Registration no. 11–377, year 1928. On it Moreno claims Bucharest as his place of birth, and 20 May 1890 as his date of birth. Beatrice Beecher was born in the USA in 1892.

'A joint project: J.L. Moreno and Beatrice B. Beecher' can be found in the Moreno archives at The Francis Countway Library of Medicine, Boston. This project (no date) was to be presented to the publishers Robert MacBride and is related to the publication of the 'Impromptu Book'.

5 A study of Moreno's relationship with Marianne reveals a lot about his personality at this time. It shows how he regarded an 'intimate' relationship, the place of children in his life, and the role of women in it as muses, partners, and lovers. There is no doubt that Marianne played a crucial role in Moreno's personal and professional development, and the way he ended the relationship does him little credit. See 'Autobiography' (1985) ch. 7: 52–3 and his letters to Marianne shown to the author by Gertrude

and Veronika Selb (see note 2). The letters from Marianne to Moreno do not seem to have been preserved. However, her family, through her sister Gertrude and her niece Veronika, have kept many memories and documents that testify to her dedication to Moreno.

6 See 'Autobiography' (1985) ch. 8: 31.

7 For the story and names associated with the impromptu work, see 'Autobiography' (1985) ch. 8: 35–42.

Chapter 6 In search of a new muse

1 See 'Autobiography' (1985) ch. 10: 11–12 and the dedication to *Psychodrama, Volume 1:* 'Dedicated to my brother William L. Moreno, sponsor of the first therapeutic theatre in Vienna, 1922 and founder of the New York theatre for psychodrama, 1942.'

2 See 'Autobiography' (1985) ch. 8: 6–8.

3 See 'Autobiography' (1985) ch. 8: 32; ch. 9: 15.

4 See 'Autobiography' (1985) ch. 9: 14–19. This information was also confirmed to the author in a personal interview with Florence Bridge.

5 For the role of Gretel Leutz, see 'Autobiography' (1985) ch. 9: 18–19. I have had many meetings with Gretel Leutz and Regina Moreno while writing this biography. Regina Moreno became a teacher, doing some psychodrama and some singing. She is married and has two children. Dr Gretel Leutz carried Moreno's work to Germany, and then around the world. She is currently the president of the International Association of Group Psychotherapy. As a sign of his confidence in her, Moreno authorized Gretel Leutz to use his name for the training institute that she founded in Germany.

6 Jonathan Moreno teaches medical ethics, but has also been active in the Association of Group Psychotherapy and Psychodrama. He leads psychodrama groups. He is part of what Moreno called the Moreno Dynasty, a dynasty that will be continued by his son Jarrett. He wrote *The First Psychodramatic Family* in association with his parents and was the main protagonist in articles written by Zerka, such as 'Psychodrama in the Crib' in *Group Psychotherapy* (1954) vii: 291–302. See also 'Autobiography' (1985) ch. 10: 10–15.

7 See 'Autobiography' (1985) ch. 10: 4–37. I must admit that one of the major problems that I have encountered while working on this biography has been in disentangling the contributions of Moreno and Zerka. After 1941, the life and work of the two were so intertwined that at times it is impossible to pinpoint who did what. It seems clear that Zerka's contribution has often been underestimated; on the other hand, rarely do we find in the history of psychiatry and psychology such a long-lived example (over thirty-five years) of a couple working so productively as a unit. It would be an interesting research project to investigate the psychology of such male-female relationships, and the conditions which promote them. Other such cooperative 'couples' have been William H. Masters and Virginia E. Johnson, Fritz and Laura P. Perls, S.H. Foulkes and Elisabeth Foulkes, but the Morenos' relationship was exceptional in the way they worked so closely together at both the personal and professional level.

Chapter 7 The development of group psychotherapy and sociometry

1 Moreno affirms the importance of *The Words of the Father* in the 'Autobiography' (1985) ch. 9: 7; for Moreno's theory of life, see Zerka T. Moreno (1969) 'Moreneans, the Heretics of Yesterday are the Orthodoxy of Today' in *Group Psychotherapy, Psychodrama and Sociometry*, xxii (1–2): 2.

2 From J.L. Moreno (1947) Psychodrama Monograph 21, *The Future of Man's World*, New York: Beacon House, 13. One of the problems in reading Moreno remains the difficulty in getting an overall and inclusive philosophical perspective, from theoretical foundations to practical applications. A book published in 1987 tried to present an overview of Moreno's writings: see Jonathan Fox (1987) *The Essential Moreno*, New York: Springer Publishing Company.

3 When invited to the first world congress on psychiatry in Paris in 1950, Moreno very typically volunteered two separate papers, one on sociometry, one on psychodrama. Confirmed in an interview with Professor Juliette Favez-Boutonier.

4 On sociatry, see J.L. Moreno (1947) Psychodrama Monograph 23, *Open Letter to Group Psychotherapists: An Introduction to Sociatry*, New York: Beacon House.

5 For further information on the work at Sing Sing and Hudson, see 'Autobiography' (1985) ch. 8: 11, 15–29; *Who shall survive?* (1934); J.L. Moreno, ed. (1945) *Group Psychotherapy: a symposium*, Beacon: Beacon House.

6 See J.L. Moreno, in collaboration with E. Stagg Whitin (1932) *Application of the Group Method to Classification*, New York: National Committee on Prisons and Prison Labor. For his later work in Hudson, see 'Autobiography' (1985) ch. 8: 23–9 and J.L. Moreno (1934) *op. cit.*

Gardner Murphy (1947) gives a good appreciation of Moreno's work in this area in *Personality: A Biosocial Approach to Origins and Structure*, New York: Harper and Brothers, in the chapter on 'Creativity, Self-enhancement and Situationism'.

7 When Moreno arrived in the United States with his invention, 'Radio-Film', he had not succeeded in selling it; however, he pioneered the use of the new technology in enhancing his teaching, research, and practice at Hudson. In 1935 he created a company 'Therapeutic Motion Pictures' to distribute the films he made there, and later at Beacon; when viewed today, these films give a good insight into his 'retraining' methods and psychodrama in the early 1940s. For further information see *Psychodrama, Volume 1* (1946) 385–419 and *Psychodrama, Volume 3* (1969) 251–4.

The motion pictures made at Hudson in 1933, while Moreno was Director of Research at the New York State Training School for Girls, were presented first to the Department of Psychology at Columbia University to Professor Gardner Murphy and Dr Kurt Lewin, and then, at the annual meeting of the American Psychiatric Association in May 1935 in Washington DC. See J.L. Moreno (1944) *Spontaneity Test and Spontaneity Training* Psychodrama Monograph 4, Beacon: Beacon House.

8 See *Who shall survive?* (1953) lxviii–lxxxv.

9 The first edition of *Who shall survive? A new approach to the Problem of Human Interrelations* was first published in 1934 with a foreword by William A. White, and was dedicated to Fannie French Morse. The revised edition published in 1953 had a different subtitle: *Foundations of Sociometry, Group Psychotherapy and Sociodrama* and was dedicated to Zerka Toeman Moreno. The 'Preludes of the Sociometric Movement' appears only in the revised edition, which explains why I refer mainly to this edition when dealing with historical material.

10 See 'Autobiography' (1985) ch. 8: 43, also many articles from newspapers around the country: these articles are kept in scrapbooks in the Harvard University Archives. See also *Psychodrama, Volume 3,* (1969) 257.

11 See 'Autobiography' (1985) ch. 11: 13–14. For the work at St Elizabeths, see Frances Herriott and M. Hagan (1941) 'The Theatre of Psychodrama at St Elizabeths Hospital' in *Sociometry* 4: 168–76; Margaret Hagan and A.M. Duval (1943) 'A Practical Red Cross Program for the Social Rehabilitation of Psychiatric Casualties in the United States Navy' in *American Journal of Psychiatry*, 100: 105–08; Winfred O. Overholser and J.M. Enneis (1959) 'Twenty years of Psychodrama at Saint Elizabeths Hospital' in *Group Psychotherapy* 12: 283–92; Dale Richard Buchanan (1981) 'Forty-one Years of Psychodrama at St Elizabeths Hospital' in *Journal of Group Psychotherapy, Psychodrama and Sociometry* 34: 134–46.

12 'Autobiography' (1985) ch. 11: 17–33.

13 For the Lewin story, see *Who Shall Survive?* (1953) xcix–cvi. This was a controversy that would need more research in order to assess correctly the contribution of the main protagonists. In my estimation, Moreno and Lewin both contributed significantly, and quite independently, to the field of social psychology. Moreno's accusations are directed mainly towards some of Lewin's students, and especially against Ronald Lippitt, a former student whose wife, Rosemary, remained very active in Morenean circles even during the controversy between Moreno and her husband.

Chapter 8 Group psychotherapy and psychodrama

1 See *Impromptu*, January 1931 (1) and (2); also the programme for the inaugural public performance of the Impromptu Theatre on 5 April 1931 (copy in the Moreno Archives, Harvard University).

2 Many accounts of the Brill controversy can be found in newspapers for 6 June 1931, for example: *The New York Times, The Washington Post, The Chicago Daily Tribune, The Los Angeles Times, The Toronto Evening Telegram, The Canadian Star, The Times,* and *Le Matin*. See also, *Who shall survive?* (1953) xliv–li and 'Autobiography' (1985) ch. 8: 12–14.

3 The controversy with S.R. Slavson raged for years and is another good example of Moreno's difficulty in dealing with other pioneers. In 1940 Slavson sent a copy of his book, *Character Education in a Democracy*, to Moreno and wrote: 'To Dr J.L. Moreno, with my deep appreciation of his pioneering work,' for Moreno's comments, see *The First Psychodramatic Family*, (1964) 18. Moreno's personal correspondence is very hard on Slavson and makes us aware of a lot of dealing behind the scenes with

other colleagues from around the world to keep Slavson out of any leadership roles. The two 'protagonists' created their own associations and their own journals and fought long and hard. At the end of his life, Moreno became somewhat less aggressive towards Slavson. A whole book could be written on this particular subject: beyond the professional rivalry a more personal side is bound to emerge. See the Moreno Archives in Harvard, and the minutes and publications of The American Group Psychotherapy Association, Inc.

4 Most of the Beacon estate has been sold and in place of the former sanatorium now stands a row of newly-built houses. The only preserved building is Moreno's own house, where Zerka still lives. The Beacon stage from the theatre has been saved, and rebuilt a few miles from the original Moreno Institute by Clare Danielson.

5 Moreno had many visitors to his Institutes. Fritz Perls was one of them, and he was quite reluctant to give any credit to Moreno, even though it is evident that his own basic technique — the monodrama — bears many similarities to psychodrama. Moreno never missed an opportunity to let people know about Perls's visit to his Institute to New York in the late 1940s, and confronted the founder of the Gestalt therapy movement directly in front of an audience of more than 1,000 people during a meeting of the American Psychological Association in 1964 in San Francisco. (Personal archive material; interview with Dr Leon Fine.)

Eric Berne, the founder of transactional analysis, and a student of Brill, did not hesitate to acknowledge his debt to Moreno. See Eric Berne (1947) *The Mind in Action*, New York: Simon and Schuster.

S.H. Foulkes, the founder of group analysis, visited Moreno in New York and developed a personal and professional relationship with him. Both were to cooperate in the development of an international association of group psychotherapists.

6 For the historical development of psychodrama at St Elizabeths hospital, see Frances Herriott and M. Hagan (1941) 'The Theatre of Psychodrama at St Elizabeths Hospital' in *Sociometry* 4: 168–76; Winifred Overholser and J.M. Enneis (1959) 'Twenty years of Psychodrama at Saint Elizabeths Hospital' in *Group Psychotherapy* 12: 283–92; Dale Richard Buchanan (1981) 'Forty-one Years of psychodrama at St Elizabeths Hospital', in *Journal of Psychotherapy, Psychodrama and Sociometry*, 34: 134–46.

7 'Before a gathering of grad students and professors that more than filled the modern, newly completed hall, Dr J.L. Moreno accepted, last monday, the presentation of his latest "child" — the Harvard Psychodrama Theatre. With Harvard as the proud mother, this addition to the clinical psychology family has, as Dr Henry Murray pointed out in his introduction, no question of paternity: for the psychodramatic techniques are Dr Moreno's great contribution to the science of social relations.' (*The Radcliffe News*, 7 October 1949, quoted in *The First Psychodramatic Family* (1964) 32.)

8 List of the first monographs published by Beacon House in the early 1940s:

Psychodrama Monographs
No. 1: *Sociodrama, a Method for the Analysis of Social Conflicts*, J. L. Moreno; No. 2: *Psychodramatic Treatment of Performance*

Neurosis, J.L. Moreno; No. 3: *The Theatre for Spontaneity*, J.L. Moreno; No. 4: *Spontaneity Test and Spontaneity Training*, J.L. Moreno in collaboration with Helen H. Jennings; No. 5: *Psychotherapy Shock Therapy*, J.L. Moreno

Sociometry Monographs
No. 1: *Developments in Social Psychology, 1930–1940*, Leonard S. Cottrell Jr and Ruth Gallagher; No. 2: *Sociometry and the Cultural Order*, J.L. Moreno; No. 3: *Sociometric Statistics of Social Configurations*, J.L. Moreno and Helen H. Jennings; No. 4: *Foundations of Sociometry*, J.L. Moreno; No. 5: *Group Method and Group Therapy*, J.L. Moreno

9 Even though Drs Moreno and Masserman cooperated for many years, their relationship deteriorated after 1960 and reached a very low point. See Masserman's correspondence with Moreno published in his book *A Psychiatric Odyssey* (1965) and the 'Masserman File' in the Moreno Archives, Harvard University.

Chapter 9 The pilgrim

1 *Who shall survive?* (1953) lxxxvii.
2 *Who shall survive?* (1953) xc and 'Autobiography' (1985) ch. 8: 15.
3 This anecdote was told me by Professor Juliette Favez-Boutonier, secretary of the Congress. For the role of Moreno in France and the development of psychodrama in France, see Anne Ancelin Schützenberger (1970) *Precis de psychodrame*, Paris: Presses Universitaires de France, 213–24; see also *Psychodrama, Volume 3* (1969) 252–3.
4 See *Who shall survive?* (1953) xci and, for the early involvement J.L. Moreno (1945) *Group Psychotherapy: A Symposium*, Beacon: Beacon House.
5 For details of Moreno's journey to Russia, see *International Journal of Sociometry and Sociatry* (1960) II (2). For correspondence between Moreno and the State of Israel, see *The First Psychodramatic Family* (1964) 108–12. In a letter sent to President Lyndon B. Johnson on 3 January 1967, Moreno states:

Dear Mr President:

I feel it is my duty to transfer to you an idea which might be helpful in the present crisis, as to what is your next step, on behalf of Vietnam. I know that you must be worried. This, and the report in *The New York Times*, that you recently employed a method which I have developed, called roleplaying, in connection with the meeting with Prime Minister Harold Wilson of Great Britain, is the reason why I am writing to you at this point.

My opinion is that you must go one step further, and arrange for a personal encounter with Mr Ho Chi Minh, President of North Vietnam. The idea in itself is simple and appeals to common-sense. But carrying it out may require, beside intuition, some counseling. No one is as well qualified to judge the situation as you are, because it is your situation, but I am a professional psychiatrist of ripe vintage, life fellow of the American Psychiatric Association, usually identified by my work in human relations, sociometry, psychodrama, role playing and group psychotherapy.

If you feel that you would like to avail yourself of my assistance, I would be glad to serve you and the country. I may be reached by letter or telephone and would be glad to come to see you in Washington or Texas, wherever you may be . . .

Correspondence between the White House and Moreno can be found in the Moreno Archives at Harvard University. No meeting took place between Moreno and Johnson.

6 A special issue of *Group Psychotherapy, Psychodrama and Sociometry* 'Honoring Dr J.L. Moreno: University of Vienna and Bad Vöslau' was published in 1969, xxii (1–2).

7 In addition, Moreno was honoured, in particular, by the American Psychiatric Association, the American Psychological Association, and the New York State Medical Association.

8 The correspondence relating to the creation of the Association can be found in the Moreno Archives at Harvard. See also *Group Psychotherapy* (1954) 7 (1 and 2).

9 See Moreno Archives, Harvard University, under International Psychodrama Conferences.

10 For instance, at a UNESCO conference he rose to his feet to speak, hesitated while the delegates grew uneasy, and then said: 'I do not want to tell you something I have already told someone else!'

10 Death and legacy

1 The different versions of the autobiography can be found in the Moreno Archives at Harvard University, see note 2, chapter 1.

2 By, among others, Carl Hollander, Lewis Yablonski, Martin R. Haskell, James M. Enneis, The Sirokas, Marcia Karp, Jonathan Moreno, Anne Ancelin Schützenberger, Ella Mae, James Sachs, Adam Biatner, David Kipper, Heida Straul, Leon Fine, Gretel Leutz.

3 From interviews with Gretel Leutz, Anne Ancelin Schützenberger, Zerka Toeman Moreno, John Nolte, and Ann Quinn.

4 Personal interview with Pierre Weil.

Select bibliography of Moreno's works

Moreno wrote over three hundred books and articles, many of them repeats. An almost complete bibliography can be found in A. Paul Hare (1986) 'Bibliography of Work of J.L. Moreno' in *Journal of Group Psychotherapy, Psychodrama and Sociometry* 39, (3): 95–128. Moreno published his work anonymously and under various forms of his name, for example Jakob Levy, Jakob Moreno Levy, or J.L. Moreno. The works listed here are the major ones, quoted frequently in the text; less important works referred to are included in the references proper.

J. Levy (1914) *Einladung zu einer Begegnung. Heft 1* (*Invitation to an Encounter, Part 1*), Vienna/Leipzig: Anzengruber/Verlag Brüder Suschitzky.

Jakob Levy (1915) *Einladung zu einer Begegnung, Heft 2* (*Invitation to an Encounter, Part 2*), Vienna/Leipzig: Anzengruber/Verlag Brüder Suschitzky.

Jakob Levy (1915) *Einladung zu einer Begegnung. Heft 3* (*Invitation to an Encounter, Part 3*), Vienna/Leipzig: Anzengruber/Verlag Brüder Suschitzky.

Jakob Levy Moreno (1918) 'Die Gottheit als Autor' ('The Godhead as Author') in *Daimon* 1, February, 3–31.

Jakob Moreno Levy (1919) 'Die Gottheit als Redner' ('The Godhead as Orator or Preacher') in *Der Neue Daimon* January, 3–18.

Jakob Moreno Levy (1919) 'Die Gottheit als Komödiant' ('The Godhead as Comedian or Actor') in *Der Neue Daimon* January, 48–63.

(anonymous) (1920) *Das Testament des Vaters* (*The Words of the Father*), in *Die Gefährten*, 3: 1–33. Berlin/Potsdam: Kiepenheuer Verlag.

(anonymous) (1923) *Der Königsroman* (*The King's Novel*), Berlin/Potsdam: Kiepenheuer Verlag.

(anonymous) (1924) *Das Stegreiftheater* (*The Theatre of Spontaneity*), Berlin/Potsdam: Kiepenheuer Verlag.

(anonymous) (1924) 'Theater ohne Zuschauer' ('Theatre without spectators') in the Catalog Programm Almanach prepared for the International Exhibition of New Theatre Techniques, Vienna: Wurthle und Sohn Verlag. This plan of a theatre stage was prepared by the

architect Rudolf Hönigfeld under Moreno's supervision.
J.L. Moreno (1932) in collaboration with E.S. Whitin, *Application of the Group Method to Classification*, New York: National Committee on Prisons and Prison Labor; reprinted with additions in 1957 as *The First Book on Group Psychotherapy*, Beacon: Beacon House.
J.L. Moreno (1934) *Who Shall Survive? A New Approach to the Problem of Human Interrelations*, Washington, DC: Nervous and Mental Disease Publishing Co.; 1953 published in a revised edition with additions, including 'A prelude to the sociometric movement', by Beacon House.
(anonymous) (1941), with a preface by J.L. Moreno, *The Words of the Father*, Beacon: Beacon House. This book is more than a translation of *Das Testament des Vaters*, since it includes additions, and long philosophical and theological explanations.
J.L. Moreno (1946) *Psychodrama, Volume 1*, Beacon: Beacon House.
J.L. Moreno (1947) *The Theatre of Spontaneity*, Beacon: Beacon House.
J.L. Moreno (1950) *Sociometry and The Science of Man*, Beacon: Beacon House.
J.L. Moreno (1951) *Sociometry. Experimental Method and the Science of Society: An Approach to a New Political Orientation*, Beacon: Beacon House.
J.L. Moreno (1955) *Preludes to my Autobiography*, Beacon: Beacon House.
J.L. Moreno (1959) *Psychodrama. Volume 2: Foundations of Psychotherapy*, Beacon: Beacon House.
J.L. Moreno (1964) in collaboration with Zerka T. Moreno and Jonathan Moreno, *The First Psychodramatic Family*, Beacon: Beacon House.
J.L. Moreno (1969) in collaboration with Zerka T. Moreno, *Psychodrama. Volume 3: Action Therapy and Principles of Practice*, Beacon: Beacon House.
J.L. Moreno (1985) (copyright Zerka T. Moreno and Jonathan D. Moreno) 'The Autobiography of J.L. Moreno, M.D.' Moreno Archives, Harvard University, Boston, USA.

References

Alexander, Franz G. (1966) *The History of Psychiatry*, New York: Harper and Row.

Ancelin-Schützenberger, Anne (1970) *Précis de Psychodrame*, Paris: Presses Universitaires de France.

Bergner, Elisabeth (1978) *Bewundert Viel und Viel Gescholten*, Munich: Bertelsmann Verlag.

Berne, Eric (1947) *The Mind in Action*, New York: Simon and Schuster.

Boria, Giovanni (1983) *Tele, Manuale di Psichidramma Classico*, Milan: Franco Angeli Editore.

Bratescu, George (1975) 'The Date and Birthplace of J.L. Moreno' in *Group Psychotherapy and Psychodrama*, 28: 2–3.

Buchanan, Dale Richard (1981) 'Forty-one Years of Psychodrama at St Elizabeths Hospital' in *Journal of Group Psychotherapy, Psychodrama and Sociometry* 34: 134–46.

Clair, Jean (1986) *Vienne 1880–1938: L'apocalypse Joyeuse*, Paris: Editions du Centre Pompidou.

Dube, Wolf-Dieter (1972) *The Expressionists*, London: Thames & Hudson.

Eloesser, Arthur (1927) *Elisabeth Bergner*, Berlin: William and Co. Verlag.

Fox, Jonathan (1987) *The Essential Moreno*, New York: Springer Publishing Company.

Freud, Sigmund (1922) *Dreams and Telepathy*, in Standard Edition, 18, London: Hogarth Press.

Freud, Sigmund (1933) *New Introductory Lectures on Psychoanalysis*, in Standard Edition, 22, London: Hogarth Press.

Friedman, Maurice (1988) *Martin Buber's Life and Work*, Detroit: Wayne State University Press.

Gay, Peter (1988) *A Life for our Time*, New York: Norton Press.

Giroud, Françoise (1988) *Alma Mahler ou L'art d'etre aimée*, Paris: Laffont.

Gomez, Alfredo (1987) 'Spain to Give Sephardic Jews Special Place in Columbus Rites' in *Los Angeles Times*, Part II, 25 July, p. 4.

Greenberg, Ira H. (1974) *Psychodrama: Theory and Therapy*, New York: Behavioral Publications.

Gurvitch, George (ed.) (1950) *Sociometry in France and in the United States*
Hagan, Margaret and Duval, A.M. (1943) 'A Practical Red Cross Program for the Social Rehabilitation of Psychiatric Casualties in the United States Navy' in *American Journal of Psychiatry*, 100: 105–08.
Hall, Murray (1985) *Österreichische Verlagsgeschichte 1918–1938* (2 vols.), Vienna: Böhlau.
Herberg, Will (1956) *The Writings of Martin Buber*, New York: Meridian Books.
Herriott, Frances and Hagan, M. (1941) 'The Theatre of Psychodrama at St Elizabeths Hospital' in *Sociometry* 4: 168–76.
Johnson, Paul E. (1959) 'Interpersonal Psychology and Religion: Moreno and Buber' in *Group Psychotherapy*, xii (3): 211–17.
Johnston, William M. (1972) *The Austrian Mind*, Berkeley: The Regents of the University of California.
Kobry, Yves et al. (1985) 'Vienne 1880–1938', in *Revue D'Esthétique*, (9).
Langer, William L. (1948) *An Encyclopedia of World History*, Boston: Houghton Mifflin Co.
Lesak, Barbara (1988) *Die Kulisse Explodiert: Friedrich Kiesler Theaterexperimente und Architekturprojekte 1923–25*, Vienna: Löcker.
MacDonald, Malcolm (1987) *Schoenberg*, London: J.M. Dent and Sons Ltd.
Marcus, Jacob R. (1938) *The Jew in the Mediaeval World: a Source Book*, New York: Atheneum.
Mahler, Alma (1985) *Ma Vie*, Paris: Hachette.
Margolis, Max L. and Alexander Marx (1927) *A History of the Jewish People*, New York: Atheneum.
Marschal, Brigitte (1988) *Ich bin der Mythe*, Vienna: Böhlau Verlag.
Masserman, Jules (1965) *A Psychiatric Odyssey.*
Moreno, J.L. (1931) *Impromptu*, 1 and 2.
Moreno, J.L. (1932) in collaboration with E. Stagg Whitin, *Application of the Group Method to Classification*, New York: National Committee on Prison and Prison Labor.
Moreno, J.L. (1944) *Spontaneity Test and Spontaneity Training*, Psychodrama Monograph 4, Beacon: Beacon House.
Moreno, J.L. (1945) *Group Psychotherapy: a symposium*, Beacon: Beacon House.
Moreno, J.L. (1947) *The Future of Man's World* Psychodrama Monograph 21, New York: Beacon House.
Moreno, J.L. (1947) *Open Letter to Group Psychotherapists: An Introduction to Sociatry*, Psychodrama Monograph 23, New York: Beacon House.
Moreno, J.L. (1960) 'Psychiatric Encounter in Soviet Russia' in *International Journal of Sociometry and Sociatry.*
Moreno, J.L., Friedmann, A., Battegay, R., and Moreno, Zerka T. (eds) (1966) *The International Handbook of Group Psychotherapy.*
Moreno, Zerka T. (1954) 'Psychodrama in the Crib' in *Group Psychotherapy*, vii: 291–302.
Moreno Zerka T. (1969) 'Moreneans. The Heretics of Yesterday are the

Orthodoxy of Today', in *Group Psychotherapy. Psychodrama and Sociometry*, xxii (1–2).
Moreno, Zerka T. (1979) 'Escape me never' in *Group Psychotherapy, Psychodrama and Sociometry*, xxxii: 5–11.
Murphy, Gardner (1947) *Personality. A Biosocial Approach to Origins and Structure*, New York: Harper and Brothers.
Nietzsche, Friedrich (1968) *Ainsi parlait Zarathustra*, Paris: Gallimard.
Overhoser, Winifred O. and Enneis, J.M. (1959) 'Twenty years of Psychodrama at Saint Elizabeths Hospital' in *Group Psychotherapy* 12: 283–92.
Pollak, Michael (1984) *Vienne 1900*, Paris: Editions Gallimard/Juillard.
Raabe, Paul (1985) *Die Autoren und Bücher des Literarischen Expressionismus*, Stuttgart: J.B. Metzlersche Verlagsbuchhandlung.
Reik, Theodor (1956) *The Search Within*, New York: Farra.
Roazen, Paul (1984) *Freud and his Followers*, New York: New York University Press.
Rosenblit, Marsha L. (1983) *The Jews of Vienna 1867–1914*, Albany: State University of New York Press.
Sachs, Joseph (1937) *Beauty and the Jew*, London: Golston Ltd.
Schnitzler, Arthur (1987) *Une jeunesse viennoise*, Paris: Hachette.
Schorske, Carl E. (1985) *Fin-du-siècle Vienna*, Cambridge: Cambridge University Press.
Semo, I. (1944) *Bejarano*, Bucharest: Institutul de Arte Grafice.
Slavson, S.R. (1940) *Character Education in a Democraty*, New York: Association Press.
Wagenbach, Klaus (1968) *Kafka*, Paris: Seuil.
Zweig, Stefan (1964) *The World of Yesterday*, London: University of Nebraska Press.

Index